ATHENE Series

General Editors

**Gloria Bowles
Renate Klein
Janice Raymond**

Consulting Editor

Dale Spender

The Athene Series assumes that all those who are concerned with formulating explanations of the way the world works need to know and appreciate the significance of basic feminist principles.

The growth of feminist research internationally has called into question almost all aspects of social organization in our culture. The Athene Series focuses on the construction of knowledge and the exclusion of women from the process—both as theorists and subjects of study—and offers innovative studies that challenge established theories and research.

ATHENE, the Olympian goddess of wisdom, was honored by the ancient Greeks as the patron of arts and sciences and guardian of cities. She represented both peace and the intellectual aspect of war. Her mother, Metis, was a Titan and presided over all knowledge. While pregnant with Athene, Metis was swallowed whole by Zeus. Some say this was his attempt to embody her supreme wisdom. The original Athene is thus twice born: once of her strong mother, Metis, and once more out of the head of Zeus. According to feminist myth, there is a "third birth" of Athene when she stops being an agent and mouthpiece of Zeus and male dominance, and returns to her original source: the wisdom of womankind.

MAKING VIOLENCE SEXY

FEMINIST VIEWS ON PORNOGRAPHY

DIANA E. H. RUSSELL, EDITOR

TEACHERS COLLEGE PRESS

Teachers College, Columbia University
New York and London

Paperback Cover Photograph:

Participants in the Feminist Perspectives on Pornography Conference by Women Against Violence and Pornography in the Media, march on Broadway in a performance by Suzanne Lacy and Leslie Labowitz. San Francisco, November, 1978. Photo by Rob Blalack.

Published by Teachers College Press, 1234 Amsterdam Avenue, New York, NY 10027

Library of Congress Cataloging-in-Publication Data

Making violence sexy : feminist views on pornography / Diana E.H. Russell, editor.
    p.   cm.
    Includes bibliographical references and index.
    ISBN 0-8077-6269-5 (alk. paper). — ISBN 0-8077-6268-7 (pbk. : alk. paper)
    1. Pornography — Social aspects. 2. Violent crimes. 3. Women — Crimes against. 4. Feminism. 5. Feminist theory. I. Russell, Diana E. H.
HQ471.M32   1993
363.4′7 — dc20   92-41999

ISBN 0-8077-6269-5
ISBN 0-8077-6268-7 (pbk.)

Printed on acid-free paper
Manufactured in the United States of America

99 98 97 96 95 94 93   7 6 5 4 3 2 1

This book is dedicated to Nikki Craft for her creative, ground-breaking, and courageous actions against pornography and violence against women; to Catharine MacKinnon and Andrea Dworkin for their brilliant reformulation of pornography as a civil rights issue and for their efforts to devise a new way of combatting some of its harmful effects; to all three women for their dedication to this issue despite the extended backlash against an anti-pornography stance; and to all the other women who are continuing the fight against this dangerous method of subjugating women.

Contents

Acknowledgments

But for Dorchen Leidholdt, this book would never have happened. In the summer of 1985, we shared bitter feelings that the feminist analysis of pornography — developed by so many of us over the prior 10 years — appeared to be obliterated after the publication of the final reports of the Attorney General's Commission on Pornography (1985). Despite the fact that *Take Back the Night*, Laura Lederer's fine anthology on feminist views of pornography, was only 5 years old and still in print, we felt that a new collection was needed to try to revitalize awareness of our unique perspective — one that is totally different from liberals, radicals, and right-wing people. Our years of hard-won progress had slipped from the public eye — years of speaking out, marches, demonstrations, conferences, educational tours, slide presentations, guerrilla theater, civil disobedience, and the formulation of important new legal strategies, especially the reconceptualization of pornography as a form of discrimination against women.

In July of 1986, Dorchen and I decided to co-edit a new feminist anthology on pornography. She was located in Palo Alto at that time, I in Berkeley, so our proximity allowed us to collaborate on a daily basis. Because of our sense of urgency, we decided to complete the anthology before Dorchen returned to law school in New York in October, and I to my teaching at Mills College in Oakland, California. The Attorney General's hearings on pornography had made this a very hot and controversial issue, so we were confident that our proposal would be snapped up with enthusiasm.

Alas, rejection letters started arriving, and we finally realized that none of our prospective publishers were willing to publish our anthology. Their reactions showed us that all anti-pornography positions were seen as right-wing, or, at best, supportive of the right-wing. Our feminist analysis was lost in the polarization of views that had developed almost overnight. We were struck by the irony that anti-pornography feminists are almost invariably accused of censorship while the publishing industry feels free to refuse to publish feminist work in the name of being anti-censorship.

In May 1987, Renate Klein, feminist writer and Athene Series editor, came to our rescue. But by this time Dorchen and I were heavily committed to other projects and we were at opposite ends of the country with no budget for long distance phone calls. Finally, Dorchen found it impossible to continue working on the book, so I took over as sole editor. Delays were also caused by Pergamon Press' move from Oxford, England, to New York, then, in 1991, their purchase by two publishers in one year: first Macmillan, then Teachers College Press. After the passing of all these years, I had to jettison most of the manuscripts for *Making Violence Sexy: Feminist Views on Pornography* that Dorchen and I had compiled.

The book title, *Making Violence Sexy*, came from John Stoltenberg's phrase "making sexism sexy." I amended his phrase to making *violence* sexy, thus providing a succinct and accurate title for this anthology.

I am very grateful to Renate Klein for her interest in publishing this book, and for her enthusiastic belief in its importance when so many other publishers shied away from its flagrantly anti-pornography stance.

I am indebted to many people who have helped by reading and commenting on one or more of my chapters in this volume: Joan Balter, Robert Brannon, James Check, Nikki Craft, Candida Ellis, Marny Hall, Angela Harraway, Dorchen Leidholdt, Anna Livia, Catharine MacKinnon, Sharon O'Connell, Suzanne Popkin, Wendy Powell, Jeanne Quint, Kris Wood, and Barbara Yoder. Thanks also to Chris Pocock for digging up some excellent articles, Roberta Harmes for locating hard-to-find publications, and Mary Anne Saunders for her assistance with word processing. Robert Brannon, in particular, has had a considerable impact on my introduction. Our dialogue has resulted in our generating a new definition of what I refer to as pornography and he calls erotomisogyny. It is a rare treat to have such a rich exchange about concepts that are important in my work.

Finally, I want to thank all the contributors whose fine work is included in this volume, and to apologize to those authors whose articles I had to exclude because of my very tiresome habit of producing manuscripts that are much longer than my contracts permit. Last, but not least, I am grateful to Sarah Biondello, my editor at Teachers College Press, for the careful and professional job she has done as she has shepherded my manuscript through its different phases. *Making Violence Sexy* would have been published years earlier had it been in the hands of Teachers College Press from the beginning.

MAKING VIOLENCE SEXY
FEMINIST VIEWS ON PORNOGRAPHY

CHAPTER 1

Introduction

Diana E. H. Russell

"Before pornography became the pornographer's speech it was somebody's life."
—Catharine MacKinnon, 1987

"These chicks are our natural enemy. . . . It is time we do battle with them. . . . What I want is a devastating piece that takes the militant feminists apart. . . . They are unalterably opposed to the romantic boy–girl society that *Playboy* promotes."
—Hugh Hefner, 1984[1]

"What would it say about one's status if the society permits one to be hung from trees and calls it entertainment—calls it what it is to those who enjoy it, rather than what it is to those to whom it is done?"
—Andrea Dworkin & Catharine MacKinnon, 1988, p. 61

In the early 1970s, Berl Kutchinsky conducted research in Denmark from which he concluded that sex crimes had decreased there after the censorship laws against pornography were repealed (1970, 1973). Although Kutchinsky's analysis was scientifically flawed, it was exceedingly influential. Ever since then I had wanted to see for myself what Danish pornography looked like. I was fortunate to have Danish anthropologist Annette Leleur as my guide and confidence-enhancer (I've never felt comfortable entering porn stores alone) as we toured the pornography shops in Copenhagen.

Brightly colored crotch shots of women's genitals were a common sight in the arcades and store windows all over downtown Copenhagen. The pornography stores were situated in the fancy parts of town, giving them an air of complete acceptability. Real women's intimate body parts had been reduced to commodities and merchandized like all the other goods in

1

the surrounding shops. Hundreds of vaginas of every shape and hue were available for free visual rapes by male passersby.

Inside the stores, the men managers insisted that their businesses were no different from others. Typically they arranged their wares in special interest categories such as large-breasted women, oral and anal sex, women having sex together, bondage and torture, rape, bestiality (I particularly remember the pictures of women sexually engaged with pigs), and "baby love," with pictures of young girls being sexually abused by adult men. I noticed that all the books of photographs on so-called baby love involved girls of color (from India, I believe). Perhaps Danish girls had not yet been sufficiently demeaned for Danes to feel comfortable about seeing their own white children sexually abused in public. But Indian girls—what did they matter? Racism can flourish in places where few people of color reside, as well as where many do.

Could this transformation of Copenhagen really have happened because one scholar did a study that purported to prove that the easy availability of pornography for men to view and masturbate to would serve to lower the rape rate? Or did a majority of Danish males want greater access to pornography, so they used Kutchinsky's study to provide a scientific rationale to legitimize their desires? Whatever the explanation, subsequent reanalysis of Kutchinsky's data by several scholars has shown that the statistics he reported actually revealed an *increase* in the incidence of rape (see for example, Bachy, 1976; Check & Malamuth, 1986; Cline, 1974; Court, 1977). The overall statistics on sex crimes appeared to have decreased only because lesser crimes such as exhibitionism, voyeurism, and homosexual prostitution were no longer recorded by the police. Hence the illusory decline in sex crimes was actually due to a change in police recording practices, not the lifting of restrictions on pornography (Harmon & Check, 1989, pp. 36–37). But the myth lingers in the minds of many people that the Danish experience proved that viewing pornography is cathartic— a safety valve that helps to prevent rape and other forms of sexual assault.

WHAT IS PORNOGRAPHY?

Feminists of the anti-pornography-equals-censorship school deliberately obfuscate any distinction between erotica and pornography, using the term erotica for all sexually explicit materials.[2] In contrast, anti-pornography feminists consider it vitally important to distinguish between pornography and erotica.

(I define *pornography* as *material that combines sex and/or the exposure of genitals with abuse or degradation in a manner that appears to endorse, condone, or encourage such behavior.* Although women's bodies are the staple of adult pornography, it is important to have a gender neutral definition that encompasses gay pornography, as well as child pornography that portrays children of both sexes. Animals are also targets of pornographic depictions.

Most of the chapters in this book will focus on *male heterosexual pornography,* which I define as *material created for heterosexual males that combines sex and/or the exposure of genitals with the abuse or degradation of females in a manner that appears to endorse, condone, or encourage such behavior.*

Erotica refers to *sexually suggestive or arousing material that is free of sexism, racism, and homophobia, and respectful of all human beings and animals portrayed.* This definition takes into account that humans are not the only subject matter of erotica. For example, I remember seeing a short award-winning erotic movie on the peeling of an orange. The shapes and coloring of flowers or hills can render them erotic. Many people find Georgia O'Keefe's paintings erotic. But erotica can also include overtly or explicitly sexual material.

The requirement of nonsexism means that the following types of material qualify as pornography rather than erotica: sexually arousing images in which women are consistently shown naked while men are clothed or in which women's genitals are displayed but not men's; or in which men are always portrayed in the initiating, dominant role. An example of sexualized racism that pervades pornography entails depictions of women that are confined to young, white bodies that fit many white men's narrow concept of beauty, that is, very thin, large breasted, blonde women.

Canadian psychologists Charlene Senn and Lorraine Radtke found the distinction between pornography and erotica to be significant and meaningful to the women subjects in their experiment (see Chapter 17 for a more detailed description of this research). Their research demonstrates that a conceptual distinction between pornography and erotica is both significant and operational.

The term *abusive* sexual behavior in my definition refers to sexual conduct that ranges from derogatory, demeaning, contemptuous, or damaging to brutal, cruel, exploitative, painful, or violent. *Degrading* sexual behavior refers to sexual conduct that is humiliating, insulting, disrespectful, for example, urinating or defecating on a woman, ejaculating in her face, treating her as sexually dirty or inferior, depicting her as slavishly taking orders from men and eager to engage in whatever sex acts a man wants, calling her insulting names while engaging in sex, such as bitch, cunt, nigger, whore.

Note all the abuse and degradation in the portrayal of female sexuality in Longino's description of typical pornographic books, magazines, and films:

> Women are represented as passive and as slavishly dependent upon men. The role of female characters is limited to the provision of sexual services to men. To the extent that women's sexual pleasure is represented at all, it is subordinated to that of men and is never an end in itself as is the sexual pleasure of men. What pleases women is the use of their bodies to satisfy male desires. While the sexual objectification of women is common to all pornography, women are the recipients of even worse treatment in violent pornography, in which women characters are killed, tortured, gang-raped, mutilated, bound, and otherwise abused, as a means of providing sexual stimulation or pleasure to the male characters. (Longino, 1980, p. 42)

What is objectionable about pornography, then, is its abusive and degrading portrayal of females and female sexuality, *not* its sexual content or explicitness.

A particularly important feature of my definition of pornography is the requirement that *it appears to endorse, condone, or encourage abusive sexual desires or behaviors.* These attributes differentiate pornography and materials that include abusive or degrading sexual behavior for educative purposes. For example, movies such as "The Accused," and "The Rape of Love," present realistic representations of rape with the apparent intention of helping viewers to understand the reprehensible nature of rape, and the agony experienced by rape victims.

I have used the expression "it appears to" instead of "it is intended to" endorse, condone, or encourage sexually abusive desires or behavior to avoid the difficult if not impossible task of establishing the intentions of producers before being able to decide whether or not material is pornographic. If some/many of the viewers of a movie, book, or pictures subsequently experience desires to degrade or abuse women, or behave in degrading or abusive ways toward women, it seems reasonable to infer that the movie, book, or pictures *did* endorse, condone, or encourage such desires or behavior, and that we are therefore dealing with pornography (Brannon, personal communication, March 11, 1992).

My definition differs from most definitions, which focus instead on terms like "obscenity" and "sexually explicit materials." It also differs from the one I have used heretofore, which limited pornography to sexually explicit materials (Russell, 1988). I decided to avoid the concept "sexually explicit" because I could not define it to my satisfaction. In addition, I chose to embrace a long-standing feminist tradition of including in the notion of pornography all types of materials that combine sex with the abuse or degradation of women. For example, members of WAVPM

(Women Against Violence in Pornography and Media—the now defunct San Francisco-based feminist anti-pornography organization) used to refer to record covers, jokes, ads, and billboards as pornography when they were sexually degrading to women, even when nudity or displays of women's genitals were not portrayed (Lederer, 1980).

Some people may object that feminist definitions of pornography that go beyond sexually explicit materials differ so substantially from common usage that they make discussion between feminists and nonfeminists confusing. First of all, there is no consensus on definitions among nonfeminists or feminists. For example, some feminists *do* include the concept of sexual explicitness as a defining feature of pornography. Andrea Dworkin and Catharine MacKinnon define pornography as "the graphic sexually explicit subordination of women through pictures and/or words" (1988, p. 36). They go on to spell out nine ways in which this overall definition can be met, for example, "(i) women are presented dehumanized as sexual objects, things, or commodities." James Check (1985) uses the term sexually explicit materials instead of pornography, presumably in the hope of bypassing the many controversies associated with the term pornography. But these scholars have not, to my knowledge, defined what they mean by sexually explicit materials.

Sometimes there can be a good reason for feminists to employ the same definition as nonfeminists. For example, in my study of the prevalence of rape, I used a very narrow, legal definition of rape because I wanted to be able to compare the rape rates obtained in my study with those obtained in government studies. Had I used a more reasonable definition that included oral and anal penetration, for example, my study could not have been used to show how grossly flawed the methodology of the government's national surveys are in determining meaningful rape rates.

But if there is no compelling reason to use the same definition as that used by those with whom one disagrees, then it makes sense to define a phenomenon in a way that best fits feminist principles. As my objection to pornography is not that it shows nudity or different methods of sexual engagement, I see no reason to limit my definition to sexually explicit material. However if, like MacKinnon and Dworkin, my goal was to formulate a definition that would be the basis for developing a new law on pornography, then my choice might have been different. But I am not a lawyer, and I do not wish to make the requirements of law the basis for my definition. This is not to say that my definition would necessarily be unsatisfactory as a basis for developing a law on pornography. I leave this for others more familiar with the requirements of generating useful legal definitions to decide.

My definition of pornography does not include all the features that commonly characterize such material. For example, pornography frequently depicts females, particularly female sexuality, inaccurately. "Pornography Tells Lies About Women" declared a bold red and black sticker designed by WAVPM to deface pornography. These distortions often have serious consequences. Some viewers act on the assumption that the depictions are accurate, and presume that there is something wrong with females who do not behave like females in pornography. This can result in verbal abuse or physical abuse, including rape, by males who consider they are entitled to the sexual goodies that they want or that they believe is their right to have. It has been shown that pornography consumers are more likely to believe that unusual sexual practices are more common than they really are (Zillmann, 1989).

Sexual objectification is another common characteristic of pornography. It refers to *the portrayal of human beings — usually women — as depersonalized sexual things such as "tits, cunt, and ass," not as multi-faceted human beings deserving equal rights with men.* As Susan Brownmiller so eloquently noted, in pornography "our bodies are being stripped, exposed and contorted for the purpose of ridicule to bolster that 'masculine esteem' which gets its kick and sense of power from viewing females as anonymous, panting playthings, adult toys, dehumanized objects to be used, abused, broken and discarded" (1975, p. 394).

The sexual objectification of females is not confined to pornography. It is also a staple of mainstream movies, ads, record covers, songs, magazines, television, art, cartoons, literature, pin-ups, and so on, as well as being a way of conceptualizing how many men learn to see women and sometimes children.

Inconsistencies in Definitions of Pornography

Many people have talked or written about the difficulty of defining pornography and erotica, declaring that, "One person's erotica is another person's pornography." This statement is often used to ridicule an anti-pornography stance. The implication is that if there is no consensus on a definition of pornography, its effects cannot be examined.

Yet there is no consensus on the definitions of many phenomena. Rape, for example. Legal definitions vary considerably in different states. The police often have their own definitions, which may differ from legal definitions. For example, if a woman is raped by someone she knows, the police often "unfound"[3] the case because they are skeptical about most acquaintance and date rapes. This skepticism does not come from the law — except sometimes in cases of marital rape.

If rape is defined as forced intercourse or attempts at forced intercourse, the problem of figuring out what exactly constitutes force remains. How does one measure it? What is the definition of intercourse? Does it include oral and anal intercourse, intercourse with a foreign object, digital intercourse, or is it limited to vaginal penetration by the penis? How much penetration is necessary to qualify as intercourse? How does one determine if an attempt at rape versus some lesser sexual assault has occurred? How does one deal with the fact that the rapist and the victim often do not believe that a rape occurred, even when the definition of rape was met? For example, many rapists do not consider that forcing intercourse on an unwilling woman qualifies as rape because they think the woman's "no" means "yes." Many victims think they have not been raped when the perpetrator is their husband or lover, even though the law in most states considers such acts rape. Fortunately, few people argue that because rape is so difficult to define and there is no consensus on the best definition of it, it should therefore not be considered a heinous act, as well as an illegal one.

Similarly, millions of court cases have revolved around arguments as to whether a killing constitutes murder or manslaughter.[4] Just because it takes a court case to decide this question, no one argues that killing should therefore not be subject to legal sanctions.

In contrast, the often-quoted statement of one judge that although he could not necessarily define pornography, he could recognize it when he saw it, is frequently cited to support the view that pornography is entirely in the eye of the beholder. Many people have argued that because there is no consensus on how to define pornography and/or because it can be difficult to determine whether or not the pornographic label is appropriate in particular cases, pornography should therefore not be subject to legal restraints, or even opprobrium.

It is interesting to note that lack of consensus did not prove to be an obstacle in making pictorial child pornography illegal. This makes it clear that the difficulty of defining pornography is yet one more strategy the pro-pornographers and their apologists employ in their efforts to derail those who oppose the harms of pornography, and to make their work appear futile.

FEMINISTS ORGANIZE AGAINST PORNOGRAPHY
IN THE UNITED STATES

In 1976 I was one of the founders of the San Francisco-based Women Against Violence in Pornography and Media—WAVPM. It was the first feminist anti-pornography action group in this country, and played a key role in developing a feminist analysis critical of pornography, and in mobilizing the women's liberation movement to include this issue on its agenda.[5]

Almost from the start of our organization, we criticized the sexist research on pornography available at that time, most of which claimed that pornography was harmless (*Technical Report of the Commission on Obscenity and Pornography*, 1970). We pointed out the misogyny and the increasing portrayal of violence against women in pornography, and we challenged some of the illogical arguments used to defend it as innocuous. For example, we argued that just as advertising succeeds in selling products, pornography sells sexism and violence against women.

Our anti-pornography theory and actions challenged the mostly male researchers to investigate the effects of pornography in a less biased fashion (for example, see Lederer, 1980). Psychologists Neil Malamuth and Edward Donnerstein are among the best known of the researchers who responded to this challenge in the 1970s. Together with their colleagues such as James Check and John Briere, these men conducted experiments that started to confirm some of our major assertions about the relationship between pornography and violence against women (for example, see Malamuth & Check, 1985 a & b, as well as Part III of this volume).

A few feminist researchers also entered the field. We started to have an impact, chiefly as critics of the work of the preponderantly male researchers — even the most well-intentioned of whom found it difficult to root out their sexism (see Lederer, 1980). More significantly, Susan Brownmiller was so inspired by WAVPM's 1978 national conference for feminists' organizing against pornography, that she, together with others, founded the New York-based Women Against Pornography (WAP). While WAVPM died several years ago, WAP became one of the major feminist anti-pornography organizations in the United States.

In the 1980s, however, it became apparent that some feminists did not agree with our view that pornography eroticizes sexism and violence against women. These feminist skeptics included a few academics, socialist feminists, feminists who supported sadomasochism for lesbians, among others (see, for example, SAMOIS Collective, 1981; Sexuality Issue Collective, 1981; Snitow, Stansell, & Thompson, 1983; Vance, 1984), and later, a group of women who signed what is known as the Feminist Anti-Censorship Task Force (FACT) brief — a statement attacking anti-pornography feminists as censors (Hunter & Law, 1987–1988).

The disagreement within the feminist movement became particularly intense in response to the successful campaigns initiated by Catharine MacKinnon and Andrea Dworkin to recast pornography as a civil rights issue (see Chapter 9). The Civil Rights Ordinance they drafted for Minneapolis in 1983 to enable victims of pornography to sue pornographers for damages was greeted by cries of "Censorship!" This has become the knee-jerk response to almost any action undertaken by anti-pornography feminists (for example, Burstyn, 1985). The reasoning of the anti-porn-equals-censorship school seems to go as follows: Censorship is bad; believing that pornography is harmful to women means being pro-censorship; therefore pornography is not harmful. This reasoning is fallacious on several grounds; most feminists who believe pornography is harmful, are not pro-censorship. But even if we were, the pros and cons of censorship are a completely separate issue from whether or not pornography is harmful. More important, trying to stop harm is not what censorship means. (See Chapter 9 for further information about the anti-anti-pornography feminists.)

FALLOUT FROM THE ATTORNEY GENERAL'S COMMISSION ON PORNOGRAPHY

The situation for anti-pornography feminists worsened after the Final Report of the Attorney General's Commission on Pornography was published in June 1986. Because the Commissioners had concluded that pornography causes violence against women, and because they advocated increasing restrictions on pornography by tightening up the obscenity laws in various ways, many liberals and radicals—including the majority of men in the publishing industry—became fearful that the government would take on the role of censor and that they would lose their right to publish and to acquire pornography. These fears caused them to ridicule the very notion that pornography could be harmful.

For example, a group called the Media Coalition, which includes the American Booksellers Association, the Association of American Publishers, the Council of Periodical Distributors, the International Periodical Distributors Association, and the National Coalition of College Stores, launched an ambitious propaganda campaign to protect sexually explicit "speech" by trying to discredit the idea that pornography causes rape and other violence against women. The Media Coalition hired a Washington, DC-based public relations firm, Gray and Company, to develop a strategy to manipulate the public to reject the evidence and to repudiate the Commission's conclusion that pornography causes harm to women.

Steve Johnson, a representative of Gray and Company, advised the Media Coalition that "a successful effort to relieve publishers, distributors and retailers from harassment will involve communicating several broad themes with which most Americans agree." One of these "themes" was as follows: *There is no factual or scientific basis for the exaggerated and unfounded allegations that sexually oriented content in contemporary me-*

dia is in any way a cause of violent or criminal behavior" (emphasis added).[6]

Steve Johnson's statement is flawed on several counts. First, he is inaccurate about the sentiments of the American people. A Gallup poll conducted July 11–14, 1986, found that nearly 75% of those surveyed supported "an outright ban on the portrayal of sexual violence in magazines, movies, and videocassettes" (Gallup, 1986, p. 6). Second, there is now well-documented evidence that pornography causes harm to women, including experimental and survey data, the application of the laws of learning, testimonies by pornography models and other survivors of pornographic abuse, and testimonies of sexual offenders and men who have worked in the pornography industry. This volume will provide examples of these different kinds of evidence for the violence-promoting effects of pornography.

However, with more than twice the budget of the entire Pornography Commission at its disposal for the first year of its campaign alone, the Media Coalition appears to have successfully bought much of the public opinion that has been permitted expression in the mass media of this nation. Under an anti-censorship banner, dissenting opinions and evidence of the harm caused by pornography have simply been suppressed, a practice that continues to this day.

Dworkin and MacKinnon cite several examples of this censorship. For instance: "A *New York Times* reporter was told by a chief editor that *The New York Times* would no longer carry news stories about the feminist political opposition to pornography" (Dworkin & MacKinnon, 1988, Part II, ch. 1, p. 78). This also became the policy of the local newspaper in Bellingham, Washington, when three of us landed in jail for tearing up pornography as a protest (see Chapter 22 for a detailed account of this action).

Dworkin and MacKinnon point out the hypocrisy of people who censor us in the name of anti-censorship: "The same people who say the pornographers must be protected because everything must be published and protected are the first to say that feminist work opposing pornography must not be published in order to protect free speech" (1988, p. 79). Elsewhere, they state this contradiction more succinctly: "Shut up to protect free speech"(p. 79). As already mentioned, *Making Violence Sexy*, started in 1985, has been a victim of this kind of censorship.

Third, the notion that pornography is harmless overlooks the fact that in many instances the actual *making* of pornography involves or even requires violence and sexual assault. This issue will be discussed in more detail in the next section.

Despite the overwhelming evidence for the causal link between pornography and sexual violence, the feminist critique of pornography as woman-hating propaganda that promotes sexism and violence against women is being silenced by respectable fronts for the pornographers and their customers, that is, the publication industry, the mass media, and their supporters in academia and the legal profession. It is ironic that most of these people do not dispute the fact that racist propaganda promotes racism and violence against people of color, that anti-Semitic propaganda promotes anti-Semitism and violence against Jews, and that homophobic propaganda promotes homophobia and violence against lesbians and gay men.

In addition, those who defend pornography in the name of sexual liberation and/or freedom of speech often strenuously oppose racist and anti-Semitic literature and movies (unless they appear in pornography). Their ostensible concern about freedom of speech seems to evaporate in such cases. Indeed, there would be a public outcry — and rightly so — if there were special nonpornographic movie houses where viewers could see whites beating up people of color, or Christians beating up Jews, and where the victims were portrayed as enjoying or deserving such treatment. But if it's called pornography and women are the victims, then it is considered sex and those who object that it is harmful to women are regarded as prudes.

It is true that pornography often does not involve explicit physical violence against women, but that does not mean that it is necessarily nonabusive. There are vehement protests when Jews are portrayed as avaricious, shrewd, and cliquey, and African-Americans as stupid, lazy, and oversexed. But when women are depicted as willing recipients of all the multiplicity of acts that male pornography consumers like to see done to their bodies, many people claim this to be cathartic, a safety valve against sex crimes, or at least harmless.

Such blatant inconsistencies are examples of faulty patriarchal logic (yet men claim that women are the illogical sex!). For if it is detrimental for Jews and African-American men and women to be depicted in stereotypic ways, as I believe it is, then it must also be detrimental when women of color and white women are depicted in stereotypic ways *as women*. If racist and anti-Semitic movies are believed to inculcate or intensify anti-Semitism and racism, then it must be granted that movies that portray sexist stereotypes also inculcate or intensify sexism.

While issues of censorship and the First Amendment are almost always raised when feminists protest against pornography, this is rarely the case when people of color protest against bigoted portrayals and verbal insults directed at them. This inconsistency is due, at least in part, to the fact that many people are using these concerns as a political ploy to confuse and intimidate anti-pornography feminists. As Andrea Dworkin and Catharine MacKinnon have so aptly observed: "The pornographers have convinced many that *their* freedom is *everyone's* freedom" (Allen, 1985, p. 1, emphasis added).

ABUSE OF WOMEN IN THE MAKING OF PORNOGRAPHY

Catharine MacKinnon points out the frequently forgotten fact (quoted in the epigraph at the beginning of this chapter) that "before pornography became the pornographer's speech it was somebody's life" (1987, p. 179). Many people, including some of the best researchers on pornography in the United States (for example, see Malamuth & Donnerstein, 1984), ignore the abuse and/or violence some pornographers use to manufacture these misogynist materials. Testimony by women and men involved in such activity provides numerous examples of this (see Part I of this volume for testimony by women who were subjected to violent sexual abuse when photographed, videotaped, or filmed to make pornography. Also see Attorney General's Commission on Pornography, 1986).

In one case, a man who said he had participated in over a hundred pornographic movies testified at the Commission hearings in Los Angeles as follows: "I, myself, have been on a couple of sets where the young ladies have been forced to do even anal sex scenes with a guy which [sic] is rather large and I have seen them crying in pain" (1986, p. 773).

Another witness testified at the Los Angeles hearings as follows:

> Women and young girls were tortured and suffered permanent physical injuries to answer publisher demands for photographs depicting sadomasochistic abuse. When the torturer/photographer inquired of the publisher as to the types of depictions that would sell, the torturer/photographer was instructed to get similar existing publications and use the depiction therein for instruction. The torturer/photographer followed the publisher's instructions, tortured women and girls accordingly, and then sold the photographs to the publisher. The photographs were included in magazines sold nationally in pornographic outlets (1986, pp. 787–788).

Peter Bogdanovich writes of *Playboy* "Playmate of the Year" Dorothy Stratten's response to her participation in a pornographic movie: "A key sequence in *Galaxina* called for Dorothy to be spread-eagled against a cold water tower. The producers insisted she remain bound there for several hours, day and night. In one shot of the completed film, the tears she cries are real" (1984, p. 59). Although this movie was not made for the so-called adult movie houses, I consider it pornography because of its sexist and degrading combination of sexuality and bondage.

A letter sent to the United States Attorney General's Commission on Pornography provides a final example of abuse in the making of pornography: "A mother and father in South Oklahoma City forced their four daughters, ages ten to seventeen, to engage in family sex while pornographic pictures were being filmed" (1986, p. 780).

It should not be assumed that violence occurs only in the making of *violent* pornography. For example, although many people would classify the movie *Deep Throat* as nonviolent pornography because it does not portray rape or other violence, we now know from Linda (Lovelace) Marchiano's two books (*Ordeal*, 1980, and *Out of Bondage*, 1986), as well as from her public testimony (for example, *Public Hearings*, 1983), that this film is in fact a documentary of rape from beginning to end (also see Chapter 2).

Although rape is illegal, the showing and distribution of actual rapes on film is protected as free speech. As Dworkin and MacKinnon (1988, p. 60) so aptly question: "If lynchings were done *in order to* make photographs, on a ten-billion-dollar-a-year scale, would that make them protected speech?" And later they ask:

> What would it say about the seriousness with which society regards lynching if actual lynching is illegal but pictures of actual lynching are protected and highly profitable and defended as a form of freedom and a constitutional right? What would it say about the seriousness and effectiveness of laws against lynching if people paid good money to see it and the law looked the other way, so long as they saw it in mass-produced form? What would it say about one's status if the society permits one to be hung from trees and calls it entertainment — calls it what it is to those who enjoy it, rather than what it is to those to whom it is done? (1988, p. 61).

Although it is disturbing that so many people ignore the harm done to the women who are used in making pornography, this kind of harm should be distinguished from the harm that occurs to the consumers and their victims (Robert Brannon, personal communication, March 11 & April 28, 1992). Either kind of harm can occur, with or without the other. The rest of this chapter will focus on the latter kind of harm.

SEPARATING THE CONSEQUENCES OF PORNOGRAPHY FROM THE ISSUE OF CENSORSHIP

Assessing the consequences of pornography is one thing; deciding what to do about it — if anything — is another. Because an assessment of the consequences *does* reveal many extremely destructive effects, the logical next question becomes how it should best be dealt with.

A common argument is that pornography may have harmful consequences, but censoring it would have even worse effects because it would
undermine freedom of speech. Therefore, the proliferation of increasingly
extreme forms of pornography must be tolerated no matter how destructive
the effects are. The fallacy here is in assuming that censorship is the only
way to try to combat pornography. There are many ways to do this that do
not involve censorship, for example, writing letters, editorials, and articles
in newspapers, magazines or books; education about the detrimental
effects of pornography; speak-outs by pornography survivors; demonstrations, marches, confrontations with pornographers and their defend-
ers; graffiti protests of pornographic ads, window displays, porn stores,
and so forth; sabotage against the property of pornographers and their
commercial outlets; tearing up pornography and other acts of civil disobedience.

It is also fallacious to think that all legal actions constitute censorship.
For example, restricting pornography in ways that are consistent with the
First Amendment is not censorship, even if it is done by government action
(C. MacKinnon, personal communication, January 1990).

The final section of this volume includes a section on feminist actions
against pornography, none of which can be considered pro-censorship.

PORNOGRAPHY'S NEW FACES

Videos have revolutionized the availability of pornography in the past
15 years. As increasing numbers of Americans have purchased videocassette recorders, the market for so-called adult videos has grown enormous-
ly. No longer do men have to find their way to the sleazy parts of town to
masturbate to pornographic movies in theater seats or porn booths, nervous that someone from the office or neighborhood might see them. They
can now watch videos in the privacy of their homes. And they have a much
better chance of getting their dates, partners, or wives to watch the videos
with them, as women have typically been even more reluctant than men to
enter porn stores and theaters. Indeed, according to a survey conducted by
Adult Video News, 15% of so-called adult tapes were rented by women in
1989 (45% by couples, both gay and straight, and 40% by men alone;
Palac, 1991, p. 13).

Another survey administered by a trade publication called *Video
Store*, found that "69 percent of general interest video outlets carry sex
tapes" (Palac, 1991, p. 13). And *Adult Video News* reported that "sales and
rentals of adult tapes in general interest video stores alone totaled over
$992 million in 1989. These figures do not include tapes purchased by mail

order or in an adult-only store" (Palac, 1991, p. 31). Pornographer Lisa Palac's statement that "the video revolution of the early 1980s turned video porn into a mainstream entertainment product" is no exaggeration (1991, p. 13).

In sociologist Lillian Rubin's study of approximately one thousand U.S. citizens, she reports that pornography "has increasingly found its way into the lives of the respectable" since the advent of the videocassette recorder (1990, p. 126). Almost two-thirds of the 600 people who returned her questionnaires and over half of the 375 people she interviewed, said that "they sometimes used pornographic films as a sexual stimulant when they were in a relationship, even if it was only a brief one" (1990, p. 126). And, "the younger the age group, the more likely this [use of pornographic videos] was to be seen as an erotic option."

Another tribute to the mainstreaming of pornography in contemporary U.S. is Rubin's finding that about 25% of her sample "said they had experimented with some form of bondage," particularly those under 35 years of age (1990, p. 128).

The fact that pornographic videos can be purchased in the same outlets as the nonpornographic fare also enhances their marketability. Some reports maintain that many women have now added the renting of pornographic videos to their shopping lists. However, Rubin points out that "More often than not, the idea to watch an X-rated film comes from the man" (1990, p. 126). Indeed, "Women far more often than men called the films boring and unimaginative," and many of them were offended by the way women in them are exploited (1990, pp. 126–127).

As an increasing number of Americans also own, or have access to, video cameras, more men are making their own pornographic home movies. It would be interesting to know in what percentage of cases women initiate the making of such videos and decide on the content. Of these women, it would also be relevant to find out, if it were possible, what proportion desire such videos for themselves, in contrast to trying to please their male partners. Because few women show any interest in the so-called adult entertainment industry, it seems likely that most home videos are made by men for their sexual satisfaction. There are, of course, many notorious cases of such home videos being filmed by femicidal murderers, such as Leonard Lake and Charles Ng. Who knows how many of the everyday amateurs are also trying or succeeding in marketing this new cottage industry.

Computer pornography has been around since the early 1980s, at a cost of about $15 to $20 a software package (Erlich, 1989, p. 7). "One Los Angeles firm reportedly offered computer porn as a free bonus with bulk purchases of other software" (Erlich, 1989, p. 7). MacPlaymat has been by far the most popular pornographic computer game for some time, selling for about $50. This is how Reese Erlich describes it: "An animated, anatomically correct woman comes on the screen and says, 'Hello, I'm Maxie, your date from MacPlaymat. Would you like to take off my clothes? I'll guide you. Start with my blouse.'" Sex toys can be plunged into Maxie's vagina, she can be handcuffed, gagged, and shackled at her spike heel-shod ankles, made to perform sex with another woman, and made to make noises to indicate sexual pleasure. There is also a panic button that can make Maxie disappear and a spreadsheet appear in her place, so that the boss, the wife, a female colleague, or any other likely source of disapproval can be kept in ignorance about it.

One woman who spoke out against MacPlaymat asked if employers would look differently at the "game," "if 'Maxie' were a Jew and the 'tool-box' were used to torture Jews in a concentration camp" (Erlich, 1989, p. 8). She observed that Germany has banned the sale of all neo-Nazi computer software.

Phone pornography is also a relatively new invention, although it is no longer as flourishing or as lucrative as it was a few years ago. Some controversial cases have forced Pacific Bell to give up its formerly laissez-faire policy toward it. For example, in a landmark 1987 court case, a family sued Pacific Bell for $10 million because their 12-year-old son had persuaded a 4-year-old girl to orally copulate him shortly after listening to $150 worth of dial-a-porn messages (Viets, 1987, p. A23). "My daughter was raped by Pacific Bell and Tele-promo" (a phone porn business in Mill Valley, California), declared the father of the young victim (Sandalow, 1987, p. A11).

Attorneys for the children's parents argued that Pacific Bell and the dial-a-porn company should be compelled to stop allowing children access to the sexually explicit phone messages, and should be financially liable for the rape. At that time, Pacific Bell was earning about $24 million in annual revenue from their dial-a-porn messages (Viets, 1987). Regrettably, the trial court dismissed the case in 1988, and the court of Appeals also ruled in 1989 that Pacific Bell was not liable in this case (Brian T. v. Pacific Bell, 1989, p. 707). Nevertheless, a federal law was passed in 1989 that required telephone companies "to block access to sex-message services unless a customer asked in writing to receive them" ("Dial-a-porn restrictions," 1992). This law was challenged by four companies in federal court in New York City, and not enforced pending the outcome of the Supreme Court's ruling on the appeal. In 1992, the Supreme Court left the law intact by declining to consider the challenge. According to one newspaper account, this decision "threatens to all but destroy the 'dial-a-porn' business" that had grown to a $2 billion-a-year industry ("Dial-a-porn restrictions," 1992).

WHY FOCUS ON PORNOGRAPHY?

People frequently ask why I focus on pornography rather than on the eroticized violence in mainstream media. Well-known pornographer researcher Edward Donnerstein said in a recent televised interview that researchers "must look at all the media," not just at pornography, as similar messages are communicated by all of them (1990). This position is comparable to rape researchers being challenged for focusing on rape rather than studying all forms of sexual assault. Researchers on mainstream media are not similarly criticized for failing to include pornography.

I would not be concerned about pornography if I thought that it played an insignificant role in the occurrence of rape and sexual assault, and if it did not promote sexism. This is true of other feminists opposed to pornography, differentiating us from the conservatives who see sex and nudity as sinful, dirty, and immoral.

I choose to focus on pornography rather than on mainstream media for several reasons. Since I became engaged with this issue in 1974, I have observed that many women find it too threatening and ugly to willingly acquaint themselves with the contents of pornography. (In contrast, many women — particularly teenagers — have voluntarily viewed woman-slashing movies.) Heterosexual women in particular find that knowing the contents and understanding the meaning of pornography often alienates them from men because of the blatant women-hatred that pervades it. Combatting pornography requires that women must stop avoiding looking at it and instead must face the women-hatred it both expresses and fosters.

For these and other reasons, research on pornography has long been monopolized by men whose studies have often suffered from a sexist bias. For example, several male researchers have blithely claimed that women's responses to pornography are the same as men's, even though tests of attitudes as well as studies of pornography consumers (who are overwhelmingly male) show that most women dislike pornography — *regardless* of their physiological response to it (see Senn, Chapter 17). Women are more often turned on by the romantic stories in women's magazines and books than they are by sexually explicit material.

Another reason I choose to focus on pornography is that much of it is designed as a masturbation tool for men (in classy pornography joints, tissues are provided to wipe up their customers' ejaculations). Because the pleasure of ejaculation becomes associated with degrading depictions of women, the sexual pleasure serves as a particularly powerful reinforcer for the masturbator, who learns to be turned on by the degradation itself. Because men's viewing of pornography frequently culminates in orgasm, the lessons of pornography are learned much faster and more tenaciously than when they view nonpornographic media. They also develop a strong stake in keeping it at their disposal. This explains the viciousness of men's fight against feminists to protect pornography. For example, pictures of well-known feminist anti-pornography activists like Gloria Steinem, Andrea Dworkin, Susan Brownmiller, and Dorchen Leidholdt have appeared in pornographic magazines under a "Most Wanted" headline parodying the FBI's most wanted list of criminals.

PROSTITUTION AND PORNOGRAPHY

One extraordinary inconsistency in United States culture is that prostitution is illegal in all states except Nevada, yet pornography that involves women selling their sexual services in front of a camera is defended as a legally protected expression of free speech. Does it really make sense that an act of prostitution in front of a camera is more acceptable than the same act performed in private? How does the use of a camera turn the act of prostitution into art or speech? These women are not simulating sex. They are literally being fucked, tied up, spread-eagled, having ejaculate sprayed over their faces and bodies, having anal, oral, and vaginal sex with three different men at the same time, being urinated on, and so on. No one knows what percentage of them are also being beaten up, tortured, raped, or even killed, before, during, or after the photographic or filming sessions.

In order to justify this doublethink, one has to ignore the fact that a real woman is being photographed and focus on the photographic image. A similar process of victim obliteration occurs when people debate whether or not pornography is harmful and ignore the sexual abuse sometimes clearly evident in the pornographic photographs.

The terms pornography "model," "porn actress," or "star" are typically used to differentiate these photographed or filmed women from other prostitutes despite the fact that they, like all prostitutes, are paid for the exploitation of their bodies. To break through these euphemistic descriptions of what these women do to earn their living, it would help to refer to them as prostitutes rather than as pornography models, actresses, or the now fashionable term sex-workers.

To my mind, because this abuse is photographed for public consumption, and because the women being photographed invariably have no control over what happens to the pictures, movies, or videos for the rest of their lives, the harm suffered by prostitutes who are used to make pornography is often significantly more severe than it is for prostitutes who do not participate in pornography.

MAKING VIOLENCE SEXY

Although titled *Making Violence Sexy*, this volume will examine nonviolent as well as violent pornography. Many people make a strong distinction between violent and nonviolent pornography, maintaining that only violent pornography is harmful. This includes researchers Neil Malamuth, Edward Donnerstein, and Daniel Linz, who stress that the research to date shows negative effects only for violent pornography (see their testimonies to the Attorney General's Commission on Pornography, 1986). This conclusion indicates that they discount the sound research of some of their colleagues. Experiments by James Check and Ted Guloien (1989), Dolf Zillmann and Jennings Bryant (1984, 1989), for example, show harmful effects from viewing nonviolent as well as violent pornography. Indeed, Check and Guloien actually found more harmful effects from abusive but nonviolent pornography than from violent pornography. Zillmann has shown that an appetite for stronger material is fostered by viewing milder fare: "Consumers graduate from common to less common forms of pornography," that is, to more violent and degrading materials (1985, p. 127).

THE ORGANIZATION OF *MAKING VIOLENCE SEXY*

It is vitally important that discussions of pornography are informed by knowledge and understanding of the experiences of victims and survivors of this industry. Hence, Part I is devoted to several first-person accounts of such experiences. Although the term *survivor* will often be used in this context, there is no way of knowing whether all these women are still alive.

Part II provides an overview of a number of major issues, including Andrea Dworkin and Catharine MacKinnon's thoughtful answers to a number of common questions people frequently raise about pornography. Other contributions focus on the meaning and significance of pornography for African-American women, an African-American man, gay men, and a personal account by a straight man.

Part III is devoted to feminist research on pornography. Part IV provides examples of different kinds of actions that anti-pornography feminists have initiated, particularly a series of actions that took place in Bellingham, Washington, in 1990 and 1991.

Part I

SURVIVORS OF PORNOGRAPHY

"WHAT'S YOUR *PLEASURE*, MISS? WOMEN *DISMEMBERED*? WOMEN *SKINNED ALIVE*? OR WOMEN *RAPED* AND *SLAUGHTERED* AT *RANDOM*?!"

Credit: Reprinted with special permission of North American Syndicate.

CHAPTER 2

The Real Linda Lovelace

Gloria Steinem

Remember *Deep Throat*? It was the porn movie that made porn movies chic; the first stag film to reach beyond the bounds of X-rated theaters and into much bigger audiences. Though it was created in 1972 as a cheap feature that took only forty thousand dollars and a few days to make, it ended the decade with an estimated gross income of six hundred million dollars from paying customers for the film itself plus its subindustry of sequels, cassettes, T-shirts, bumper stickers, and sexual aids. In fact, so much of the media rewarded it with amusement or approval that *Deep Throat* entered our language and our consciousness, whether we ever saw the film or not. From the serious Watergate journalists of the Washington *Post* who immortalized "Deep Throat" by bestowing that title on their top-secret news source, to the sleazy pornocrats of *Screw* magazine — a range that may be, on a scale of male supremacy, the distance from *A* to *B* — strange media bedfellows turned this cheap feature into a universal dirty joke and an international profit center.

At the heart of this dirty joke was Linda Lovelace (née Linda Boreman) whose innocent face and unjaded manner was credited with much of the film's success. She offered moviegoers the titillating thought that even the girl next door might love to be the object of porn-style sex.

Using Linda had been the idea of Gerry Damiano, the director-writer of *Deep Throat*. "The most amazing thing about Linda, the truly amazing thing," she remembers him saying enthusiastically to Lou Peraino, who bankrolled the movie, "is that she still looks sweet and innocent." Nonetheless, Peraino (who was later arrested by the FBI as a figure in alleged organized-crime activities in the illicit-film industry) complained that Linda wasn't the "blond with big boobs" that he had in mind for his first porn flick. He continued to complain, even after she had been ordered to service him sexually.

In fact, watching Linda perform in public as a prostitute had given Damiano the idea for *Deep Throat* in the first place. He had been at a party where men lined up to be the beneficiaries of the sexual sword-swallower trick Linda had been taught by her husband and keeper, Chuck Traynor. By relaxing her throat muscles, she learned to receive the full-length plunge of a penis without choking; a desperate survival technique for her, but a constant source of amusement and novelty for clients. Thus creatively inspired, Damiano had thought up a movie gimmick, one that was second only to Freud's complete elimination of the clitoris as a proper source of female pleasure and invention of the vaginal orgasm. Damiano decided to tell the story of a woman whose clitoris was in her throat and who was constantly eager for oral sex with men.

Though his physiological fiction about *one* woman was far less ambitious than Freud's fiction about *all* women, his porn movie had a whammo audiovisual impact; a teaching device that Freudian theory had lacked.

Literally millions of women seem to have been taken to *Deep Throat* by their boyfriends or husbands (not to mention prostitutes who were taken by their pimps) so that each one might learn what a woman could do to please a man *if she really wanted to*. This instructive value seems to have been a major reason for the movie's popularity and its reach beyond the usual male-only viewers.

Of course, if the female viewer were really a spoilsport, she might identify with the woman on screen and sense her humiliation, danger, and pain — but the smiling, happy face of Linda Lovelace could serve to cut off empathy, too. *She's there because she wants to be. Who's forcing her? See how she's smiling? See how a real woman enjoys this?*

Eight years later, Linda told us the humiliating and painful answer in *Ordeal*, her autobiography. She described years as a sexual prisoner during which she was tortured and restricted from all normal human contact.

Nonetheless, it's important to understand how difficult it would have been at the time (and probably still is, in the case of other victims) to know the truth.

At the height of *Deep Throat*'s popularity, for instance, Nora Ephron wrote an essay about going to see it. She was determined not to react like those "crazy feminists carrying on, criticizing nonpolitical films in political terms." Nonetheless, she sat terrified through a scene in which a hollow glass dildo is inserted in Linda Lovelace's vagina and then filled with Coca-Cola, which is drunk through a surgical straw. ("All I could think about," she confessed, "was what would happen if the glass broke.") Feeling humiliated and angry, but told by her male friends that she was "over-reacting," that the Coca-Cola scene was "hilarious," she used her license as a writer to get a telephone interview with Linda Lovelace. "I totally enjoyed myself making the movie," she was told by Linda. "I don't have any inhibitions about sex. I just hope that everybody who goes to see the film . . . loses some of their inhibitions."

So Nora wrote an article that assumed Linda to be a happy and willing porn queen who was enjoying " . . . $250 a week . . . and a piece of the profits." And she wrote off her own reaction as that of a "puritanical feminist who lost her sense of humor at a skin flick."

What she did not know (how could any interviewer know?) was that Linda would later list these and other answers as being dictated by Chuck Traynor for just such journalistic occasions; that he punished her for show-ing any unacceptable emotion (when, for instance, she cried while being gang-banged by five men in a motel room, thus causing one customer to refuse to pay); in fact, that she had been beaten and raped so severely and regularly that she suffered rectal damage plus permanent injury to the blood vessels in her legs.

What Nora did not know was that Linda would also write of her three escape attempts and three forcible returns to this life of sexual servitude: first by the betrayal of another prostitute; then by her own mother who was charmed by Chuck Traynor's protestations of remorse and innocence into telling him where her daughter was hiding; and finally by Linda's fears for the lives of two friends who had sheltered her after hearing that she had been made to do a sex film with a dog, and outside whose home Traynor had parked a van that contained, Linda believed, his collection of hand grenades and a machine gun.

Even now, these and other facts about Traynor must be read with the word "alleged" in front of them. Because of Linda's long period of fear and hiding after she escaped, the time limitations of the law, and the fact that Traynor forced her to marry him, legal charges are difficult to bring. Linda's book documents her account of more than two years of fear, sad-ism, and forced prostitution. Traynor has been quoted as calling these charges "so ridiculous I can't take them seriously." He has also been quoted as saying: "when I first dated her she was so shy, it shocked her to be seen nude by a man. . . . *I created Linda Lovelace.*"

Linda's account of being "created" includes guns put to her head, turning tricks while being watched through a peephole to make sure she couldn't escape, and having water forced up her rectum with a garden hose if she refused to offer such amusements as exposing herself in restau-rants or to passing drivers on the highway.

Ordeal is a very difficult book to read. It must have been far more difficult to write. But Linda says she wanted to purge forever the idea that she had become "Linda Lovelace" of her own free will.

Was profit a motive for this book? Certainly she badly needs money for herself, her three-year-old son, her imminently expected second baby, and her husband, a childhood friend named Larry Marchiano, whose work as a TV cable installer has been jeopardized by his co-workers' discovery of Linda's past. For a while, they were living partially on welfare. But Linda points out that she has refused offers of more than three million dollars to do another porn movie like *Deep Throat*. (For that filming, Linda was paid twelve hundred dollars; a sum that, like her fees for turning tricks as a prostitute, she says she never saw.)[1] "I wouldn't do any of that again," she says, "even if I could get fifty million dollars."

A different motive for writing *Ordeal* is clear from Linda's response to a postcard written by a young woman who had been coerced into prostitution, a woman who said she got the courage to escape after seeing Linda on television. "Women have to be given the courage to try to escape, and to know that you *can* get your self-respect back," she says. "It meant the whole world to me to get that postcard."

Ironically, her own hope of escape came with the surprising success of *Deep Throat*. She had become a valuable property. She had to be brought into contact with outsiders occasionally, with a world that she says had been denied to her, even in the form of radio or newspapers. Now, she says soberly, "I thank God today that they weren't making snuff movies back then. . . . "

She says she escaped by feigning trustworthiness for ten minutes, then a little longer each time, until, six months later, she was left unguarded during rehearsals for a stage version of *Linda Lovelace*. Even then, she spent weeks hiding out in hotels alone, convinced she might be beaten or killed for this fourth try at escape, but feeling stronger this time for having only her own life to worry about. It took a long period of hiding, with help and disguises supplied by a sympathetic secretary from Traynor's newly successful Linda Lovelace Enterprises (but no help from police, who said they could do nothing to protect her "until the man with the gun is in the room with you"), before the terror finally dwindled into a nagging fear. Traynor continued to issue calls and entreaties for her return. He filed a lawsuit against her for breach of contract. But he had also found another woman to star in his porn films — Marilyn Chambers, the model who appeared in a comparatively nonviolent porn movie called *Behind the Green Door*.

And then suddenly, she got word through a lawyer that Traynor was willing to sign divorce papers. The threats and entreaties to return just stopped.

Free of hiding and disguises at last, she tried to turn her created identity into real acting by filming *Linda Lovelace for President*, a comedy that was supposed to have no explicit sex, but she discovered that producers who offered her roles always expected nudity in return. She went to a Cannes Film Festival but was depressed by her very acceptance among celebrities she respected. "I had been in a disgusting film with disgusting people. . . . What were they doing watching a movie like that in the first place?"

Once she started giving her own answers to questions and trying to explain her years of coercion, she discovered that reporters were reluctant to rush into print. Her story was depressing, not glamorous or titillating at all. Because she had been passed around like a sexual trading coin, sometimes to men who were famous, there was also fear of lawsuits.

Only in 1978, when she was interviewed by Mike McGrady, a respected newspaper reporter on Long Island where she had moved with her new husband, did her story begin the long process of reaching the public. McGrady believed her. In order to convince publishers, he also put her through an eleven-hour lie-detector test with the former chief polygraphist of the New York district attorney's office, a test that included great detail and brutal cross-questioning. But even with those results and with McGrady himself as a collaborator, several major book publishers turned down the manuscript. It was finally believed and accepted by Lyle Stuart, a maverick in the world of publishing who often takes on sensational or controversial subjects.

One wonders: Would a male political prisoner or hostage telling a similar story have been so disbelieved? *Ordeal* attacks the myth of female masochism that insists women enjoy sexual domination and even pain, but prostitution and pornography are big businesses built on that myth. When challenged about her inability to escape earlier, Linda wrote: "I can understand why some people have such trouble accepting the truth. When I was younger, when I heard about a woman being raped, my secret feeling was *that could never happen to me,* I would never *permit* it to happen. Now I realize that can be about as meaningful as saying I won't permit an avalanche."

There are other, nameless victims of sexual servitude: the young blonds from the Minnesota Pipeline, runaways from the Scandinavian farming towns of Minnesota, who are given drugs and "seasoned" by pimps and set up in Times Square; the welfare mothers who are pressured to get off welfare and into prostitution; the "exotic" dancers imported from poorer countries for porn films and topless bars; the torture victims whose murders were filmed in Latin America for snuff movies popular here, or others whose bodies were found buried around a California filmmaker's shack; the body of a prostitute found headless and handless in a Times Square hotel, a lesson to her sisters. Perhaps some of their number will be the next voiceless, much-blamed women to speak out and begin placing the blame where it belongs. Perhaps Linda's example will give them hope that, if they return, some of society will accept them. Right now, however, they are just as disbelieved as rape victims and battered women were a few years ago.

To publicize her book, Linda is sitting quiet and soft-spoken on TV's "Phil Donahue Show." Under her slacks she wears surgical stockings to shield the veins that were damaged by the beatings in which she curled up, fetuslike, to protect her stomach and breasts from kicks and blows: this she explains under Donahue's questioning. Probably, she will need surgery after her baby is born. The silicone injected in her breasts by a doctor (who, like many other professionals to whom she was taken, was paid by Linda's sexual services) has shifted painfully, and surgery may be necessary there, too.

Yet Donahue, usually a sensitive interviewer, is asking her psychological questions about her background: How did she get along with her parents? What did they tell her about sex? Didn't her fate have something to do with the fact that she had been pregnant when she was nineteen and had given birth to a baby that Linda's mother put up for adoption?

Some of the women in the audience take up this line of questioning, too. *They* had been poor. *They* had strict and authoritarian parents; yet *they* didn't end up as part of the pornographic underground. The air is thick with self-congratulation. Donahue talks on about the tragedy of teenage pregnancy, and what parents can do to keep their children from a Linda-like fate.

Because Traynor did have a marriage ceremony performed somewhere along the way (Linda says this was to make sure she couldn't testify against him on drug charges), she has to nod when he is referred to as "your husband." On her own, however, she refers to him as "Mr. Traynor."

Linda listens patiently to doubts and objections, but she never gives up trying to make the audience understand. If another woman had met a man of violence and sadism who "got off on pain," as Linda has described in her book, *she might have ended up exactly the same way.* No, she never loved him: he was the object of her hatred and terror. Yes, he was very nice, very gentlemanly when they first met. They had no sexual relationship at all. He had just offered an apartment as a refuge from her strict childlike regime at home. *And then he did a 180-degree turn.* She became, she says quietly, a prisoner. A prisoner of immediate violence and the fear of much more.

She describes being so isolated and controlled that she was not allowed to speak in public or to go to the bathroom without Traynor's permission. *There was no choice. It could happen to anyone.* She says this simply, over and over again, and to many women in the audience the point finally comes through. But to some, it never does. Donahue continues to ask questions about her childhood, her background. What attracted her to this fate? How can we raise our daughters to avoid it? If you accept the truth of Linda's story, the questions are enraging, like saying, "What in your background led you to a concentration camp?"

No one asks how we can stop raising men who fit Linda's terrified description of Chuck Traynor. Or what attracted the millions of people who went to *Deep Throat*. Or what to do about the millions of "normal" men who assume that some violence and aggression in sex are quite okay.

A woman in the audience asks if this isn't an issue for feminism. Linda says that yes, she has heard there are anti-pornography groups, she is getting in touch with Susan Brownmiller who wrote *Against Our Will*. That definitive book on rape has led Brownmiller to attack other pornographic violence against women.

But it's clear that, for Linda, this is a new hope and new connection.

For women who want to support Linda now and to save others being used sexually against their will, this may be the greatest sadness. At no time during those months of suffering and dreams of escape, not even during the years of silence that followed, was Linda aware of any signal from the world around her that strong women as a group or feminists or something called the women's movement might be there to help her.

Surely, a victim of anti-Semitism would know the Jewish community was there to help, or a victim of racism would look to the civil rights movement. But feminist groups are not yet strong enough to be a public presence in the world of pornography, prostitution, and gynocide; or in the world of welfare and the working poor that Linda then joined. Even now, most of her help and support come from sympathetic men: from McGrady who believed her life story, from her husband who loses jobs in defense of her honor, from the male God of her obedient Catholic girlhood to whom she prayed as a sexual prisoner and prays now in her daily life as homemaker and mother.

Even her feelings of betrayal are attached to her father, not her mother. During her long lie-detector test, the only time she cried and completely broke down was over an innocuous mention of his name. "I was watching that movie *Hardcore*," she explained, "where George C. Scott searches and searches for his daughter. Why didn't my father come looking for me? He saw *Deep Throat*. He should've known. . . . He should've done something. Anything!"

After all, who among us had mothers with the power to rescue us, to *do something?* We don't even expect it. In mythology, Demeter rescued her daughter who had been abducted and raped by the King of the Underworld. She was a strong and raging mother who turned the earth to winter in anger at her daughter's fate. Could a powerful mother now rescue her daughter from the underworld of pornography? Not even Hollywood can fantasize that plot.

But Linda has begun to uncover her own rage, if only when talking about her fears for other women as pornography becomes more violent. "Next," she says quietly, as if to herself, "they're going to be selling women's skins by the side of the road."

And women have at least begun to bond together to rescue each other as sisters. There are centers for battered women, with publicized phone numbers for the victims but private shelters where they cannot be followed. It's a system that might work for victims of prostitution and pornography as well, if it existed, and if women knew it was there.

In the meantime, Linda takes time out from cleaning her tiny house on Long Island ("I clean it twice a day," she says proudly) to do interviews, to send out her message of hope and strength to other women who may be living in sexual servitude right now, and to lecture against pornography with other women, who are now her friends. She keeps answering questions, most of them from interviewers who are far less sympathetic than Donahue.

How could she write such a book when her son will someday read it? "I've already explained to him," she says firmly, "that some people hurt Mommy — a long time ago." How can her husband stand to have a wife with such a sexual past? ("It wasn't sexual. I never experienced any sexual pleasure, not one orgasm, nothing. I learned how to fake pleasure so I wouldn't get punished for doing a bad job.") And the most popular doubt of all: *If she really wanted to, couldn't she have escaped sooner?*

Linda explains as best she can. As I watch her, I come to believe the question should be different: *Where did she find the courage to escape at all?*

Inside the patience with which she answers these questions — the result of childhood training to be a "good girl" that may make victims of us all — there is some core of strength and stubbornness that is itself the answer. She *will* make people understand. She will *not* give up.

In the microcosm of this one woman, there is a familiar miracle: the way in which women survive — and fight back.

And a fight there must be.

Deep Throat plays continuously in a New York theater and probably in many other cities of the world. Bruises are visible on Linda's legs in the film itself, supporting her testimony that she was a prisoner while she made it. Do viewers see the bruises or only her smile?

So far, no invasion of privacy or legal means has been found to stop this film. Money continues to be made.

Deep Throat has popularized a whole new genre of pornography. Added to all the familiar varieties of rape, there is now an ambition to rape the throat. Porn novels treat this theme endlessly. Some emergency-room doctors believe that victims of suffocation are on the increase.

As for Chuck Traynor himself, he is still the husband and manager of Marilyn Chambers.

Larry Fields, a columnist for the Philadelphia *Daily News*, remembers interviewing them both for his column a few years ago when Marilyn was performing a song-and-dance act in a local nightclub. Traynor bragged that he had taught Linda Lovelace everything she knew, but that "Marilyn's got what Linda never had — talent."

While Traynor was answering questions on Marilyn's behalf, she asked him for permission to go to the bathroom. Permission was refused. "Not right now," Fields remembers him saying to her. And when she objected that she was about to appear onstage: "Just sit there and shut up."

When Fields also objected, Traynor was adamant. "I don't tell you how to write your column," he said angrily. "Don't tell me how to treat my broads."

CHAPTER 3

A Portrait of Angel:
The Life of a Porn Star

Bebe Moore Campbell

When I pass the X-rated section of the video store, I often wonder about the anonymous faces I see on the boxes. When the women are Black, the proverbial question always comes to mind: What's a nice girl like that doing in a place like this? The answer, I've learned recently, is usually the greater part of the tragedy.

Angel Kelly is not anonymous. She is the most famous Black adult actress in the multimillion-dollar hardcore pornographic video business and the lead in more than 150 adult videos. Her fame is intact, even though in the last two years she has made only one feature and has left the business. She considers her former profession vastly superior to that of a prostitute, pointing out that she chooses her sex partners; ironically, the vast majority of these have been white, as there are very few Blacks in the adult industry and far fewer men than women.

In her films Angel has engaged in oral sex, masturbation, lesbian sex, and heterosexual sex, and in one film she has sex with three white men simultaneously. She says she has never engaged in anal sex. When making adult videos, she used a contraceptive sponge to fight against infection, as well as for birth control, and she was tested regularly for venereal diseases and HIV. As she described her business to me on the telephone, Angel sounded intelligent, articulate and upbeat. She spoke of being a success and of working hard. "I have fans," she said. "I'm a star."

But Angel Kelly was sad the morning we met for breakfast. A tall, strikingly pretty woman with smooth toffee-colored skin and luminous brown eyes that stared at me unhappily from across the table, she told me

Reprinted from *Essence*, November 1990, pp. 63–64, 121–122, by permission of the author.

that the previous day a close friend of hers had placed a gun in her mouth and pulled the trigger.

"I just don't understand her death," she said, pain and confusion clouding her face. "Meagan was such a gentle soul."

The dead woman was also an actress who worked exclusively in adult videos. But when I suggested that there was a connection between having sex in front of a camera and suicide, Angel recovered her telephone poise. Her air of fragile vulnerability, so evident when she spoke of her dead friend, vanished. "I'm not ashamed of what I've done," she declared. "I'm the first successful Black adult video actress."

Although Angel said she was a star, she reminded me of a wounded child grieving for the loss of her innocence. The more I listened to her, the more I wondered if becoming a porn star is what happened to her after something in her life had gone wrong.

"I grew up the eldest of three children in a very middle-class family. My mother and father were both professionals," she told me. But the more we talked, the less convinced I was that her family life had been as *Brady Bunch*-perfect as she described it. Girls who grow up like that usually don't end up as porn stars. Angel seemed too composed, too glib. In frustration, I pressed the only button that let me see inside her: Did she know of any other adult actresses who had committed suicide?

When Angel answered, her voice faltered a little. "It's hard to be an adult actress in this business," she admitted, "especially if you're Black. The industry looks upon us with such disgust; I've never been recognized with awards and magazine covers. Black women are hired to play hookers and maids, and I've never really earned residuals. Sometimes companies have put sex scenes I've done in one video in completely different videos, and I've never earned a dime on them.

"There was another suicide three years ago. She couldn't reach out to us." The "us" Angel referred to is the Pink Ladies Social Club, a self-help organization for women involved in the making of adult videos, which Angel and other women working in the industry helped to found in 1987. The organization puts out a bimonthly newsletter and offers emotional support and medical information. The Pink Ladies also offers a suicide hot line.

"I had a pretty rough time three years ago," Angel said. "That's when I helped form the organization. It gave me some strength to fight and helped make the industry a better place for the ladies who wanted to get involved. We're so defeated and confused."

Upon further reflection and some coaxing on my part, Angel revealed that her idyllic childhood hadn't been so perfect. "Lansing, Michigan, where I grew up, was an overwhelmingly white town," she recalled. "I was one of maybe three Black kids in high school, and because the elite white crowd didn't accept me, I hung around with the bad white kids. I was wild, into partying. I was expelled from school three times for not doing homework, for smoking, cutting classes and drinking. My father was hard on me. He would never let me go anywhere. I wasn't even allowed to have a boyfriend. He kicked me out of the house when I was 16, and by the time I was 18 I didn't want to hear anything he had to say.

"I got married when I was 19 to an 18-year-old white boy I'd dated for a year and a half," she continued. "For a while he worked as a model and for a lawn-care company, then he lost his job. After six months, my husband disappeared. Someone told me later he was gay.

"Anyway, at the age of 19 I had no money and no job. I went back to my mother's house, because by this time she and my dad were divorced. A girlfriend of mine was doing totally nude exotic dancing in a booth at Cinema X, and she suggested that I work there. All I had to do was masturbate in a booth in front of men on the other side of a glass partition. It sounded so easy, and I needed money. Men put money in a slot in the glass partition. Everything was cash, and everything that came through that slot was mine. The first time I took my clothes off in that booth, I remember feeling a rush. It was pleasing to me to be able to turn men on. Not everyone can do that," she said with pride.

But six months of having men ejaculate against the glass partition changed Angel. "I began to look cheaper and sleazier," she said. "I guess that's the way I felt about myself. I began to see men in their truest form, and they are unbelievably sick."

She worked in the booth for two years before she became a dancer in a topless bar. "By then nothing offended me," she said. After seeing her dance, a photographer from a skin magazine asked her to do a nude layout. Angel agreed, and after her pictures appeared in *Players* and *Cheri* she received offers to make adult videos. In 1985 she and a friend moved to California to work in the adult-film industry.

"The first time I made a video I was very scared," Angel said. "I had to meet the director in the parking lot of a store and be taken to the set. The set was very tacky. I just closed my eyes and did what I had to do; I went numb. But after the first time, I thought, 'Hey, this isn't so bad.' I didn't feel forced. I did enjoy having the sex; I'd have orgasms."

I wondered how Angel could have orgasms and feel numb at the same time. I noticed that numb was a word she used a lot. Where had she learned to feel nothing?

Because of the popularity of interracial videos and the dearth of Black adult stars, Angel found herself in great demand and soon was earning

$1,000 a day. From 1986 until the end of 1987 she worked nonstop, earning several hundred thousand dollars; often she completed two or more videos a week. And as her features became recognized she was invited to perform exotic dancing at various clubs, where she earned up to $3,500 a week. While dancing in the nude during one such appearance, she was attacked onstage by a man who forced his tongue into her vagina. Neither the club's management nor the patrons came to her aid. The public rape left her traumatized and humiliated. Eventually she found a new and dangerous way to become anesthetized.

"I got caught up in drugs," Angel said flatly. "There was a lot of pressure to do cocaine. My friends did it, and because I had money I tried it and got hooked. Drugs were an escape."

While addicted to cocaine, Angel became pregnant. She opted for an abortion. "When I found out I was pregnant I almost freaked out. I still get depressed about the abortion."

Angel quit cocaine cold turkey when she became pregnant, something she described as very difficult. It was after the abortion that Angel began to think about creating a new life for herself. "I decided it wasn't all right for me to have sex in front of the camera anymore."

Our conversations were nearly over, but I still had unanswered questions. Why would a pretty, obviously bright young woman end up having sex on film for money? She wasn't telling me everything; something was missing. My mind kept returning to her childhood. I sensed the answers were there.

"Were you good in school?" I asked.

The question surprised her. "Yes," she said softly. "When I was in elementary school I made very good grades. I loved to read and write. I didn't start messing up until fifth or sixth grade."

"What happened then?"

Angel averted her eyes. "I'm ashamed to say," she said after a long pause. She took a deep breath and continued. "My time with my father wasn't right." She looked at me with a pain-filled expression, and suddenly all my questions were answered.

"The first time something happened I was 11. My father showed me a porn movie. Then he had me giving him massages. He touched me and I got nauseated. I didn't like it, but the abuse continued for six months. I told my mother, but she didn't believe me. And then after that he was always angry with me. One time he beat me up. Then he put me out of the house.

"A couple of years after he kicked me out, my parents and I went to a therapist. I described everything, and that's when my mother realized I wasn't lying. My father denied it all. I hated him so much. I don't know if there is a connection between what happened with my father and my being in the industry. I really don't know why I did what I did."

Many experts report that victims of sexual abuse often shut down emotionally in order to cope. Angel's affinity for numbness made sense. She told me that many of her fellow adult actresses were also molested as children.

It may be difficult for Angel to kick the sex industry, but it won't be impossible. At 27, Angel Kelly is a survivor, and she's determined to make her life work.

"I would like to go back to school," said Angel, who completed two years at a community college. "I am learning about producing and directing, and I'm learning a lot behind the camera. I don't want to be 30 years old and still taking my clothes off."

But unlike many other 27-year-olds, Angel has a past that can haunt her. "I met a Black guy recently and we liked each other," she said. "We started dating, but then one of his friends told him who I was and he stopped calling. That's going to keep happening. Even after I'm dead, my videos will be out there. I've been swallowed up by the adult-video industry. I feel used and cheated."

CHAPTER 4

Surviving Commercial
Sexual Exploitation

Evelina Giobbe

I was forced into prostitution at age 13. I was one of many girls who ran away from home during the sixties. The first night I ran away, I was raped. The second night I was gang raped. The third night I was wandering around the streets in a daze when I was befriended by an adult man. I confided my problems to him and he offered to take me in. He was kind, fed me, and feigned concern. He also kept me drugged, spoke glowingly about prostitution, and took nude photographs of me.

After a few weeks, he sold me to a pimp. I didn't understand what was happening at the time. He introduced me to a man who attempted to seduce me. When I resisted he raped me and told me that I would work for him as a prostitute. When I refused, he repeatedly battered and sexually assaulted me. He threatened my life and the lives of my family. He threatened to contact my mother and tell her I was a prostitute. He also threatened to turn me over to the authorities, whom he said would lock me up until my 21st birthday. The scandal, he said, would destroy my family. I believed him.

My pimp controlled every aspect of my life. He dyed my hair, changed my name, bought the food I ate and the clothes I wore. I never had any money. I was never out of his sight, except when I was "working" and then he wasn't far away.

Sometimes he took me to a bar where other pimps showed off "their women." We weren't allowed to speak or leave our pimps' sides. We were traded from pimp to pimp. They'd use us to pay off their debts to each other. We were often kidnapped, sometimes at gunpoint. If a woman was

Edited testimony from the U.S. Attorney General's Commission on Pornography, June 19, 1985. Reprinted by permission of the author.

recaptured by her original pimp, he would savagely punish her for "running away" with her abductor. To be without a man left a woman vulnerable to often more brutal pimps who considered her fair game since she didn't belong to anyone.

I tried on many occasions to escape my first pimp. As a teenager without any resources, isolated from friends and family and believing that I was a criminal, I was an easy mark. Each time he would track me down and force me back. He would drag me down streets, out of restaurants, even into taxis, all the while beating me while I protested, crying and begging passersby for help. No one wanted to get involved.

The men who bought me—the tricks—knew I was an adolescent. Most of them were in their 50s and 60s. They had daughters and granddaughters my age. They knew a child's face when they looked into it. It was clear that I was not acting of my own free will. I was always covered with welts and bruises. They found this very distasteful and admonished me. It was even clearer that I was sexually inexperienced. So they showed me pornography to teach me and ignored my tears as they positioned my body like the women in the pictures, and used me.

One of my regular customers had a vast collection of both adult and child pornography, including photographs of prepubescent children in bondage. He was a theater producer and had video equipment in his home long before it was mass produced. He made pornographic videotapes of myself and another woman on the average of once a week for about a year.

My pimp sent me to "stag parties" attended by as many as twenty men. They took place in catering halls, bars, and union halls. Initially, the men watched porn films. Afterwards another girl and I would have to have sex with them. I was also sent to business conventions held at major hotels in New York. The series of events was always the same. Porn films followed by myself and other women having sex with the men. The films most often set the tone for the kinds of acts we were expected to perform.

I was often sent to an apartment on the West Side. There were usually two or three men there. After I had sex with them, they'd take pictures of me in various pornographic poses. I didn't have the vocabulary to call them pornographers. I used to think photography was their hobby. Today, I realize that the studio apartment, furnished with a bed and professional camera equipment, was in fact a commercial pornography mill.

One time, two of us were taken to an apartment in New Jersey to meet some men. We were told that they were gangsters; that we "should be nice to them." When we arrived we were taken into a room containing a large bed surrounded by lighting and film equipment. We were told to act out a lesbian scene. After about 15 minutes we were told to get dressed, that they couldn't use us. We returned to New York unpaid. Looking back, I realized that I'd been used in a commercial porn loop.

A lot of people assume that women and girls like me consent to this abuse. Consent, however is not a possibility for a girl who was delivered into the hands of organized crime figures in New Jersey. Others wonder why I didn't turn to the police. As a matter of fact, I didn't have to walk to our local precinct to speak to the police. They were at our apartment every week for their payoff — me.

When I was 16 I was picked up by the police. The courts labeled me as incorrigible. I was remanded to a juvenile detention center. My incarceration was a nightmare of sexual abuse at the hands of the males employed to "guard" us. When I was transferred to a less secure facility, I escaped. There was no place left for me to go except back to prostitution.

My last pimp was a pornographer and the most brutal of all. He owned about three women or girls at any given time. Every night he'd run stag films after which he'd choose one of us for sex. The sex always duplicated the pornography. He used it to teach us to service him. He made pornography of all of us. He also made tape recordings of us having sex with him and of our screams and pleas when he beat us, often threatening us with death. Later he would use these recordings to humiliate us by playing them for his friends in our presence, for his own sexual arousal and to terrorize us or other women he brought home.

One morning I came in to find the walls of our bedroom covered with blood and a semiconscious woman lying on the floor covered with bruises and welts. Her eyes were swollen shut and blood was running down her legs. My pimp had raped her with a broom. I was told to guard her but when he fell asleep I freed her. I paid dearly for that. He beat me with a riding crop and raped me. He made a tape recording of that entire night and delighted in playing it over and over.

This man recruited adult women by advertising for models. When a woman answered his ad, he'd offer to put her portfolio together for free, be her agent, and make her a "star." He'd then use magazines like Playboy to convince her to pose for "soft-core" porn. He'd then engage her in a love affair and smooth talk her into prostitution. "Just long enough," he would say, "to get enough money to finance your career as a model." If sweet talk didn't work, violence and blackmail did. She became one of us.

I escaped prostitution by chance. I had been taking drugs since I was recruited into prostitution to numb my physical and emotional pain. As I destroyed myself with heroin, my marketability declined. I was no longer usable by pimps or tricks, so I was freed. After five years of prostitution, I was penniless, homeless, and addicted to heroin. My thighs are permanently scarred from repeated beatings. Many of my teeth are missing and cracked from blows to my face. I am infertile due to chronic venereal disease and a massive infection I contracted at age 15 because my pimp forced me to turn tricks during a miscarriage induced by a beating he had subjected me to.

I am a rare survivor. Most women who have shared my experiences are not as fortunate. It took close to 20 years to undue the physical and emotional trauma of being used in prostitution and pornography. Today I am an activist in the feminist anti-pornography movement. But the pornography that was made of me still exists. I know the men who made it. I know where some of them are. But there is nothing I can do about it. I live knowing that at any time it could surface and be used to humiliate me and my family. It can be used to ruin my professional life in the future. Because pornography is a profitable multi-billion-dollar-a-year industry, I also know that what happened to me will continue to happen to other women and girls. They will continue to be used and hurt in the same way that I was. And if they should be fortunate enough to escape, they will live under the same threat of exposure and blackmail that I do.

These were my first, very personal thoughts about the sexual exploitation to which I was subjected in the sex industry. Over seven years have passed since I gave my testimony to the Attorney General's Commission on Pornography. I was shielded by a curtain and a pseudonym (Sarah Wynter), while the pornographers sat openly in the hearing room shielded by their lawyers and the first amendment. Subsequently, as I continued to speak at feminist conferences, I began to receive letters from women all over the country describing their experiences in the sex industry as violent, degrading, and dehumanizing. From those letters, I published a newsletter to document our lives. Since its inception the WHISPER (Women Hurt in Systems of Prostitution Engaged in Revolt) newsletter has grown from a small grassroots response to the myths about prostitution, to a nationally respected organization that educates the public about prostitution as a system of exploitation and abuse, and advocates for service provision to its victims. Based on our advocacy and organizing efforts we have developed an analysis of prostitution as a system of oppression that differentially harms women and children. By listening to survivors describe the tactics of control that kept them trapped in the sex industry and comparing this to our knowledge of battering, we've joined with battered women's shelters and sexual assault programs in defining prostitution as violence against women. By documenting the violence and manipulation used to recruit and trap women in the sex industry, we've begun to educate the public that prostitution is not a "career choice" or a "victimless crime," but rather that prostitution creates an environment in which crimes against women and children are defined as a commercial enterprise.

On a more personal note, as time passed I chose to give up the illusion of safety that a pseudonym gave me, understanding that no woman was safe as long as systems of prostitution are allowed to continue. I took this action in defiance of the pimps and pornographers who sell women's bodies and steal their souls, and the johns who think they can turn child sexual abuse, rape, and battery into a job by throwing money at their victims. These men can no longer coerce my silence by threatening to distribute the degrading photographs and films they took of me because they only serve as evidence of my abuse. I hope my personal/political choice will contribute to other women speaking out and organizing to end commercial sexual exploitation.

A supporter of a waitress at Bette's Diner in Berkeley, CA, in 1990. The waitress refused to serve a customer while he read *Playboy*. This conveys the view that *Playboy* is a "White Boy's Magazine" that fosters men's sense of entitlement, as well as their violent behavior toward women.

Credit: Photographed by Simon Nathan

CHAPTER 5

Testimony on Pornography and Incest

Katherine Brady

"It is my belief that if we confront this abuse and degradation openly, we will be able to find a way to stop it."

My name is Katherine Brady. I was born in Dubuque, Iowa and I was
educated and married and lived for over 23 years in Green Bay, Wisconsin.
I am a single parent with two daughters, aged 12 and 13. I am testifying
here today as both an incest survivor and a child abuse prevention activist.

My father incestuously abused me for a period of 10 years, from the
time I was 8 years old until I was 18. . . . During the early stages of the
molestation, my father used pornographic materials as a way of coercing
me into having sex with him. In the beginning, the pornography consisted
of materials he confiscated from inmates of two state institutions where he
worked. He was employed as a prison guard at the Central State Mental
Hospital, Waupun, Wisconsin, and subsequently worked as a training and
corrections officer at the Reformatory for Boys in Green Bay, Wisconsin.

My father used the pornography for several purposes. First of all, he
used it as a teaching tool — as a way of instructing me about sex and about
what he wanted me to do with him. When he showed me the pictures, he
would describe the acts in detail: "This is fellatio," "this is what you do
with intercourse," and so forth.

Second, my father used the pictures to justify his abuse and to convince me that what we were doing was normal. The idea was that if men
were doing it to women in the pictures, then it was OK for him to do it to
me.

Finally, he used the pornography to break down my resistance. The
pornography made the statement that females are nothing more than ob-

This is a slightly edited version of Brady's testimony to the Senate Subcommittee on
Juvenile Justice, August 8, 1984.

jects for men's sexual gratification. How could I refuse my father when the pornography showed me that sex is what women and girls are for?

My father first told me about pornography when I was 9 years old. Then he sneaked it to me for private viewings after sending my mother and brother away. He would send my mother away on errands as if she were a child. Our family was typical in his being the authority, the head of the household. . . . When I was about 10 he told me not to tell my mother anything about what he was doing with me.

When he showed me the pornography for the first time, this is what it was like: As I sat down on the bed, he spread out the pictures of men and naked women in all sorts of sexual positions with each other. Looking at them, I felt a rush spread through my body. . . . I felt intense sexual desire, total revulsion, increasing excitement, abandonment of reason, a sense of sin and guilt, the shame of it all, and a resolve to forget it until next time.

The following passage is an excerpt from my book, *Father's Days* [1979]. My body developed early—when I was in the sixth grade—and I menstruated in grade school. Once I was in puberty, my father escalated the molestation. By that time, his use of pornography had subtly coerced me into submission. I had learned from his lessons with pornography that I had to submit to his abuse. Because I was afraid of his physical power and verbal authority, it never occurred to me to challenge his use of pornography or his abuse. The pornography frightened me, it confused me, and yet it excited me. I felt trapped. My only means of surviving psychologically was to become detached—to send my mind off—to pretend that the abuse was happening to someone else. I pretended for many years that I had a "normal family." The truth is that the pornography trained me to respond to my father's sexual demands.

Years later I married, and several years into the marriage, my now exhusband introduced me to other forms of pornography—popular so-called men's magazines like *Playboy*. Although the pictures in these magazines were sleek and glossy—unlike those of my father's home-made pornography—their message about women and girls was basically the same. Like my father, my husband was using pornography to tell me what he wanted me to be and do. Like my father, my husband was telling me that females were just sexual playthings. The introduction of pornography into my marriage perpetuated the damage to my self-image and self-esteem. It brought into our love-making an element of violence. It made me think of my body as an object of abuse. Ultimately, it contributed to the deterioration of what might have been a joyous emotional and sexual relationship.

It would be comforting to think that my experiences of sexual abuse in childhood and sexual degradation in marriage are very rare experiences for girls and women. But since the publication of my story, I helped found the Katherine Brady Foundation, which is a national clearinghouse for victims of child sexual abuse, and I began to work actively with Women Against Pornography [in New York]. I encountered hundreds and hundreds of survivors of sexual abuse, as well as dozens of mental health professionals. I learned that my experiences of abuse through pornography were not unusual.

Pornography is frequently found in homes and other places where children have been sexually abused. The incest perpetrator will show the child pornographic pictures of smiling girls or women and say, "Look at them. They like it. So what is the matter with you?"

One factor that contributes to children's reluctance to report sexual abuse is that pornography persuades the child that the acts are normal. Although I do not know exactly what role pornography played in my father's sexual and psychological development—he is very reticent about such matters—his perceptions of women and girls are straight out of pornography. He used to tell me stories about the acts that he saw when he was in World War II, for example, a story about a donkey raping a child. He also developed a game which he showed me. He pretended he was wiring my breasts together. It was almost like a setup for an S & M kind of attitude in my psyche. And I think now: Where did he get that game? It was a violent sexual act that he did to me.

It is only recently that survivors of sexual abuse and pornography have been given the opportunity—and the support—to speak publicly about their injuries. It is my belief that if we confront this abuse and degradation openly, we will be able to find a way to stop it.

CHAPTER 6

Testimony on Pornography and Marital Brutality

Rev. Susan Wilhem

I had not realized the extent of the harm pornography has done to me until recently, when I was working on a photo-montage of pornography for an educational forum. I came across a picture of a position my ex-husband had insisted we try. When we did, I hemorrhaged for three days. My bruised cervix is still a problem after ten years.

My father used pornography like *Argosy, True, Saga, Stag,* and *Cavalier*. They are adventure story magazines, different from the slicks. I was not supposed to read them, but I did. The women in them were either short dumpy fishwives with their hair in curlers or beautiful sexy available creatures. The short dumpy ones were also sexually used, but men did not really enjoy them. That was my education on what women were like.

Most of my sex life with my ex-husband was sexually abusive. He had a lot of pornography around the house, both the slicks and the hard core. It made him expect that I would want to do crazy things. He kept saying our sex life was, and I was, dull and unfun. When we were first married, he didn't use pornography or drink. Later he started to drink, and, after he started using pornography, sex became especially abusive. He got his ideas from the pornography. Having sex, how he wanted it, was nonnegotiable.

He had a fetish about hating pubic hair. He used to shave his and mine. Once he slipped and slit my clitoris. He claimed it was an accident.

If he decided I liked something, he would try to kill it, like the dogs we had. I am convinced he tried to kill me more than once. There are also more subtle ways of killing the spirit.

He exposed me to the pornography too. Once we saw an X-rated film that showed anal intercourse. After that, he pressed me to try it. I agreed

---

Testimony in support of an Anti-Pornography Civil Rights Ordinance in New York City.

46

to once, but found the experience very painful, but he kept trying to do it again. He told me my vagina had become as sloppy as an old sow's and he could not get pleasure any other way. He also used to pinch and bite me. When I said "it hurts," he would say, "no, it doesn't." I became numb. I lost track of my own feelings. One time, he said "It's *supposed* to hurt." After that, something started to change for me.

We, the victims of pornography, are paying with our lives. We should have some place to go to complain about how pornography is part of making our husbands into rapists.

CHAPTER 7

Testimony from Public Hearings on the Ordinance to Add Pornography as Discrimination Against Women

The following are slightly edited excerpts from the transcripts of Public Hearings on Ordinance to Add Pornography as Discrimination Against Women, Committee on Government Operations, City Council, Minneapolis, Minnesota, December 12–13, 1983, organized by Catharine MacKinnon and Andrea Dworkin.

PORNOGRAPHY AND CHILD RAPE—MS. L.

I am going to talk about being raped and how pornography was involved in that rape. When I was 13 I was camping with the Girl Scouts in Northern Wisconsin. It was 10 years ago in November. I was walking through the forest outside the camp in mid-afternoon when I came upon three deer hunters who were reading magazines and talking and joking around.

I turned to walk away and one of the men yelled, "There is a live one." I thought they meant a deer, so I ducked and tried to run away. Then I realized that there weren't any deer in sight and that they meant me. So I started running and they ran after me. I tripped. The forest was covered with pine needles and leaves, and they caught me.

I told them that I would go away and to please leave me alone. They said, "You are not going anywhere," and forced me to get up. They pulled my hair and started looking at me up and down, calling me a little Godiva (I had long hair then), a golden girl, and making jokes. They told me to take my clothes off, so I did. It was very cold. They told me to lie down and not to say anything; that if I made a sound, they would kill me. They would blow my head off.

All three men had hunting rifles. Two of them held their guns at my head, and the first man hit my breast with his rifle while they continued to laugh. Then the first man raped me. When he was finished they started

48

making jokes about how I was a virgin. I didn't know how they knew that. And they made jokes about how they could use something like this when they were in boot camp and they made jokes about being in the military. Then the second man raped me.

None of the men attempted to kiss me or touch my breasts; they simply wanted to have intercourse. When the second man was finished, the third man was not able to get an erection. The other men told me to give him a blow job but I didn't know what a blow job was. The third man then forced his penis into my mouth and told me to do it. I didn't know what I was supposed to be doing. He started swearing at me and calling me a bitch and a slut and saying that I had better do it right and that I wasn't even trying. He started getting very angry and one of the men pulled the trigger on his gun so I tried harder. When he had an erection, he raped me.

They continued to make jokes about how lucky they were to have found me when they did and about my being a virgin. Then they started kicking me and kicking leaves and pine needles on to me, and they told me that if I wanted more I could come back the next day. When they started walking away I put my clothes back on. Then I looked down and saw that they had been reading pornographic magazines with nude women on the covers.

I walked a fair amount away and then broke down and cried under a tree. I went back to the camp but I didn't tell anyone that I had been raped. I went to the bathroom and saw that I had bled on my underwear, so I assumed that I had gotten my period. I didn't know that virgins bleed. I didn't find that out until a few years later. I didn't seek any medical help and I didn't tell anyone that I had been raped until I was 20 years old. I didn't feel I could tolerate having anyone think it was my fault or blaming me or not understanding. And I couldn't tolerate having no control over who had the information once I told someone. I knew that my mother would most likely tell a great many people.

Ms. Dworkin: Had you seen pornography before?

Ms. L: Yes, my father and my older brothers all had pornography. They kept it under their mattresses and under their beds. I had looked at the pornography in my home when I was growing up.

Ms. MacKinnon: What do you remember about what you were thinking they would do to you at the time?

Ms. L: When I was being raped, I thought they were going to kill me.

PORNOGRAPHY AND CALLOUS SEX—MS. N.

I am afraid to be here and afraid not to be here. What brought me here is that I know a lot of women who have stories to tell about how pornography has hurt them, and how they are trying to recover from the destruction it has brought into their lives. They can't be here today because they are still working through a lot of that pain. Testifying here is also a way of purging my own shame about what happened to me. I will say "fuck" three times in my testimony because I believe in calling something what it is.

I was 21 years old at the time. It was March or April 1980. I had a sexual relationship with this man for about a year. He had gone to a stag party, and I was home alone in my apartment. He called me on the telephone and he said that he had seen several short pornographic films and that he felt very horny. He asked if he could come over to have sex with me. I said yes because at the time I felt obligated as his girlfriend to satisfy him. I also felt that a refusal would be indicative of sexual "hang-ups" on my part and that I was not "liberal" enough.

When he arrived, he informed me that the other men at the party were envious that he had a girlfriend to fuck. They wanted to fuck too after watching pornography. He then took off his clothes and had me perform fellatio on him. I did not do this of my own volition. He put his genitals in my face and said "Take it all." Then he fucked me on the couch in the living room. All this took about five minutes. When he was finished he dressed and went back to the party. I felt ashamed and numb and I also felt very used.

This encounter differed from previous ones. It was much quicker, it was somewhat rougher, and he was not aware of me as a person. There was no foreplay. It is my opinion that his viewing of pornography served as foreplay for him.

There was no lasting detrimental effects on me from this experience alone. It was simply an intensification of the ordinary treatment I received from him, which resulted in feelings of low self-esteem, depression, confusion, and a lot of shame.

I do not have any knowledge of him purchasing pornography at any time in our relationship. But I know that the friends he got together with twice a week had it in their homes, so he was exposed to it regularly.

I feel what I have to say here is important. He went to this party, saw pornography, got an erection, then inflicted his erection on me. There is a direct causal relationship here.

PORNOGRAPY AND SEXUAL TERRORISM—MS. O.

I am unable to state what my relationship is to the people I am going to talk about because many of them are still victims whose lives are in danger.

For the majority of my life, I lived with a divorced woman and her children in the house that she owned. Her ex-husband also lived there. He would not leave. He threatened to kill the woman if she ever tried to get help in getting away from him.

Over a period of 18 years the woman was regularly raped by this man. He brought pornographic magazines, books, and paraphernalia into the bedroom with him and told her that if she did not perform the sexual acts in the "dirty" books and magazines, he would beat her and kill her. I know this because my bedroom was right next to hers. I could hear everything they said. I could hear her cries and screams. In addition, since I did most of the cleaning in the house, I would often come across the books, magazines, and paraphernalia that were in the bedroom and other rooms. The magazines had pictures of mostly women and children and some men. Eventually, the woman admitted to me that her ex-husband used pornographic materials to terrorize and rape her.

Not only did I suffer through the torture of listening to the rapes and tortures of a woman, but I could see what grotesque acts this man was performing on her from the pictures in the pornographic materials. I was also able to see the systematic destruction of a human being taking place before my eyes.

At the time I lived with the woman, I was completely powerless to help her and her children to get away from this man. I was told by him that if I ever told anyone about the things he did or if I ever tried to run away, he would beat me, he would break and cut off my arms and legs, and he would cut up my face so that no man would ever want to look at me. He also said that he would kill me, and that he would make me sorry that I ever told on him.

During the time that I was held captive by that man, I was physically and psychologically abused by him. I was whipped with belts and electrical cords. I was beat[en] with pieces of wood. I was usually forced to pull my pants down before I was beaten. I was touched and grabbed where I did not want him to touch me. I was also locked into dark closets and the basement for many hours at a time, and I was often not allowed to speak or cry.

The things that this man did to me were also done to the children of the woman, except that they suffered from even worse abuse. Part of the psychological abuse I suffered from was from the pornographic materials that the man used to terrorize us. I knew that if he wanted to, he could do more of the things that were done in those magazines, to me. When he looked at the magazines, he made hateful, obscene, violent remarks about women in general and about me. He told me that because I am female I am here to be used and abused by him, and that because he is a male he is the master and I am his slave.

I was terrorized into keeping silent and it wasn't until three years after I escaped from him that I was psychologically and emotionally strong enough to tell anyone what had happened to me. Pornography caused that man to do those things to me and to other women and children. Pornography is an extension of the violence and hatred against women that already exists in this society. Getting rid of pornography would get rid of part of the violence against women that permeates this society. Pornography makes a mockery of torture, beatings, rapes, mutilations, degradations, and killings that I and other women have suffered from, all for men's sexual gratification.

Every time I walk into a neighborhood grocery store or drug store I am reminded that if I don't watch my step and do what I'm told, keep silent or stay in my place, that I could end up like one of the women in the pornographic material being sold in those stores. I believe what those magazines say because it has happened to me.

The last statement that I have to make is a political one. If someone wants to study the condition of women in this society, all that person has to do is view a pornographic book, magazine, or movie. Pornography is a blueprint for how to degrade a woman. Pornography tells the truth about women's condition in this society. But pornography lies about how we think and feel about our condition.

PORNOGRAPHY AND THE DESTRUCTION
OF A MARRIAGE—MS. M.

I am here today to share with you some of the ways in which the presence of pornography is directly related to physical, sexual, and psychological abuse in my life. . . .

During the second year of marriage my husband started reading more and more pornography. He started out by reading *Playboy*, then magazines like *Penthouse* and *Forum*. I would come home from work and fix dinner while he read excerpts from the magazines about group sex, wife swapping, anal intercourse and bondage. I was really repulsed by the things he was reading to me and . . . I kept saying "People are just making these things up for this magazine. I don't believe it." He bought more and more magazines to prove to me that people weren't making it up, and that they were saying how wonderful these things were.

We started meeting his friends at wet T-shirt contests and amateur strip nights. We would meet together as a group and go to pornographic adult theaters or live sex shows. Initially I argued that the women on stage looked very devastated, like they were disgusted and hated it. I felt devastated and disgusted watching it. I was told by the men that if I wasn't so smart and if I would be more sexually liberated and more sexy, I would get along a lot better in the world and that they and a lot of other men would like me more.

About this time I started feeling very terrified. I realized that this wasn't a joke anymore; that this was something that he [husband] was really serious about. I called my mother and told her that things were happening in my marriage around sex that I really didn't like. She told me that divorce was something that she didn't want in our family — that it was very disgraceful. She knew how competent I was and she said, "I know you can hang in there and give it your best."

To numb myself I did a lot more drinking with my husband and with our friends. When people came to dinner, a lot of alcohol was consumed. Then my husband would bring out the drinking and stripping game. He asked people to live out the various scenarios in the magazines that he had been reading to me. They participated in these scenarios a few times. I stayed a couple of times, and once I left.

My husband and I had incredible arguments about this. I told him that I loved him and wanted to be a good wife. I wanted our marriage to work. But I didn't want to be with these other people. It was *he* I wanted to be with and no one else. He told me that if I loved him I would do these things, and that, as I could see from the things that he had read to me in the magazines, a lot of times women didn't like it initially, but if I tried it enough, I would probably like it or learn to like it. Then he read me stories where women learned to like it.

Once when I was asleep at night and a friend of his was over, he asked the friend to come into our room and sleep with us. I woke up finding his friend in bed with us. When his friend realized I was not a willing participant, he apologized to me and left.

To prevent more of these group situations, which I found very humiliating and very destructive to my self-esteem and to my feelings of self-worth, I agreed to act out in private a lot of the scenarios that my husband read to me. These depicted bondage and different sexual acts that I found very humiliating to do. Things were getting really terrible and I was feeling suicidal and very worthless as a person. Any dreams I had of a career in medicine were totally washed away. I could not think of myself any more as a human being.

Then, because of my husband's job, we were transferred overseas. The pornography that he and his friends had been reading was much more violent overseas. . . . He started taking me to sex shows where there were women and animals, especially snakes. We went to sex shows called "banana lady shows," and shows where men participated in sex acts with women on stage.

About this time my husband started having to go away a lot so I was alone. I started studying karate and I also started feeling that I had some kind of control over my body again. I started feeling in touch with the fact that I am a person. I did a lot of traveling by myself and I started feeling more and more courageous.

One night when I was in one of the pornographic institutions, I sat with a couple of people I knew and watched the women on stage and the different transactions and acts going on, and the sale of the women, and I realized that my life wasn't any different from those women except that what I did was done in the name of marriage. I could see how I was being seasoned by the use of pornography and I could see what would come next. I could see more violence and I could see more humiliation, and I knew at that point I was either going to die from it or I would kill myself or I would leave. And I felt strong enough to leave.

I spent the next few years of my life healing myself with the help of therapy, education, and friends. But I know the memories and the scars will remain. Pornography is not a fantasy. It was my life. Reality. It involved abuse to my body.

If what I said today can help prevent one woman from experiencing the pain I was involved in, it is worth it.

Ms. Dworkin: How old are you now and how old were you when you left your marriage?

Ms. M.: I am 29. I was 25 when I left my husband, and my divorce papers came through when I was 26.

Ms. Dworkin: Did your husband talk to you about making films and making the kinds of things that he was seeing with you as a participant?

Ms. M.: Yes he did. When we would go to the amateur nights, he would try to get me up on stage, but I refused. Husbands trafficking their wives, making them have sex with another man, became a theme for a while in the magazines. I remember various stories. One was about a woman in a cabin. A man would be hiding, and her husband would also be in hiding to photograph his wife with this man. My husband tried to get me to do that several times.

Ms. Dworkin: During this period of time, were you actually raped in your marriage?

Ms. M.: Yes, I was. I actually refer to my whole marriage as marital rape. Several times, especially following the incidents where my husband asked our friends to come to bed with us when I was already asleep, he felt it was his privilege if he was at all sexually turned on or needing to be gratified, to rape me. Most of the time I would wake up. Sometimes I would just keep my eyes closed and try to tolerate it. Several times when I confronted him about this he said if I refused to have him do this, then he had to masturbate. I know that with his religious background that is a sin.

Ms. Dworkin: When you were living in the Orient you said that the porn was very much more violent. Could you describe what was actually in it?

Ms. M.: The pornography had mostly Oriental and black women in it, and it depicted women as animals. It showed women having sex with animals, and women in cages. There were a lot of whips. I guess some of it was S and M pornography. Women were led around with collars on. They showed women being penetrated anally. They showed more gang rapes than here. It was more abusive in that the women were not portrayed as these glamorous perfect women. They were portrayed more as slaves.

Ms. MacKinnon: Could you describe in a couple of words what you see to be the relationship between the pornography and the things that your husband asked you to do?

Ms. M.: He read the pornograpy like a textbook, like a journal. When he finally convinced me to be bound, he read in the magazine how to tie the knots and bind me in a way that I couldn't escape. Most of the scenes where I had to dress up or go through different fantasies were the exact same scenes that he had read in the magazines.

Ms. MacKinnon: Did your husband remarry?

Ms. M.: He remarried in the year that we got divorced to a woman who was almost 10 years younger than him. When I saw him to finalize our divorce and to get some of my last possessions he said, "Do you want to see what she looks like?" Then he showed me pictures of her naked, in pornographic poses.

PORNOGRAPHY AND RACISM—MS. U.

When I was first asked to testify I resisted because the memories are so painful and so recent. I agreed because of my four-year-old daughter and other Indian children. I want them to grow up in a more healthful and loving society.

I was attacked by two white men. From the beginning they let me know they hated my people, even though it was obvious from their remarks that they knew very little about us. And they let me know that the rape of a "squaw" by white men was practically honored by white society. In fact, it has been made into a video game called *Custer's Last Stand* [The correct name for this video game is *Custer's Revenge*]. And that's what they screamed in my face as they threw me to the ground, "This is more fun than *Custer's Last Stand!*"

They held me down, and as one was running the tip of his knife across my face and throat, he said, "Do you want to play *Custer's Last Stand?* It's great. You lose, but you don't care, do you? You like a little pain, don't you, squaw?" They both laughed and then he said, "There is a lot of cock in *Custer's Last Stand*. You should be grateful, squaw, that all-American boys like us want you. Maybe we will tie you to a tree and start a fire around you."

They made other comments like, "The only good Indian is a dead Indian." "A squaw out alone deserves to be raped." These words still terrorize me today.

It may surprise you to hear stories that connect pornography and white men raping women of color, but it doesn't surprise me. I think pornography, racism, and rape are perfect partners. They all rely on hate. They all reduce a living person to an object. A society that sells books, movies, and video games like *Custer's Last Stand* on its street corners, gives white men permission to do what they did to me. Like they said, I'm scum. It is a game to track me down, rape and torture me.

So I bring my screams of that night here to you today, hoping that they will help you decide to stand against the dehumanization and violence of pornography. I would like to end with a poem that I wrote about my nightmares after my attack.

I used to welcome the first shadows of the night as they slid along the edge of day. The thunderbird closing her eyes slowly, softly pulling us all into the beauty of the darkness and the dream.

Now the shadows hide danger and hatred. The thunderbird screams her warning of the terror of the darkness and the nightmare.

The hoop of the universe is broken. Sacred eagle feathers are strewn on the ground where they throw me, naked, to play out *Custer's Last Stand*.

Knives slash red streaks. Mean, twisted faces, large rough hands, swirl and chase me through the darkness. I struggle awake just as the owl calls my name.

PORNOGRAPHY AND SEXUAL HARASSMENT—MS. R.

I am going to relate what happened to me about four years ago on my job. For the past six years I have been training as a plumber. About four years ago I got stuck on a job that was almost completed. I don't know if you understand construction set-ups, but generally in the winter, certain trades get together in a little shack inside a building where they eat lunch and have coffee and everything else.

When I came on the job, three of the trades had set up a nice little shack. It was a real shock when I walked in. Three of the four walls in the room were completely decorated with pictures from magazines like *Hustler*, *Playboy*, *Penthouse*, and *Oui*. Some of them were regular pinups but some were very, very, explicit, showing women with their legs spread wide and men and women performing sex acts and women in bondage. It was very uncomfortable for me to go there and have dinner and lunch with about 20 men while facing all these pictures and hearing these men talking. The only thing they talked about was women, their old ladies, their girlfriends, and all their conquests over the weekend.

I put up with it for about a week, but I finally got to the point where I could no longer tolerate sitting there. I felt totally naked in front of these men. Being one of only two women on the job and being rather new at it and not knowing of any alternatives, I got pissed off one day and ripped all the pictures off the wall. Well, it turned out to be a real unpopular move. I came back in at lunch time and half the pictures were back up again. They pulled them out of boxes and stuck them on the wall and proceeded to call me names and otherwise ignore me. There was one electrician who had it in for me. He always said, "Hey, bitch," or some other term that didn't really sit with me too well. It was very, very hostile.

After lunch I went back in and took all the pictures down again. When I went back the next morning, some of them were back up again. At that point I decided that I no longer wanted to eat with all these men and I began to eat my lunch at other places in the building. I was totally boycotted at work. The men wouldn't talk to me. I was treated like I had done something terrible. It was really uncomfortable. I felt no support from any of the men. I approached my boss one time and said, "I don't like these things," and he said, "I can't do anything about it. These men do what they want to do." And I said, "Piss on it. *I* will do what *I* want to do."

Just by happenstance, I was at a meeting that weekend and was relating my story to some women and one of them worked for the Affirmative Rights Office in Minneapolis. She said, "We can help you out." She organized three other women and herself to make an unannounced inspection. I said, "I don't want them to know that I had anything to do with this because I'm scared."

The women came and took note of all the pictures that were up on the walls. I hadn't tampered with them again, so they were all up again. Then they wrote letters to each of the companies involved.

I came out of work one day and my car door was bashed in. It wasn't parked anywhere near where any other car would have hit it. The electrician was extremely angry at me and I have no proof that he did it, but I have a sneaky suspicion that he did. He was subsequently removed from his job.

After the LEAP [Affirmative rights] officers had written letters to send out to various employers, my boss, who owned the company, called me up one day and said, "Look, I heard you are having a little trouble down there. Why don't you just calm down a little bit. Don't make such a mess. We don't need any trouble down there. Just ignore it." I said, "Hey, I can't ignore it. I don't have to. It's already done."

A couple of days later my boss got the letter. He was told that the company did not comply with the [affirmative] action guidelines. In the meantime, I had asked for a transfer and my transfer came through. It came a lot faster because they decided I was making too much trouble and they had to get me out of there.

Ms. MacKinnon: Do you have any idea what their stake in it [the pornography] was; why they kept putting it up over and over?

Ms. R.: Being the only woman on the job doing men's work, I have encountered pretty much hostility in the last six years. I was a legal threat on that particular job because I had replaced one of the men who was causing trouble. . . . I think they were doubly angry at me because of that.

PORNOGRAPHY AND PROSTITUTION—MS. S.

I am speaking for a group of women in Minneapolis who are all former prostitutes. All of us feel very strongly about the relationship between pornography and prostitution. Many of us wanted to testify at this hearing but are unable to because of the consequences of being identified as former whores.

It is absolutely incredible to me that prostitution is seen as a victimless activity. Many prostitutes are rightly terrified of breaking their silence, fearing harassment to themselves and their families and loss of their jobs. We have started to meet together to make sense of the abuse we have experienced in prostitution and how pornography endorses and legitimizes that abuse.

One of the very first commonalities we discovered was that we were all introduced to prostitution through pornography, and we were all under 18 at the time. Pornography was our textbook. We learned the tricks of the trade by men exposing us to pornography; we tried to mimic what we saw. I cannot stress enough what a huge influence we feel this was. These pictures were of real men and women who appeared to be happy consenting adults, engaged in human sexuality.

One of us had the experience of being paid by a client to go to a house where she found a group of physically disabled men, and another group of physically able men. Everyone was watching pornographic films: movies of men fucking women, women doing oral sex on men, and women being penetrated by animals. The movies were played continuously. The able-bodied men were joking and making comments like, "That's how real men do it," instructing the handicapped men, teasing them that if they watched enough of these movies they would be able to perform normally. Then the disabled men were undressed by the able men. The woman refused to engage sexually with the disabled men, so she was forced to. She was held down by the physically able men while everyone watched and the movies kept going.

These men had various physical deformities. Some were amputees, some paraplegics. Some were able to perform, some weren't. After this, the able-bodied men said they were going to show the handicapped men how "real men" do it. They forced the women to act simultaneously with the movie. In the movie at this point, a group of men were urinating on a naked woman. All the men in the room were able to perform this task, so they all started urinating on the woman who was now naked. Then the able-bodied men had sex with the woman while the disabled men watched.

Another woman met a man in a hotel room. When she got there she was tied up while sitting on a chair nude. She was gagged and left alone in the dark for what she believed to be an hour. When the man returned with two other men, they burned her with cigarettes and attached nipple clips to her breasts. They had many S and M magazines with them and showed her many pictures of women appearing to consent, enjoy, and encourage this abuse. She was held for twelve hours while she was continuously raped and beaten. She was paid $50 or about $2.33 per hour.

Another woman was in a room with two clients. One of the men told her that he had seen some pictures of women who had shaved their pubic hair and that it had turned him on. They then proceeded with a jackknife to remove the woman's pubic hair, plucking and burning what the knife had missed. They made comments on how her hairless vagina reminded them of their young daughters' genitals. They then engaged in intercourse.

Women in our group were forced constantly to enact specific scenes that men had witnessed in pornography. Men would direct women to copy postures and poses of things they had seen in magazines and then they would take pictures of the women. If pornography was not actually in the room with the client, there would be a constant reference to it.

One man paid a woman $35 to recruit another woman so he could direct them in a lesbian scenario he had seen in a movie. When *Deep Throat* was released, we experienced men joking and demanding oral sex.

It is very amazing to me what happens when a group of ex-prostitutes get together in one room and tell their stories. We discovered that the men we had serviced were very powerful in this community. Especially interesting to us are the numbers of men involved in the media who use prostitutes and pornography. These are the same men that perpetuate the myth that Minneapolis is a clean city with exceptional morals and a high quality of life.

In my experience, there was not one situation where a client was not using pornography while he was using me or that he had not just watched pornography or he referred to it verbally. Men constantly witness the abuse of women in pornography and if they can't engage in that behavior with their wives, girlfriends, or children, they force a whore to do it. My wish is that you could see with my eyes just for a day how clear the relationship is between pornography and the systematic abuse of women. I'm petrified for young women today. I believe the pornography that is published today is more brutal and dangerous than when I was involved in prostitution. I worry about how this will affect your daughters, who I know will be victims of this pornography in one way or another. I also worry about the prostitutes on the street who are being used by the pornographic industry.

A young woman who works at the University of Minnesota and could not come here to speak for herself, told the following story. She was involved in prostitution between 1970 and 1974.

> I remember a house on Second Avenue South, which a trick asked me to go to. He told me that I would be able to make a lot of money there. It turned out to be the same house that my pimp had been urging me to go to where young pretty girls could get tied up, beaten and burned with cigarettes and earn $500 for a short half hour's work. I had steadily refused to go, but when my pimp found out I had been invited, I *had* to go.
>
> The woman who ran the place lived there with her children. She kept a room upstairs for the tricks to use. It had a projector to show porn films and there was stacks of pornographic material in the room. The tricks would go in there, look at the porn to get psyched up, and then a girl would be sent into the room. The youngest girl I know about who went there was only thirteen.
>
> When I went into the room, the trick said that I was almost too old. But he was pleased with me because I looked young. He stripped me, tied me spread-eagled on the bed so that I could not move, and

then began to caress me very gently. Then, when he thought I was relaxed, he squeezed my nipple really hard. I did not react. He held up a porn magazine with a picture of a beaten woman and said, "I want you to look like that. I want you to hurt." He then began beating me. When I did not cry fast enough, he lit a cigarette and held it right above my breast for a long time before he burned me. I told him that as God was my witness, he had better kill me or untie me right now, because if he didn't, I would turn him into the police, and that I would call his wife and tell his family about him. He believed me and let me go. But I know that this house continued to provide that service for those who could pay.

When I worked at massage studios, the owners had subscriptions to *Playboy*, *Penthouse*, *Penthouse Forum*, and the like. These magazines were arranged in the waiting area of most of the massage places which I worked in. If a girl was not inside with a trick, she was expected to sit out in front with the men who were waiting or who were undecided, and to look at the magazines with them in order to get them titillated. The men would ask me questions like, "Do you really like it when more than one man fucks you?" "Do you really like to suck men off, like this hot little number who wrote the letter to *Forum*?" They used the soft porn to help them work up the courage to try the acts described in the magazines with the prostitutes at the massage studio.

At one point, I was on the company payroll of a couple of well-known businesses in Minneapolis. One of these companies, an insurance firm, kept an apartment in Edina which was used as a place to entertain big clients when they came to town. The place was very expensively furnished, had parquet oak floors, a well-stocked bar, and in the closets, stacks of pornographic films and magazines and pictures as well as lingerie for the women to wear.

What usually happened was that the man who was in charge of entertainment would invite some local associates who wanted to have a good time, along with visiting big shots who needed or wanted to be entertained. The men who got there first started drinking and watching porn movies. Then three or four women — always fewer than the men — would arrive. They would ask us to get into the lingerie and maybe show another film or bring out pictures. And then the intercourse would start, all in one room, so that some men would watch. This was all straight sex and the men were never coercive, but I got paid extra money if I could find prostitutes who were willing to have anal sex or who were willing to perform oral sex on another woman in front of the men.

This is a story of a woman who is currently working downtown in Minneapolis.

I was the main woman of a pimp who filmed sexual acts almost every night in our home. The dope man supplied us with free cocaine in exchange for arranged orgies. He was a really freaky man. The men arranged to have women — who I assumed were forced to be there — to have sex with dogs, and filmed those acts. There were stacks of films all over the house, which my pimp used to blackmail people with.

One morning I came downstairs in time to see a very young girl run naked out of the house. I found her friend, also naked, tied up in the closet. The one who ran away, after being forced to perform sexually all night, went to the police. I don't know what my pimp did with the other girl. I do know that he had kidnapped them and felt safe in doing so because they were foreign and alone. The girl came back with the police, but nothing ever happened. My pimp continued to make films of people doing every kind of sex act in the living room of our home. He was never involved in the acts, he got off by watching.

Ms. Dworkin: Could you describe a little more about the relationship between the pornography shown and the pictures actually taken of the young woman that it was being shown to?

Ms. S.: Young women would be picked up off the street. Everyone's first experience was always the same. The men would either show a woman magazines or take her to a movie. Then afterwards he instructed her to act in the way that the magazines or the film had depicted. I call it the training period. Then these men, or different men, would set up scenarios, usually with more than one woman, to copy scenes that they had seen portrayed in magazines and books. Then they would make their movies using home video equipment and Polaroid cameras for their own libraries of pornography.

Part II

OVERVIEW

An anti-pornography banner was set aflame at a Take Back the Night march in San Francisco in November 1990. In the background women carry signs bearing the pictures and names of the victims of the Massacre in Montreal.

Credit: Jane Philomen Cleland, San Francisco

CHAPTER 8

Pornography and Freedom

John Stoltenberg

There is a widespread belief that sexual freedom is an idea whose time has come. Many people believe that in the last few decades we have gotten more and more of it — that sexual freedom is something we can carve out against the forces of sexual repressiveness, and that significant gains have been won, gains we dare not give up lest we backslide into the sexual dark ages, when there wasn't sexual freedom, there was only repression.

Indeed, many things seem to have changed. But if you look closely at what is supposed to be sexual freedom, you can become very confused. Let's say, for instance, you understand that a basic principle of sexual freedom is that people should be free to be sexual and that one way to guarantee that freedom is to make sure that sex be free from imposed restraint. That's not a bad idea, but if you happen to look at a magazine photograph in which a woman is bound and gagged and lashed down on a plank with her genital area open to the camera, you might well wonder: Where is the freedom from restraint? Where's the sexual freedom?

Let's say you understand that people should be free to be sexual and that one way to guarantee that freedom is to make sure people can feel good about themselves and each other sexually. That's not a bad idea. But if you happen to read random passages from books such as the following, you could be quite perplexed:

> "Baby, you're gonna get fucked tonight like you ain't never been fucked before," he hissed evilly down at her as she struggled fruitlessly against her bonds. The man wanted only to abuse and ravish her till she was totally broken and subservient to him. He knelt between her wide-spread legs and gloated over the cringing little pussy he was about to ram his cock into. (Baker, 1978, p. 132)

Reprinted by permission of the author from Michael S. Kimmel (Ed.), (1990), *Men confront pornography*. New York: Penguin USA/Meridian, pp. 60–71.

And here's another:

> "Bitch," he snapped, pulling away from her, yanking his dick out of her mouth. "You're trying to make me come before I'm ready. You know I like to fuck your ass before I come! You inconsiderate bitch!" he spat, knowing how she ate up that kind of talk. (Mixer, 1977, p. 103)

Passages such as these might well make you wonder: Where are the good feelings about each other's body? Where's the sexual freedom?

Let's say you understand that people should be free to be sexual and that one way to guarantee that freedom is to make sure people are free from sexualized hate and degradation. But let's say you come upon a passage such as this:

> Reaching into his pocket for the knife again, Ike stepped just inches away from Burl's outstretched body. He slid the knife under Burl's cock and balls, letting the sharp edge of the blade lightly scrape the underside of Burl's nutsac. As if to reassert his power over Burl, Ike grabbed one of the bound man's tautly stretched pecs, clamping down hard over Burl's tit and muscle, latching on as tight as he could. He pushed on the knife, pressing the blade into Burl's skin as hard as possible without cutting him. "Now, you just let us inside that tight black asshole of yours, boy, or else we're gonna cut this off and feed it to the cattle!" (Robeson, 1981, p. 27)

After reading that, you might well ask: Where's the freedom from hatred? Where's the freedom from degradation? Where's the sexual freedom?

Let's say you understand people should be free to be sexual and that one way to guarantee that freedom is to make sure people are not punished for the individuality of their sexuality. And then you find a magazine showing page after page of bodies with their genitals garroted in baling wire and leather thongs, with their genitals tied up and tortured, with heavy weights suspended from rings that pierce their genitals, and the surrounding text makes clear that this mutilation and punishment are experienced as sex acts. And you might wonder in your mind: Why must this person suffer punishment in order to experience sexual feelings? Why must this person be humiliated and disciplined and whipped and beaten until he bleeds in order to have access to his homoerotic passion? Why have the Grand Inquisitor's most repressive and sadistic torture techniques become what people do to each other and call sex? Where's the sexual freedom?

If you look back at the books and magazines and movies that have been produced in this country in the name of sexual freedom over the past decade, you've got to wonder: *Why has sexual freedom come to look so much like sexual repression? Why has sexual freedom come to look so much like unfreedom?* The answer, I believe, has to do with the relationship between freedom and justice, and specifically the relationship between *sexual* freedom and *sexual* justice. When we think of freedom in any other sense, we think of freedom as *the result* of justice. We know that there can't truly *be* any freedom until justice has happened, until justice exists. For any people in history who have struggled for freedom, those people have understood that their freedom exists on the future side of justice. The notion of freedom *prior to* justice is understood to be meaningless. Whenever people do not have freedom, they have understood freedom to be that which is arrived at by achieving justice. If you told them they should try to have their freedom without there being justice, they would laugh in your face. Freedom *always* exists on the far side of justice. That's perfectly understood — except when it comes to sex.

The popular concept of sexual freedom in this country has never meant sexual justice. Sexual-freedom advocates have cast the issue only in terms of having sex that is free from suppression and restraint. Practically speaking, that has meant advocacy of sex that is free from institutional interference; sex that is free from being constrained by legal, religious, and medical ideologies; sex that is free from any outside intervention. Sexual freedom on a more personal level has meant sex that is free from fear, guilt, and shame — which in practical terms has meant advocacy of sex that is free from value judgments, sex that is free from responsibility, sex that is free from consequences, sex that is free from ethical distinctions, sex that is essentially free from any obligation to take into account in one's consciousness that the other person is a *person*. In order to free sex from fear, guilt, and shame, it was thought that institutional restrictions on sex needed to be overthrown, but in fact what needed to be overthrown was any vestige of an interpersonal ethic in which people would be real to one another; for once people are real to one another, the consequences of one's acts matter deeply and personally; and particularly in the case of sex, one risks perceiving the consequences of one's acts in ways that feel *bad* because they do not feel *right*. This entire moral-feeling level of sexuality, therefore, needed to be undone. And it was undone, in the guise of an assault on institutional suppression.

Sexual freedom has never really meant that individuals should have sexual self-determination, that individuals should be free to experience the integrity of their own bodies and be free to act out of that integrity in a way that is totally within their own right to choose. Sexual freedom has never really meant that people should have absolute sovereignty over their own erotic being. And the reason for this is simple: Sexual freedom has never really been about *sexual justice between men and women*. It has been about maintaining men's superior status, men's power over women; and it has been about sexualizing women's inferior status, men's subordination of women. Essentially, sexual freedom has been about preserving a sexuality that preserves male supremacy.

What makes male supremacy so insidious, so pervasive, such a seemingly permanent component of all our precious lives, is the fact that erection can be conditioned to it. And orgasm can be habituated to it. There's a cartoon; it's from *Penthouse*: A man and woman are in bed. He's on top, fucking her. The caption reads: "I can't come unless you pretend to be unconscious." The joke could as well have taken any number of variations: "I can't get hard unless — I can't fuck unless — I can't get turned on unless — I can't feel anything sexual unless — " Then fill in the blanks: "Unless I am possessing you. Unless I am superior to you. Unless I am in control of you. Unless I am humiliating you. Unless I am hurting you. Unless I have broken your will."

Once sexuality is stuck in male supremacy, all the forms of unjust power at its heart become almost physically addictive. All the stuff of our primitive fight-or-flight reflexes — a pounding heart, a hard sweat, heaving lungs — these are all things the body does when it is in terror, when it is lashing out in rage, and these are all things it is perfectly capable of doing during sex acts that are terrifying and sex acts that are vengeful. Domination and subordination — the very essence of injustice and unfreedom — have become culturally eroticized, and we are supposed to believe that giving eroticized domination and subordination free expression is the fullest flowering of sexual freedom.

Prepubescent boys get erections in all kinds of apparently nonsexual situations — being terrified, being in physical danger, being punished, moving perilously fast, simply being called on to recite in class. A boy's body's dilemma, as he grows older, as he learns more about the cultural power signified by the penis and how it is supposed to function in male-supremacist sex, is how to produce erections reliably in explicitly heterosexual contexts. His body gets a great deal of help. All around him is a culture in which rage and dread and hazard and aggression are made aphrodisiacs. And women's bodies are made the butt of whatever works to get it up.

The sexuality of male supremacy is viscerally committed to domination and subordination, because those are the terms on which it learned to feel, to feel anything sexual at all. Its heart pounds and its blood rushes and its autonomic nervous system surges at the thought and/or the action of forced sex, bullying sex, violent sex, injurious sex, humiliating sex, hostile sex, murderous sex. The kind of sex that puts the other person in their place. The kind of sex that keeps the other person *other*. The kind of sex that makes you know you're in the presence of someone who is palpably a man.

Some of us know how male-supremacist sexuality feels better than do others. Some of us know how that sexuality feels inside because we do it, or we have done it, or we would like to do it, or we would like to do it more than we get a chance to. It's the sexuality that makes us feel powerful, virile, in control. Some of us have known how that sexuality feels when someone else is doing it to us, someone who is having sex with us, someone whose body is inhabited by it, someone who is experiencing its particular imperative and having male-supremacist sex against our flesh. And some of us don't really know this sexuality directly; in fact, our bodies haven't adapted to male supremacy very successfully at all — it is not the sexuality that moves us, that touches us, that comes anywhere near feeling as good as we imagine we want our sexual feelings to feel. We don't recognize a longing for anything like it in our own bodies, and we've been lucky so far — very lucky — not to have experienced it *against* our bodies. Nonetheless, we know that it exists; and the more we know about pornography, the more we know what it looks like.

PORNOGRAPHY AND MALE SUPREMACY

Male-supremacist sexuality is important to pornography, and pornography is important to male supremacy. Pornography *institutionalizes* the sexuality that both embodies and enacts male supremacy. Pornography says about that sexuality, "Here's how": Here's how to act out male supremacy in sex. Here's how the action should go. Here are the acts that impose power over and against another body. And pornography says about that sexuality, "Here's who": Here's who you should do it to and here's who she is: your whore, your piece of ass, yours. Your penis is a weapon, her body is your target. And pornography says about that sexuality, "Here's why": Because men are masters, women are slaves; men are superior, women are subordinate; men are real, women are objects; men are sex machines, women are sluts.

Pornography institutionalizes male supremacy the way segregation institutionalizes white supremacy. It is a practice embodying an ideology of biological superiority; it is an institution that both expresses that ideology and enacts that ideology — makes it the reality that people believe is true, keeps it that way, keeps people from knowing any other possibility, keeps certain people powerful by keeping certain people *down*.

Pornography also *eroticizes* male supremacy. It makes dominance and subordination feel like sex; it makes hierarchy feel like sex; it makes force and violence feel like sex; it makes hate and terrorism feel like sex; it makes inequality feel like sex. Pornography keeps sexism sexy. It keeps sexism *necessary* for some people to have sexual feelings. It makes reciprocity make you go limp. It makes mutuality leave you cold. It makes tenderness and intimacy and caring make you feel like you're going to disappear into a void. It makes justice the opposite of erotic; it makes injustice a sexual thrill.

Pornography exploits every experience in people's lives that *imprisons* sexual feelings — pain, terrorism, punishment, dread, shame, powerlessness, self-hate — and would have you believe that it *frees* sexual feelings. In fact, the sexual freedom represented by pornography is the freedom of men to act sexually in ways that keep sex a basis for inequality.

You can't have authentic sexual freedom without sexual justice. It is only freedom for those in power; the powerless cannot be free. Their experience of sexual freedom becomes but a delusion borne of complying with the demands of the powerful. Increased sexual freedom under male supremacy has had to mean an increased tolerance for sexual practices that are predicated on eroticized injustice between men and women: treating women's bodies or body parts as merely sexual objects or things; treating women as utterly submissive masochists who enjoy pain and humiliation and who, if they are raped, enjoy it; treating women's bodies to sexualized beating, mutilation, bondage, dismemberment. . . . Once you have sexualized inequality, once it is a learned and internalized prerequisite for sexual arousal and sexual gratification, then anything goes. And that's what sexual freedom means on this side of sexual justice.

PORNOGRAPHY AND HOMOPHOBIA

Homophobia is absolutely integral to the system of sexualized male supremacy. Cultural homophobia expresses a whole range of antifemale revulsion: It expresses contempt for men who are sexual with men because they are believed to be "treated like a woman" in sex. It expresses contempt for women who are sexual with women just *because* they are women and also because they are perceived to be a rebuke to the primacy of the penis.

But cultural homophobia is not merely an expression of woman-hating; it also works to protect men from the sexual aggression of other men. Homophobia keeps men doing to women what they would not want done to themselves. There's not the same sexual harassment of men that there is of women on the street or in the workplace or in the university; there's not nearly the same extent of rape; there's not the same demeaned social caste that is sexualized, as it is for women. And that's thanks to homophobia:

Cultural homophobia keeps men's sexual aggression directed toward women. Homophobia keeps men acting in concert as male supremacists so that they won't be perceived as an appropriate target for male-supremacist sexual treatment. Imagine this country *without* homophobia. A woman raped every three minutes *and a man* raped every three minutes. Homophobia keeps that statistic at a manageable level. The system is not foolproof, of course. There are boys who have been sexually molested by men. There are men who have been brutalized in sexual relationships with their male lovers, and they too have a memory of men's sexual violence. And there are many men in prison who are subject to the same sexual terrorism that women live with almost all the time. But for the most part — happily — homophobia serves male supremacy by protecting "real men" from sexual assault by other real men.

Pornography is one of the major enforcers of cultural homophobia. Pornography is rife with gay-baiting and effemiphobia. Portrayals of allegedly lesbian "scenes" are a staple of heterosexual pornography: The women with each other are there for the male viewer, the male voyeur; there is not the scantest evidence that they are there for each other. Through so-called men's sophisticate magazines — the "skin" magazines — pornographers outdo one another in their attacks against feminists, who are typically derided as *lesbians* — "sapphic" at best, "bull dykes" at worst. The innuendo that a man is a "fairy" or a "faggot" is, in pornography, a kind of dare or a challenge to prove his cocksmanship. And throughout pornography, the male who is perceived to be the passive orifice in sex is tainted with the disdain that "normally" belongs to women.

Meanwhile, gay male pornography, which often appears to present an idealized, all-male, superbutch world, also contains frequent derogatory references to women, or to feminized males. In order to give vent to male sexual aggression and sadism in homosexual pornography and also to circumvent the cultural stigma that ordinarily attaches to men who are "treated like a woman" in sex, gay male pornography has developed several specific "codes." One such code is that a man who is "capable" of withstanding "discipline" — extremely punishing bondage, humiliation, and fist-fucking, for instance — is deemed to have achieved a kind of supermasculinity, almost as if the sexual violence his body ingests from another man enhances his own sexual identity as a man. (This is quite the reverse in heterosexual pornography, where sexual sadism against a woman simply confirms her in her subordinate status.) Another code common in gay male pornography, one found frequently in films, is that if a man is shown being ass-fucked, he will generally be shown ass-fucking someone else in turn — this to avoid the connotation that he is at all feminized by being fucked. Still another code in gay male pornography is that depictions of mutuality are not sustained for very long without an intimation or explicit scene of force or coercion — so you don't go limp out of boredom or anxiety that you've been suckered into a scene where there's no raw male power present.

There is, not surprisingly, an intimate connection between the male supremacy in both heterosexual and homosexual pornography and the woman-hating and effemiphobia in them both as well. That connection is male-supremacist sex — the social power of men over women acted out as eroticized domination and subordination. The difference is that gay male pornography invents a way for men to be the *objects* of male-supremacist sex without seeming to be its *victims*. In its own special fashion, gay male pornography keeps men safe from male-supremacist sex — by holding out the promise that you'll come away from it more a man.

Needless to say, for heterosexual men who don't buy this, it's repellent and a crock. Needless to say, for homosexual men who *do* buy into this, it can become a really important part of one's sexual identity as a gay man. Because if you think the problem facing you is that your masculinity is in doubt because you're queer, then the promise of gay male pornography looks like forgiveness and redemption. Not to mention what it feels like: communion with true virility.

Now this is the situation of men within male supremacy: Whether we are straight or gay, we have been looking for a sexual freedom that is utterly specious, and we have been looking for it through pornography, which perpetuates the very domination and subordination that stand in the way of sexual justice. Whether we are straight or gay, we have been looking for a notion of freedom that leaves out women; we have been looking for a sexuality that preserves men's power over women. So long as that is what we strive for, we cannot possibly feel freely, and no one can be free. Whatever sexual freedom might be, it must be after justice.

SEXUAL JUSTICE AND THE LAW

The question is how to get justice. The question is how to effect it.

There are many necessary ways to achieve sexual justice in society. The law ought to be an important one. Justice, after all, is supposed to be among the law's primary functions. But the law has had a very sorry record on that score. Historically, laws have served to perpetuate injustice — slavery, for example — as often as, or more often than, they have served to undo it. And laws about sex have been especially unhelpful, for they tend to serve the interests of the powerful and betray those who are powerless. Rape laws, for instance, have maintained the right of husbands to rape.

Obscenity laws have perpetuated a belief in the vileness of women's bodies and protected men from their sexual shame in relation to other men. Sodomy laws have legitimized the persecution of those whose very existence would seem to jeopardize men's hold on the superior status of their sex. If anything, law has functioned to defend male supremacy, to reinforce sexual injustice.

In the fall of 1983, in Minneapolis, a new legal theory was invented that might actually defy male supremacy and materially effect sexual justice. This legal theory was contained in antipornography legislation that would allow civil lawsuits against pornographers on the grounds that pornography is a violation of women's civil rights — because pornography subordinates women as a class and thereby creates sex discrimination. The law was written by two radical feminists who had been co-teaching a course on pornography at the University of Minnesota Law School — Catharine A. MacKinnon, the constitutional-law professor who pioneered the legal definition of sexual harassment as sex discrimination, and Andrea Dworkin, the author of *Woman Hating* and *Pornography: Men Possessing Women* (see Dworkin & MacKinnon, 1988). The ordinance they drafted at the invitation of the Minneapolis City Council would essentially give to those who had been the victims of male-supremacist sex in the form of pornography a cause of action — for the first time, this law would allow a woman to go into court to try to prove that she had been injured or victimized by having pornography forced on her, by being coerced into a pornographic performance, or because pornography was used in some sexual assault on her. The ordinance would also allow a woman to sue traffickers in pornography on the basis of the proven harm pornography does to the civil rights of women as a class. The fact is, these things happen, as became horrifyingly clear in public hearings before the city council during which testimony was given by both victims and victim-service providers. And the fact is, there is nothing yet on the lawbooks that would let anyone to whom these things have happened get any justice whatsoever.

The civil-rights antipornography ordinance has absolutely nothing to do with police action, morals squads, or a censorship board; it would function entirely in the form of complaints and civil suits brought by individual plaintiffs, not through prosecutions brought by the state. Under the ordinance, a woman could not get anyone arrested or put in jail, the police could not conduct a raid, and there could not be a criminal prosecution. What kind of justice, then, could a woman get? If she proved her case in a trial, she could get money damages and removal of the particular pornography from sale in the city. And that's after a court fight.

By making possible certain civil lawsuits against pornographers and traffickers in pornography, this ordinance would actually *extend* civil liberties to victims who are now outside the law; it would grant a right of speech to those victims, a right to speak in a court of law. And though the ordinance is based in laws against sex discrimination, anyone — a woman, a child, a man, or a transsexual — could sue under it if they could prove that they had been a victim of pornography.

Needless to say, what happened in Minneapolis became a national astonishment. Shock waves went out. Many allegedly progressive people had a basic problem with the ordinance. It took a stand against eroticized domination and subordination; it took a stand against male-supremacist sex; it took a stand against the very sexual conduct that makes injustice feel sexy. There was a rather widespread horror at the notion that a woman, a mere woman, might ever enter a courtroom and possibly prove — through cumbersome and expensive litigation — that a particular manifestation of male-supremacist sex had injured her and that her injury had specifically to do with the fact that she was a woman. The new law would let a woman prove that a particular instance of male-supremacist sex had done what male-supremacist sex is *supposed* to do: make her inferior and harm her, make her subordinate, make her suffer the sexual freedom of men. So it became a question of community standards: How much justice could a city tolerate?

Opponents raised an issue of freedom of speech that was really an issue about freedom of sex. Their argument was really an argument for the sexuality that feels its freedom most exquisitely when it is negating someone else's freedom. It was about wanting to keep safe the style of sexual subordination to which they had become accustomed, the sexual freedom that abhors sexual justice, the sexuality that can get hard and come only when it is oblivious to another person's rights. And it was an argument to keep off the public record any acknowledgment that male-supremacist sex is dangerous, especially to women.

Remember the cartoon: "I can't come unless you pretend to be unconscious."

Perhaps most profoundly, the civil-rights antipornography ordinance would help make victims *conscious* — conscious of their civil rights. The existence of this ordinance would have an important effect symbolically in terms of helping carve out social consciousness about what equal rights for women really must mean. Just as the existence of laws against marital rape has a "ripple effect" on people's minds — sending out the message that women are not to be raped in marriage, even to those who don't use the laws against it — this ordinance would be a community's declaration that women have civil rights that pornography may not trample on. And that would have a radical effect: That would shake male supremacy to its core, because that would make male-supremacist sex not feel so sexy.

Linda Marchiano, who as Linda Lovelace was coerced into making the pornographic film *Deep Throat* — the highest-grossing pornographic film in history — would be able to sue under this ordinance. As it becomes law in community after community, more and more victims of pornography can be expected to come forward. At last there will be the possibility of some legal recourse. At last there will be an instrument of justice available to those who are now most silenced by pornographers' freedom of so-called speech.

PORNOGRAPHY AND MEN

I want to address those of us who live in male supremacy as men, and I want to speak specifically to those of us who have come to understand that pornography does make sexism sexy; that pornography does make male supremacy sexy; and that pornography does define what is sexy in terms of domination and subordination, in terms that serve *us as men* — whether we buy it or not, whether we buy into it or not — because it serves male supremacy, which is exactly what it is for.

I want to speak to those of us who live in this setup as men and who recognize — in the world and in our very own selves — the power pornography can have over our lives: It can make men believe that anything sexy is good. It can make men believe that our penises are like weapons. It can make men believe — for some moments of orgasm — that we are just like the men in pornography: virile, strong, tough, maybe cruel. It can make men believe that if you take it away from us, we won't have sexual feelings.

But I want to speak also to those of us who live in this setup as men and who recognize the power that pornography has over the lives of women: because it can make us believe that women by nature are whores; because it can make us believe that women's body parts belong to us — separately, part by part — instead of to a whole, real other person; because it can make us believe that women want to be raped, enjoy being damaged by us, deserve to be punished; because it can make us believe that women are an alien species, completely different from us so that we can be completely different from them, not as real as us so that we can be men. I want to talk to those of us who know in our guts that pornography can make us believe all of that. We know because we've watched it happen to men around us. We know because it has happened in us.

And what I want to say is simply this: We've got to make some serious changes, and we've got to get busy and *act*. If we sit around and don't do anything, then we become the ones who are keeping things the way they are. If we sit around and all we do is intellectual and emotional dithering, then we stay in the ranks of those who are the passive enforcers of male supremacy. If we don't take seriously the fact that pornography is a radical political issue and an issue about *us*, and if we don't make serious progress in the direction of *what we're going to do about it*, then we've just gone over to the wrong side of the fight — the morally wrong, historically wrong side of a struggle that is a ground swell, a grass-roots *people's* movement against sexual injustice.

We've got to be telling our sons that if a man gets off by putting women down, *it's not okay*.

We've got to be telling merchants that if they peddle women's bodies and lives for men's consumption and entertainment, *it's not okay*.

We've got to be telling other men that if you let the pornographers lead you by the nose (or any other body part) into believing that women exist to be tied up and hung up and beaten and raped, *it's not okay*.

We've got to be telling the pornographers that whatever they think they're doing in our names as men, as entertainment for men, for the sake of some delusion of so-called manhood . . . well, it's not okay. It's not okay with *us*.

FREEDOM AND EQUALITY

Historically, when people have not had justice and when people have not had freedom, they have had only the material reality of injustice and unfreedom. When freedom and justice don't exist, they're but a dream and a vision, an abstract idea longed for. You can't really know what justice would be like or what freedom would feel like. You can only know how it feels *not* to have them, and what it feels like to hope, to imagine, to desire them with a passion. Sexual freedom is an idea whose time has *not* come. It can't possibly be truly experienced until there is sexual justice. And sexual justice is incompatible with a definition of freedom that is based on the subordination of women.

Equality is still a radical idea. It makes some people very angry. It also gives some people hope.

When equality is an idea whose time has come, we will perhaps know sex with justice, we will perhaps know passion with compassion, we will perhaps know ardor and affection with honor. In that time, when the integrity within everyone's body and the whole personhood of each person is celebrated whenever two people touch, we will perhaps truly know the freedom to be sexual in a world of real equality.

According to pornography, you can't get there from here. According to male supremacy, you should not even want to try.

Some of us want to go there. Some of us want to be there. And we know that the struggle will be difficult and long. But we know that the passion for justice cannot be denied. And someday — *someday* — there will be both justice and freedom for each person — and thereby for us all.

CHAPTER 9

Questions and Answers

Andrea Dworkin & Catharine MacKinnon

Q: What is the difference between hard-core and soft-core pornography?

A: Before pornography became an above-ground industry, the distinction was pretty simple. "Hard-core" was pornography in which an erect penis was shown. The penis could belong to a man or to an animal. For this reason, the pornography of bestiality, which usually showed a male animal penetrating a woman, was considered to be "hard-core." There was a real taboo against showing the erect penis on the screen or in magazines. Police were more likely to make arrests and to confiscate material if the erect penis was graphically shown.

As pornography became more mainstream, with more legal protection, people inside and outside the pornography industry began to obfuscate the meaning of "hard-core." People outside the pornography industry, many of whom were not consumers of pornography but felt that they knew what was in it, began to use "hard-core" to refer to explicitly debasing or violent material and "soft-core" to refer to material they thought was purely sexual. "Hard-core" came to mean the worst pornography, "soft-core" the most benign.

Because *Playboy* and *Penthouse*, for instance, were the most available and most legitimate pornography, they became the standard for "soft-core," material that was supposedly purely sexual, not misogynist or violent. Currently in popular usage, "soft-core" is virtually a synonym for *Playboy* and *Penthouse*. In one sense, both magazines are "soft-core": neither shows the erect penis; in fact, with rare exception, neither shows nude men. But in a more important sense, "soft-core" is a misnomer, because both magazines show violent and violating uses of women's bodies; both magazines include overtly violent material; both magazines have material that promotes rape and child sexual abuse.

As used by most people, the two terms are fairly meaningless. Most often, "soft-core" means pornography that someone thinks is okay; "hard-core" is pornography that someone thinks is the real stuff, dirty, mean, and at least a little abusive and repulsive. "Hard-core" has the aura of breaking taboos around it and pornographers use it in advertising as a point of pride.

The terms tell us nothing about how women are used in pornography and nothing about how the pornography itself is then used on women or children.

Q: How can you object to *Playboy*?

A: *Playboy* is a bona fide part of the trade in women.

The format of *Playboy* was developed to protect the magazine from prosecution under obscenity law. Writing from recognized writers was published to meet a standard of worth that would get the magazine First Amendment protection. The First Amendment was then used by *Playboy* to protect its sexual exploitation of women. *Playboy* sells women.

The use of women as objects in *Playboy* is part of how *Playboy* helps to create second-class status for women. Women in *Playboy* are dehumanized by being used as sexual objects and commodities, their bodies fetishized and sold. The term "bunny" is used to characterize the woman as less than human — little animals that want sex all the time, animals that are kept in hutches.

The women in *Playboy* are presented in postures of submission and sexual servility. Constant access to the throat, the anus, and the vagina is the purpose of the ways in which the women are posed.

Playboy has made a speciality of targeting women for sexual harassment: working women, including nurses, police, and military personnel; and presumptively educated women, including university students and lawyers.

Underlying all of *Playboy*'s pictorials is the basic theme of all pornography: that all women are whores by nature, born wanting to be sexually accessible to all men at all times. *Playboy* particularly centers on sexual display as what women naturally do to demonstrate this nature.

Playboy, in both text and pictures, promotes rape.

Playboy, especially in its cartoons, promotes both rape and child sexual abuse.

There is also some amount of overtly violent material in *Playboy*. The text often enthusiastically promotes various acts of violence against women, including gang-rape. The pictures usually include some pictures that show sadomasochism: women are hurt in them or are in some physical danger. (For example, a woman is naked with acupuncture needles all over her body, including in her breasts; or a woman is chained to a pole and surrounded by laser beams.)

Hugh Hefner founded *Playboy* in 1953. An early issue used an employee as a centerfold; as her employer, Hefner had sex with her too. This has remained the pattern, the women who work for *Playboy*, especially the centerfolds, being Hefner's own primary preserve of women. As the *Playboy* empire has increased in power and wealth, Hefner's personal use of the women in the magazine has continued and expanded. He uses them and he sells them. Now the women are brought to him by lesser pimps; he need not do the recruiting himself. For instance, Linda Marchiano, known as Linda Lovelace in the pornographic film "Deep Throat," was pimped to Hefner by her then-husband, Chuck Traynor. Hefner sodomized her and tried to have her have intercourse with a dog. Dorothy Stratten, a *Playboy* centerfold who was sodomized, tortured, murdered, then raped after she was dead by her pimp-husband, Paul Snider, was tricked and intimidated into photo sessions by Snider, who then sold the photos and access to Dorothy herself to Hefner. Ms. Stratten said she was sexually molested by Hefner. After her death, Hefner was made aware that Ms. Stratten had hated the pornography made of her and had hated posing for it. He responded by issuing more videotapes of Ms. Stratten posing. Dorothy Stratten's estate entered a brief in her behalf in support of the Indianapolis Ordinance. The brief outlined how Ms. Stratten had been pressured into pornography. The hope of her estate was that the Ordinance could be used to recover and destroy videotapes and photographs (primarily in back issues of *Playboy*) that are still being trafficked in.

The women used by Hefner personally and in the magazine are rarely much over eighteen. Ms. Stratten was underage when she was initially pimped to Hefner.

The sexual exploitation of women is what the magazine is, what it does, what it sells, and how it is produced.

Q: Pornography is the fault of the women who pose for it. Why don't they just stop posing?

A: The women in pornography are most often victims of child sexual abuse. Some studies show that 65 to 75 percent of the current population of women in prostitution and pornography (overlapping experiences for the same pool of women) have been abused as children, usually in the home. People who work with women who are in pornography and prostitution to provide social services or counselling, some of whom have been in pornography or prostitution themselves, believe the percentage is much, much higher. Children run away from home, from the sexual abuse, to cities where they are picked up by pimps, raped, beaten, drugged, and forced into prostitution or pornography.

Women in pornography are poor women, usually uneducated. Pornography exists in a society in which women are economically disadvantaged. The only professions in which women make more money than men are modeling and prostitution — and in prostitution, the pimps keep most if not all of it. Women's economic value is determined largely by sexual value: how much the woman's body is worth in the marketplace as a commodity.

Many women are forced into pornography as children by fathers who sexually abuse them; pornography is made of them as part of the sexual abuse they experience as children. Many women are forced into pornography by husbands, many of whom are violent (battery of married women being the most commonly committed violent crime in the country). Many women are photographed by lovers and find the photographs published as pornography in revenge or retaliation. Aspiring actresses and models are photographed nude, almost a trade practice, and find the photographs published against their will and without their knowledge in pornography.

When a woman has been forced into pornography, the pornography itself is used to keep her in a life of sexual exploitation and abuse. Think of what happens when a battered wife asks for help. She is doing what society says women should do: she is married, and the sustained battery is proof that she has been loyal to her husband, she has stayed with him, the way women are supposed to. She may be badly hurt over a period of years. When she leaves home, she is often treated as a pariah, told the brutality is her own fault. Now think of the woman forced into prostitution. She is without the so-called protections of a respectable life. She has been abandoned, if not injured in the first place, by her family. Society has no place for her and despises her for what she has been doing. The photographs of her engaging in violating sex acts — violating of *her* — usually show her smiling, as if she enjoyed being used or hurt. Where can she turn? Where can she run? Who will believe her? Who will help her? Will you? (If you won't, don't assume anyone else will.)

The pimp or pornographer will come after her. If he is her husband or her father, he will have a legal right to her. He will be violent toward her and toward anyone who tries to help her. She will be terribly hurt from the life she has been leading: she will be injured from the pornography and prostitution; she may be addicted to many drugs; she will be filled with anger and self-hate and despair.

Battered women's shelters, of which there are not enough, many of which are understaffed, will probably not offer her shelter. They are afraid of the pimps and they are afraid of the host of antisocial behaviors that the woman herself may demonstrate. Rape crisis centers do not have resources to offer shelter at all but they are also not prepared to counsel prostitutes, even though most have been raped many times and suffer the trauma of multiple rape.

The women in pornography are the first victims of pornography. The pornographers, not the women they hurt, are responsible for pornography. The men who buy and use the pornography are responsible for pornography, not the women who are violated to make the product they so enjoy. And the society that protects the pornography is responsible for pornography: the courts that value the so-called rights of the pornographers over the humanity, the dignity, the civil equality of women; the publishers and writers who keep protecting the trafficking in women as if the commercial violation of women were a basic right of publishing; the lawyers, the politicians, the media, who congregate to chant self-righteous litanies in worship of the Constitution while women are raped for fun and profit under its protection.

Q: Isn't pornography just a symptom, not a cause, of misogyny? Pornography didn't *cause* patriarchy, did it? It's not really important, is it?

A: An incredible double standard is always applied to thinking about or doing anything about pornography.

If pornography hurts women now, doesn't something need to be done about it? If women are hurt in making pornography, doesn't something need to be done? If pornography is used to choreograph and execute rape, incest, battery, and forcing women into prostitution, doesn't something need to be done? If pornography actually creates attitudes and behaviors of bigotry and aggression against women, as many laboratory studies demonstrate, doesn't something need to be done? If pornography causes rape, or sexualized torture, or increases sadism against women, or plays a role in serial murders, or contributes substantially to legitimizing violence against women, isn't it important to do something about pornography? If pornography spreads woman hating and rape as mass entertainment, how can feminists ignore or be indifferent to it as a political issue of equality? Think about the maxim "Equal pay for equal work." We understand that women are hurt by being paid less than men for doing the same work. Lower pay keeps us poorer, which debases the quality of our lives, and keeps us dependent, which does the same. Pay discrimination did not cause patriarchy. Pay discrimination is a symptom of women's lower status. It is a result of misogyny, not a cause. At the same time, pay discrimination perpetuates women's lower status (by keeping us poor) and confirms men in their misogyny (the conviction that women are worth less than men). No one would suggest that feminists abandon the fight, including the legal fight, for equal pay because it is "only a symptom," not a cause, of patriarchy itself.

Now, in fact, feminists want equal pay for work of comparable worth. Because the job market is still highly sex-segregated and the jobs women do are economically devalued because women do them, feminists are proposing that men and women should be paid the same if their jobs, though different, have similar economic and social value. We have gotten legislation passed in some places mandating equal pay for comparable work. We have claimed economic equity as a right and we want society to be reorganized so that we can realize that right. The economic disparity between men and women is a symptom of male supremacy, but, however symptomatic it is, it injures women, so we want to stop it. In getting rid of this symptom of male supremacy, we also know that we would make male supremacy a little less supreme.

Have you ever had a very high fever — 104° or 105° — just the symptom of a serious, underlying disease or infection? You had better believe that the first order of business is to reduce the fever because, even though it is a symptom, it may well jeopardize your life and on its own can irreparably damage your health. And you will feel very sick with the fever and less sick without it.

Some symptoms are pretty terrible, and it is important to try to get rid of them.

With pornography, there is massive evidence that pornography is not only a symptom of misogyny but an active agent in generating woman-hating acts and second-class status for women. Pornography sexualizes inequality and the hatred of women so that men get sexual pleasure from hurting women and putting women down. It creates bigotry and aggression. It desensitizes men to rape and other forms of sexual violence against women so that they do not recognize the violence as violence, or they believe the woman provoked and enjoyed it. Pornography is used as a blueprint for sadism, rape, and torture. It is used to force women and children into prostitution. It is used to coerce children into sex. Sex offenders use it to plan their crimes and to prime themselves to commit their crimes. It is implicated in the biographies of serial murderers and in the commissions of the murders themselves. It is more than a very high fever. It does as much damage as low pay. How can we justify not doing something about it, whether it is a symptom or a cause?

Some people claim that pornography is irrelevant to violence against women. They say that pornography is new and contemporary and that

rape, battery, and prostitution are old. They say that pornography cannot
be a cause of violence against women because violence against women
existed long before pornography.

This is not true, but suppose it were.

Even if pornography is a cause now, and never was before, we would
have to do something about it now. Think about environmental pollution.
It causes various kinds of cancer (though those who make the pollution
don't think so). Cancer existed long before the kinds of environmental
pollution that come from highly industrialized societies. But this does not
mean that pollution in our society does not cause cancer in our society.

In fact, pornography has a long history in Western civilization (and in
Asian and other civilizations too). Its history is as long as the documented
history of rape and prostitution (the so-called oldest profession, the misogynist meaning being that as long as there have been women, women
have prostituted themselves). We can trace pornography without any difficulty back as far as ancient Greece in the West. Pornography is a Greek
word. It means the graphic depiction of women as the lowest, most vile
whores. It refers to writing, etching, or drawing of women who, in real
life, were kept in female sexual slavery in ancient Greece. Pornography has
always, as far back as we can go, had to do with exploiting, debasing, and
violating women in forced sex. Drawings, etchings, and writings were
made of or about the female sex slaves performing forced sex acts. Women
were used in brothels to create live pornography for men.

The invention of the camera changed the social reality of pornography. First, it created a bigger market for live women because live women
were required to make the photographs. Someone could make a drawing
out of his imagination or memory. A photograph turned a living woman
into an exploited pornographic commodity. Pornography less and less existed in the realm of drawing, contiguous with art and imagination, and
more and more it existed in the purposeful and exciting realm of documented sexual violation. Photographs acquired commercial primacy, and
this meant that pornography required the sexual exploitation and violation
of real women to exist in a world redefined by the camera. Second, mass
means of producing the photographs democratized pornography. As writing, etching, or drawing, or as live shows in brothels, it had been the
domain of rich men, aristocrats. Now the technology made it available to
all men. Video has remarkably furthered this trend, bringing pornography
into the home, both the product itself and the video camera that allows the
man to make his own pornography of his wife or lover or child.

The role of written or drawn pornography in sexual abuse before the
invention of the camera was not studied. The rights of women did not
matter. The rights of women in brothels were not an issue. Violence

against women did not matter. The use of women in live pornographic scenarios or as models for pornographic drawings did not matter to the men who used them or to the society that allowed these uses of women. If written or drawn pornography was used in the sexual abuse of women, prostitutes, or children, it did not matter. None of them had any legal rights of personhood.

The proliferation of pornography in our society, its use in sexual assault, its widespread legitimacy, its legal impunity, its accessibility, the need for real women to make the product in a market constantly expanding in size and sadism, have presented the contemporary women's movement with an emergency of staggering proportions: sexual sadism against women is mass entertainment; sexual exploitation of women is protected as and widely understood to be a civil liberty of men; the sexual violation of women in the pornography itself is protected by the courts as "speech."

It's a hell of a symptom, isn't it?

Q: Okay, we try to dismiss pornography by saying it's a symptom, not a cause, and we fight for pay equity even though low pay is a symptom. What other evidence is there of a double standard?

A: In opposing pornography, feminists have been accused of being essentially right-wing, or giving aid and comfort to the political Right, or being in an alliance with the Right. These charges were made long before the existence of the Ordinance. They were made as soon as feminists began to speak out about the woman hating in pornography and as soon as feminists began to organize pickets and demonstrations to protest the production and distribution of pornography. In 1970, feminists committed civil disobedience by sitting in at the offices of Grove Press to protest the publication of pornography there and the way Grove treated its women employees. The super-radical-leftist publisher/owner of Grove Press not only had the feminists arrested by the then very brutal New York City Police Department for criminal trespass on his private property — he also accused them of working for the C.I.A. You can't get a bigger charge of collusion than that one; who cares that the man who made it was defending his profits, his pornography, his mistreatment of women workers (a/k/a "workers")? Certainly, the Left saw him as a radical, not as a capitalist. The Left continues to see pornographers as radicals, not as capitalists. With the emergence of Jerry Falwell on the national scene, feminists who opposed pornography were likened to Mr. Falwell. Feminist leaders were characterized as demagogues and puritanical opportunists in ongoing campaigns of character assassination. Mr. Falwell came to represent all that the Left detested in religion and politics and feminists who opposed pornography were robbed of their own political identities and convictions and caricatured as having his. Since Mr. Falwell had supported segregation in the 1960's, had supported the Viet Nam War, currently does support the regime in South Africa and the militarism of Cold War anticommunism, opposes abortion rights and gay rights, and since the feminist leaders of the antipornography movement hold opposite views on each and every issue, this was an extraordinary slander. But it was repeated as fact in mainstream newspaper articles and in the feminist press.

We don't believe that this is done to people on other issues. Take, for example, the often vituperative debate on the existence of the state of Israel. One of the women most active in calling feminists who oppose pornography right-wing has written eloquently on behalf of the continued existence of the state of Israel. Mr. Falwell also supports the continued existence of the state of Israel. We know that the reasons of this particular woman are different in kind and in quality from Mr. Falwell's reasons. Since Mr. Falwell's expressions of support for Israel sometimes have an anti-Semitic edge and always have a Cold War rationale, it would be slanderous to say the same position, broadly construed, means the same politics, or that her position does not exist independent of his. *The New York Times*, which repeatedly denounces feminists who oppose pornography and repeatedly links us with Mr. Falwell or his Moral Majority, also supports the existence of the state of Israel. We know their reasons are not Mr. Falwell's. We know their politics are not Mr. Falwell's. We do not liken Nobel Peace Prize winner Elie Wiesel to Mr. Falwell because both support the state of Israel, or Natan Sharansky, or Jacobo Timmerman. The New Jewish Agenda, a leftist group, supports the existence of the state of Israel, but its politics are opposed to, not the same as, Mr. Falwell's.

Specious analogizing is ludicrous, no less on pornography than on Israel. It is fair to say that there are many issues that can be articulated broadly enough — pro or con — so that a strange spectrum of folks seem to be on the same side. Supporting Israel is one; opposing pornography is another. But this has only been done to those of us who oppose pornography from a feminist perspective of radical equality. We have had to try to survive in an environment saturated with this kind of intellectual lie and political slander. We never expected feminist media to fall for this propagandistic nonsense, but they did, repeating it over a period of years. We never expected the Left to descend to this gutter level of intellectual corruption but they did, apparently without a second thought and with no remorse. Ultimately the effect was to erase our political identities. Women, of course, are used to being erased from political dialogue and history but not by folks who apply the word *feminist* to themselves.

The double standard was also alive and well when feminists who opposed pornography were told to shut up to protect free speech. Again, from the very beginning, before feminists created or endorsed any legal strategies against pornography, we were told repeatedly that anything we said or did against pornography would endanger free speech. For instance, when we were protesting the film "Snuff" in New York City in February 1976, one civil-liberties stalwart wrote in his regular newspaper column that we should stop picketing the film because our picketing endangered free speech. His reasoning was that in response to the pickets a theater manager might decide not to show "Snuff." This was the danger our picketing created. Picketing, of course, is a quintessential exercise of free speech. The whole idea of free speech is that someone might change their mind and their behavior. At least, this is the whole idea of picketing. Picketing is not usually friendly and compliant and supportive speech. Usually it is speech in opposition to what is going on, and it is speech that wants results. This civil libertarian believed that the showing of "Snuff" was vital to free speech and our picketing was not. Over a period of years, in newspaper articles, on editorial pages, in debates, we were told, usually with polite condescension, sometimes in a holy rage, that we were endangering free speech by talking about pornography: that is, by articulating a political opposition to it. A *New York Times* reporter was told by a chief editor that *The New York Times* would no longer carry news stories about the feminist political opposition to pornography. This occurred in 1978, after the reporter had published a superb news story objectively describing a major conference on pornography at New York University Law School. The chief editor said that such news stories created a feeling against pornography that threatened the First Amendment. *The New York Times* itself published an editorial denouncing the feminists reported on in the news story, characterizing our positions as "shrill" and "hysterical." News stories disappeared from those pages for many years. When impossible to suppress, such stories have been carried, usually slanted against us. Feminist authors writing on pornography have been repeatedly told that such books would not be published because they endangered First Amendment rights. Magazine editors have rejected numerous articles by feminist authors opposing pornography on the same grounds: that to publish the articles would jeopardize the First Amendment. The same people who say the pornographers must be protected because everything must be published and protected are the first to say that feminist work opposing pornography must not be published in order to protect free speech.

The feminist version of this pernicious nonsense has been the insistence on having a propornography side represented whenever antipornography politics are expressed, in published or spoken forums. There are feminist right-to-life activists, but no one in the women's movement has been insisting that they get equal time, let alone that they speak wherever and whenever prochoice politics are expressed. These feminist right-to-life groups began on the radical Left, in fact, in the nonviolence movement. Now there are also more politically moderate feminists who are prolife and at the same time for the Equal Rights Amendment and the rest of the feminist agenda. Not only is their participation not required at feminist events; they are not allowed in the door. It is only on the issue of pornography that those who support the pornography industry in the name of what they call feminism must speak whenever those who oppose pornography speak. Since pornography is a distillation of woman hating, linked in women's experience to rape, battery, incest, and forced prostitution, it is impossible to understand how the moral and political imperative developed to have so-called feminists speak in behalf of pornography. This can only be understood as the feminist version of shut up.

The mainstream says: shut up to protect free speech. Feminists say shut up because if you speak we will have other women here calling themselves feminists to defend this exploitation of women. In this way, we will wipe out what you have said. We don't do this to anyone else who stands up for the rights of women, but we will do this to you because we want you to shut up. You make us feel bad. We can't stand up to the pornographers. They are too mean, too real, and too powerful. We want to celebrate women. We don't want to have to face how powerless we are in the face of organized, profit-making male cruelty. It has been hard enough for us to face rape, incest, and battery. So we are having these women in here who say they are feminists but enjoy calling themselves "girls," and they want us to have fun having sex now, and they say pornography is just part of liberated sex, and if they say so it must be true for them so you aren't even right when you say pornography hurts women because it doesn't hurt all women (it doesn't hurt these "girl"-women), and if we listen to them we don't have to listen to you, which means, shut up.

And that is the sad consequence of yet another double standard. Large numbers of feminists listened with serious and honorable attention to women who exposed rape, incest, and battery; but not as many feminists have listened with serious and honorable attention to women who have been exploited in pornography or raped or tortured or violated because of it.

Finally, feminist lawyers are responsible for yet another double standard, this one cynical in the extreme. Feminist lawyers especially seem not to want to do anything real about pornography. They tell audiences of feminists that law isn't the answer, that law can do nothing, and that women should not go to the male state. These women spend their lives and make their livings (substantial for women) going to the male state. These women take other sex-discrimination issues to the male state. These feminists have clients who must think the law is some of the answer. These feminists who appear on behalf of their clients in court must have empirical proof that law can do something. They win sometimes. It is not just that they oppose a specific legal remedy — for instance, the Ordinance. It is that they say as political truth that law is useless and make women feel like fools for doing something as ridiculous as contemplating "going to the male state." Either these women lie to their clients or they lie to their audiences. If they are lawyers and they practice sex-discrimination law and they go into court, how dare they tell other feminists it is silly to do any of the above? They have used these broad and basically indefensible arguments to undercut support for the Ordinance in particular, but they do not have the courage to say that (1) they use male law, (2) they use sex-discrimination law, (3) they make money practicing law in the male courts, (4) law is essential to social change, which is partly why they practice it; *but* they do not believe that women hurt by pornography should have legal remedies. Instead they breeze through debates speaking as lawyers making anarchist arguments and speaking as female functionaries of the male courts making separatist arguments. What they say and what they do never meet on the plane of reality. They are especially dishonorable in the double standard they apply to pornography because they are specially qualified to help women who have been hurt by it.

All of these various applications of a double standard to pornography happen sometimes, not all the time. Small numbers of people, their voices and arguments enhanced by the purposeful support of the pornographers, manipulate everyone's sense of reality or sense of justice.

Most women hate pornography; all pornography hates women; and the masses of feminists here and in other countries are not confounded by these strategic uses of the double standard in defense of pornography. We note when a double standard is used and try to understand how it works politically. The acceptance of a double standard for pornography is particularly painful when it happens within the scope of the women's movement. But the real political damage is done when a double-standard tactic is used by those who have real power: media, politicians, lawyers, publishers.

Q: Why are you dividing the women's movement? The pornography issue is too divisive.

A: There have been many angry splits in the women's movement over the years. The arguments and antagonisms have been aired, often in what seems like perpetuity, in the feminist press. What is different about pornography is that the pornographers have used the so-called feminists who defend pornography to defend it in mainstream forums and in mainstream media. Feminists who oppose pornography are under constant attack from the pornographers, who have their own magazines, of course, and also tremendous influence with newspapers, other periodicals, and radio and television producers. Women who defend pornography are picked up by the pornographers and spotlighted. Often, they find that their careers, including academic careers, are advanced. They suddenly have available to them many public forums in which to express propornography politics usefully (for the pornographers) disguised as a mutation of feminism. Some of them take the vast sums of money the pornographers offer and publish attacks on feminists fighting pornography in the pornography itself. They attack feminists opposing pornography for the pornographers in forums opened up to them by the pornographers. They have allowed themselves to become the chicks-up-front through choices they have made.

There are hundreds of thousands of us, only a tiny number of them. But the tiny number of them tend to be privileged and well-placed: lawyers, academics, journalists. The hundreds of thousands of us are women in all walks of life, but not particularly well-placed. We tend to be poorer. Some of us have been prostitutes or in pornography or have suffered some other form of egregious sexual violation.

We wish that they would stop, of course. One reason is that the pornographers get so much political mileage out of them. But another reason is that we feel ashamed for them. They dishonor women.

The so-called feminist split on pornography would have the quality of a tempest in a teapot if not for the media exposure choreographed by the pornographers. We fight the pornographers. Propornography women, calling themselves "feminists," fight us. In and of itself, this is suspect as a practice of feminism.

Since 1968, feminists have been fighting the way the male world objectifies women and turns women into sexual commodities. Since 1970, we have been fighting pornography. There is no viable propornography feminism. Our legitimate differences center on *how* to fight pornography. Without the active interference of the pornographers, we would have been able to resolve these differences — or we might have agreed to let a thousand flowers bloom. Because of the complicity of the propornography women with the pornographers, feminism itself stands in danger of being irrevocably compromised and the rights of women being hurt by pornography taking second place to public spectacles of what appears to be internecine conflict. The pornographers love it.

Q: What is the role of the American Civil Liberties Union?

A: The ACLU has been very active in defending the pornographers in the media. The ACLU has been very active in defending pornography as a genre of expression that must have absolute constitutional protection: this they have done in the courts.

The ACLU has taken money for a long time from the pornographers. Some money has been raised by showing pornography. The ACLU's economic ties with the pornographers take many different forms, ranging from taking money from the Playboy Foundation to being housed for a nominal rent ($1 per year) in a building owned by pornographers. Sometimes lawyers represent the ACLU in public debate and as individuals work for pornographers in private. Their personal incomes, then, are largely dependent on being retained by the pornographers. In public they are spokesmen for high-and-mighty principles; in private, they do whatever the pornographers need done. For instance, one such lawyer represented the ACLU in many debates with feminists on pornography. He talked about the importance of free speech with serious elegance and would brook no exceptions to what must be protected because, he said repeatedly, if any exceptions were made, "feminist and gay" speech would suffer. Then, as the private lawyer for a pornographer, he sued Women Against Pornography for libel because on television a member denounced the pornographer for publishing cartoons that pornographized children. This is one way the ACLU helps pornographers wage war on feminists: high-toned in public; political destruction in private by use of money, power, and ACLU lawyers. The ACLU itself also has a record of defending child pornography by opposing any laws against it as constitutionally prohibited incursions on free speech.

The ACLU has also provided money and office space for FACT, a group that calls itself feminist, opposes the Ordinance, and defends pornography as a significant expression of women's free sexuality. One ACLU staff person was instrumental in founding FACT and often represents FACT in public while continuing to rise on the ACLU staff. Perhaps the most telling detail, a picture to hold in your mind, is this one: ACLU men and FACT women sat with representatives of *Penthouse* at a meeting of the Attorney General's Commission on Pornography in New York City in 1986. All three factions together heckled a feminist speaker whose subject was the sexual abuse of women.

The ACLU's stated commitment is to protect the Bill of Rights, the first ten amendments to the Constitution, not pornography as such, though it's hard to tell sometimes. Without a commitment to real equality of the same magnitude as its commitment to those first ten amendments, the ACLU defends power, not rights. No matter how notorious the exploitation, as for instance in child pornography, the ACLU ends up substantively defending those who exploit the powerless. The ACLU demands a literal reading of those first ten amendments, especially the First Amendment, especially its speech provision. This is an exceptionally conservative position both philosophically and politically and it has a conservative political outcome: it keeps already established patterns of inequality intact.

The ACLU has refused to consider the role of sexual abuse in keeping women silent, or how poverty keeps women, Blacks, and other minorities from having access to the means of communication. The ACLU refuses to accept responsibility for the fact that in the United States speech has to be paid for in money. The ACLU defends the power of corporations who own and control the means of speech against the aspirations of dissidents who have been excluded from the circle of protected speech by sex or race.

We also frankly abhor the ACLU's defenses of Klan and Nazi groups. The ACLU has a long history of protecting the most virulent racism. In protecting pornography, this purposeful policy continues. Pornography sexualizes racist hatred. It uses racially motivated violation, torture, and murder as sex acts that lead to orgasm. We believe that racist pornography is one source of the violence against Blacks and other minorities that is ongoing in this society. We believe that it is a *dynamic* source of racist violence.

The pornographers rank with Nazis and Klansmen in promoting hatred and violence. Their targets are always sex-based and sometimes race-based. Like the Nazis and the Klansmen, they commit the acts of violence they promote. They conduct a war against women that spreads terror.

We have asked the ACLU repeatedly over many years to protect the rights enumerated in the Bill of Rights by taking the cases of powerless or disenfranchised people, not exploiters, abusers, or purveyors of genocide. The ACLU has remained indifferent to this idea.

Q: But, under the Ordinance, won't gay and lesbian materials be the first to go?

A: In some places, under obscenity laws, graphic sexually explicit materials presenting homosexual acts are made illegal *per se*. The Ordinance does not do this. The Ordinance requires proof of actual harm before any materials can be found illegal. The harm cannot be a moral one—say, that someone is offended by the materials or believes they are not proper family entertainment or finds that they violate their religious beliefs. The harm proven must be a harm of coercion, assault, defamation, or trafficking in sex-based subordination. The fact that the participants in the sex acts shown are of the same sex is not itself a form of sex-based subordination. Only materials that can be *proven harmful* can be reached, and only by their victims, not by the government. The particular question of lesbian and gay materials under the Ordinance then becomes: if any lesbian or gay material can be proven to do harm to direct victims, is there a good reason that it ought to be exempt under the Ordinance simply *because* the materials show gay or lesbian sex?

All pornography, from *Playboy* to "Snuff," is part of somebody's sexuality, their authentic sexuality as they understand it. Their pornography is a sexual experience; it is sex to them. Not surprisingly, these same people want to be reassured that their favorite pornography is exempt from the Ordinance. For example, when men say, You can't mean *Playboy*! they are saying, I use it, I enjoy it, I have a right to it, you are not going to take it away from me, I don't care whom it hurts. This simply means, because I like it, nobody should be able to do anything about it. It is special pleading pure and simple. There is necessarily someone who feels this way about every part of the Ordinance's definition of pornography.

The broader question the Ordinance poses, then, is, Does *anyone* have a right to materials that are produced through coercion, that will be forced on others, that are the cause of assaults, that defame individuals, and that are integral to the second-class status of half the population? Is *anyone's* sexuality — however conventional or unconventional, however sincere — more important than the lives that must be, will be, ground up and spit out in little pieces in the making and use of the pornography so that the consumer's sexuality can be provided with what it needs, wants, or enjoys? Is the sexuality of the pedophile more important than the freedom from sexual exploitation of the child? Is the sexuality of the woman hater more important than the freedom from sexual slavery of the woman coerced to model for sadomasochistic pornography? for forced fellatio? Is the sexuality of the nice but lonely guy more important than the unequal life chances of all the women whose lives are endangered, made hollow, reduced a little or reduced a lot, because what he wants he gets? Is some gay men's access to pictures of subordinating gay sex more important than the right of men or boys not to be raped or violated so that pictures can be made of them, or the desire of other gay men to shape a community free of eroticized self-hatred? The point of considering all these questions at once is this: if harm is done, and it is based on gender, neither the particular sex acts performed nor the gender of those who get hurt should determine whether their civil rights are protected or not.

Because the particular acts do not change the damage done, and because harm is still harm when done by women to women and by men to men, there is no special exemption in the Ordinance for gay and lesbian materials. We are frankly mystified as well as anguished that there are lesbians who identify with and defend the pornographers' woman-hating so-called lesbian sexuality. All lesbians have necessarily suffered from the pornographers' definition of lesbian that is so central to the violence, hatred, contempt, and discrimination directed against lesbians in society. All lesbians in societies saturated with pornography must live with the fact that the pornographers have made lesbianism into a pornographic spectacle in the eyes of men.

The Ordinance does not direct itself specifically against same-sex materials as obscenity law has (with very little effect in the United States). As a matter of fact, it may be difficult to persuade courts to apply the Ordinance to same-sex materials for the same reason that sex-discrimination law has been so useless to advancing the civil rights of gay men and lesbians: sex-discrimination law, of which the Ordinance is a part, has been largely obsessed with what it calls "the gender difference" as defining its concerns. This implicit heterosexual bias to its definition of gender means that it has been difficult for courts to see sex discrimination in a same-sex context. If the attempt to apply the Ordinance to harmful gay and lesbian pornography succeeds, it would provide a precedent that could be used to apply sex-discrimination prohibitions to other civil-rights violations of gay men and lesbians. It would become part of a sexual politics and a civil-rights law that connects a feminist critique of male supremacy with a politics of gay and lesbian liberation.

Q: What do the American people think?

A: First, we have to tell you that a lot of people haven't been asked or haven't been listened to. The women and children who have been hurt through pornography — used to make it or had it used on them in sexual assault — are still a largely unidentified population, in part because the pornographers retaliate. We will give you just one example. In Minneapolis, women went before the City Council to say how they had been hurt in or by pornography. The experiences were horrible. They included rape, gang-rape, battery, torture, rape by animals, and more. Subsequently, one nationally distributed pornography magazine published an article that identified the women by name and used direct quotes from their testimony — quotes highlighted and chosen to emphasize graphic sexual violence. As a result of this article, the women without exception were harassed by obscene phone calls, followed, spied on, tormented by anonymous notes and phone calls, threatened over the phone and by notes and letters. One woman had to move because her tormentor clearly followed all her movements, including inside her own house. Those who have the most to tell have good reason never to speak in public.

Polls tell us that most Americans believe that there is a causal link between pornography and sexual violence. In a *Newsweek* poll conducted in March 1985, 73 percent of those polled believed that "sexually explicit" material (the euphemism of choice in mainstream media for pornography) leads some people to commit rape or sexual violence; 76 percent said that this same material leads some people to lose respect for women.

Time magazine conducted a similar poll in July 1986. We found the questions more confusing, with more vague or double meanings, than those reported in the *Newsweek* poll; but still the results are startling: 56 percent of all those polled, and 63 percent of the women polled, believed that "sexually explicit movies, magazines, and books" lead people to commit rape; 54 percent of all those polled, and 64 percent of the women polled, believed that sexually explicit material leads people to commit acts of sexual violence (apparently as distinct from rape). The *Time* poll found that pornography was much more troubling to women than to men: 50 percent of women were "very concerned"; only 27 percent of men figured in this category of highest concern. A total of 61 percent of the people polled believed pornography encourages people to consider women as sex objects: 50 percent of men thought this was true, 71 percent of women.

A survey conducted by the American Bar Association in September 1984 (in response to the Indianapolis Ordinance) and published in the *ABA Journal* in March 1985 queried 600 lawyers, half of whom were ABA members, half of whom were not. 66 percent of the total, and 82 percent of the women, thought that some pornography contributes to violent crimes against women; 70 percent of the total, and 89 percent of the women, thought that some pornography is discrimination against women.

The most astonishing and important survey was done by a mainstream women's magazine geared largely to homemakers, *Woman's Day*, in January 1986. 90 percent of the 6,100 respondents believed that pornography encourages violence against women. 25 percent said that they had been sexually abused by someone they knew as a direct result of his access to pornography. This 25 percent did not represent those who had been sexually abused in ways not involving pornography; nor did it represent those who had been abused, even if pornography were involved, by a stranger. This is a staggering percentage of pornography-caused abuse to come out of this or any other population of women.

80 percent of the *Woman's Day* respondents wanted all pornography outlawed. Less than 2 percent of this pool of people thought that freedom of speech was more important than the violence against women generated by pornography. In the *Time* poll, 72 percent wanted the government to crack down harder on pornography (no separate figure is given for women). Asked if magazines with nude pictures should be outlawed in local stores, 59 percent said yes — 49 percent of men, 67 percent of women. In the *Newsweek* poll, 73 percent thought that magazines that show sexual violence should be totally banned (as compared, for instance, with 21

percent who thought that showing nudity should be totally banned). 68 percent wanted a total ban on movies that depict sexual violence. 63 percent thought that the sale or rental of videos featuring sexual violence should be totally banned.

The ABA did not ask lawyers any questions about total bans. Instead, lawyers were asked about the Indianapolis Ordinance. Only 24 percent of those polled thought that the Ordinance constituted any form of censorship. 30 percent thought it was over-broad and 25 percent thought it was too vague. Both overbreadth and vagueness would be legal grounds for finding the Ordinance unconstitutional, but neither has anything to do with the basic principles of the Ordinance itself — so that, for instance, a redrafted version might not elicit these same objections from these same people. (In fact, the Seventh Circuit did not find the Ordinance to be either vague or over-broad.) 26 percent of all the lawyers polled thought the Indianapolis Ordinance was constitutional as drafted. 30 percent said it would be constitutional as drafted if studies proved conclusively that pornography leads to violence against women. (Presumably, then it would not be "over-broad" or "too vague.") 42 percent of the lawyers fifty-five or older were in favor of the Ordinance.

All of these polls and surveys have one element overwhelmingly in common: people, and especially women (whether, for instance, in the sample of women lawyers or readers of *Woman's Day*) believe, know, understand, that commercially available pornography causes sexual violence against women.

CHAPTER 10

Pornography and
Black Women's Bodies

Patricia Hill Collins

> For centuries the black woman has served as the primary pornographic "out-
> let" for white men in Europe and America. We need only think of the black
> women used as breeders, raped for the pleasure and profit of their owners. We
> need only think of the license the "master" of the slave women enjoyed. But,
> most telling of all, we need only study the old slave societies of the South to
> note the sadistic treatment — at the hands of white "gentlemen" — of "beauti-
> ful young quadroons and octoroons" who became increasingly (and were
> deliberately bred to become) indistinguishable from white women, and were
> the more highly prized as slave mistresses because of this. (Walker, 1981,
> p. 42)

Alice Walker's description of the rape of enslaved African women for
the "pleasure and profit of their owners" encapsulates several elements of
contemporary pornography. First, Black women were used as sex objects
for the pleasure of white men. This objectification of African-American
women parallels the portrayal of women in pornography as sex objects
whose sexuality is available for men (McNall, 1983). Exploiting Black
women as breeders objectified them as less than human because only animals can be bred against their will. In contemporary pornography women
are objectified through being portrayed as pieces of meat, as sexual animals
awaiting conquest. Second, African-American women were raped, a form
of sexual violence. Violence is typically an implicit or explicit theme in
pornography. Moreover, the rape of Black women linked sexuality and
violence, another characteristic feature of pornography (Eisenstein, 1983).
Third, rape and other forms of sexual violence act to strip victims of their

Excerpted from Collins, Patricia Hill. (1990). *Black feminist thought*. Boston: Unwin
Hyman, pp. 167–173. Reprinted by permission of the author.

will to resist and make them passive and submissive to the will of the rapist. Female passivity, the fact that women have things done to them, is a theme repeated over and over in contemporary pornography (McNall, 1983). Fourth, the profitability of Black women's sexual exploitation for white "gentlemen" parallels pornography's financially lucrative benefits for pornographers (Eisenstein, 1983). Finally, the actual breeding of "quadroons and octoroons" not only reinforces the themes of Black women's passivity, objectification, and malleability to male control but reveals pornography's grounding in racism and sexism. The fates of both Black and white women were intertwined in this breeding process. The ideal African-American woman as a pornographic object was indistinguishable from white women and thus approximated the images of beauty, asexuality, and chastity forced on white women. But inside was a highly sexual whore, a "slave mistress" ready to cater to her owner's pleasure.[1]

Contemporary pornography consists of a series of icons or representations that focus the viewer's attention on the relationship between the portrayed individual and the general qualities ascribed to that class of individuals. Pornographic images are iconographic in that they represent realities in a manner determined by the historical position of the observers, their relationship to their own time, and to the history of the conventions which they employ (Gilman, 1985). The treatment of Black women's bodies in nineteenth-century Europe and the United States may be the foundation upon which contemporary pornography as the representation of women's objectification, domination, and control is based. Icons about the sexuality of Black women's bodies emerged in these contexts. Moreover, as race/gender-specific representations, these icons have implications for the treatment of both African-American and white women in contemporary pornography.

I suggest that African-American women were not included in pornography as an afterthought, but instead, form a key pillar on which contemporary pornography itself rests. As Alice Walker points out, "the more ancient roots of modern pornography are to be found in the almost always pornographic treatment of black women who, from the moment they entered slavery . . . were subjected to rape as the 'logical' convergence of sex and violence. Conquest, in short" (1981, p. 42).

One key feature about the treatment of Black women in the nineteenth century was how their bodies were objects of display. In the antebellum American South white men did not have to look at pornographic pictures of women because they could become voyeurs of Black women on the auction block. A chilling example of this objectification of the Black female body is provided by the exhibition, in early nineteenth-century Europe, of Sarah Bartmann, the so-called Hottentot Venus. Her display formed one of the original icons for Black female sexuality. An African woman, Sarah Bartmann was often exhibited at fashionable parties in Paris, generally wearing little clothing, to provide entertainment. To her audience she represented deviant sexuality. At the time European audiences thought that Africans had deviant sexual practices and searched for physiological differences, such as enlarged penises and malformed female genitalia, as indications of this deviant sexuality. Sarah Bartmann's exhibition stimulated these racist and sexist beliefs. After her death in 1815, she was dissected. Her genitalia and buttocks remain on display in Paris (Gilman, 1985).

Sander Gilman explains the impact that Sarah Bartmann's exhibition had on Victorian audiences:

> It is important to note that Sarah Bartmann was exhibited not to show her genitalia — but rather to present another anomaly which the European audience . . . found riveting. This was the steatopygia, or protruding buttocks, the other physical characteristic of the Hottentot female which captured the eye of early European travelers. . . . The figure of Sarah Bartmann was reduced to her sexual parts. The audience which had paid to see her buttocks and had fantasized about the uniqueness of her genitalia when she was alive could, after death and dissection, examine both. (1985, p. 213)

In this passage Gilman unwittingly describes how Bartmann was used as a pornographic object similar to how women are represented in contemporary pornography. She was reduced to her sexual parts, and these parts came to represent a dominant icon applied to Black women throughout the nineteenth century. Moreover, the fact that Sarah Bartmann was both African and a woman underscores the importance of gender in maintaining notions of racial purity. In this case Bartmann symbolized Blacks as a "race." Thus the creation of the icon applied to Black women demonstrates that notions of gender, race, and sexuality were linked in overarching structures of political domination and economic exploitation.

The process illustrated by the pornographic treatment of the bodies of enslaved African women and of women like Sarah Bartmann has developed into a full-scale industry encompassing all women objectified differently by racial/ethnic category. Contemporary portrayals of Black women in pornography represent the continuation of the historical treatment of their actual bodies. African-American women are usually depicted in a situation of bondage and slavery, typically in a submissive posture, and often with two white men. As Bell observes, "this setting reminds us of all the trappings of slavery: chains, whips, neck braces, wrist clasps" (1987, p. 59). White women and women of color have different pornographic images applied to them. The image of Black women in pornography is almost consistently one featuring them breaking from chains. The image of Asian women in pornography is almost consistently one of being tortured (Bell, 1987, p. 161).

The pornographic treatment of Black women's bodies challenges the prevailing feminist assumption that since pornography primarily affects white women, racism has been grafted onto pornography. African-American women's experiences suggest that Black women were not added into a preexisting pornography, but rather that pornography itself must be reconceptualized as an example of the interlocking nature of race, gender, and class oppression. At the heart of both racism and sexism are notions of biological determinism claiming that people of African descent and women possess immutable biological characteristics marking their inferiority to elite white women (Gould, 1981; Fausto-Sterling, 1989; Halpin, 1989). In pornography these racist and sexist beliefs are sexualized. Moreover, for African-American women pornography has not been timeless and universal but was tied to Black women's experiences with the European colonization of Africa and with American slavery. Pornography emerged within a specific system of social class relationships.

This linking of views of the body, social constructions of race and gender, and conceptualizations of sexuality that inform Black women's treatment as pornographic objects promises to have significant implications for how we assess contemporary pornography. Moreover, examining how pornography has been central to the race, gender, and class oppression of African-American women offers new routes for understanding the dynamics of power as domination.

Investigating racial patterns in pornography offers one route for such an analysis. Black women have often claimed that images of white women's sexuality were intertwined with the controlling image of the sexually denigrated Black woman: "In the United States, the fear and fascination of female sexuality was projected onto black women; the passionless lady arose in symbiosis with the primitively sexual slave" (Hall, 1983, p. 333). Comparable linkages exist in pornography (Gardner, 1980). Alice Walker provides a fictional account of a Black man's growing awareness of the different ways that African-American and white women are objectified in pornography: "What he has refused to see—because to see it would reveal yet another area in which he is unable to protect or defend black women—is that where white women are depicted in pornography as 'objects,' black women are depicted as animals. Where white women are depicted as human bodies if not beings, black women are depicted as shit" (Walker, 1981, p. 52).

Walker's distinction between "objects" and "animals" is crucial in untangling gender, race, and class dynamics in pornography. Within the mind/body, culture/nature, male/female oppositional dichotomies in Western social thought, objects occupy an uncertain interim position. As objects white women become creations of culture—in this case, the mind of white men—using the materials of nature—in this case, uncontrolled female sexuality. In contrast, as animals Black women receive no such redeeming dose of culture and remain open to the type of exploitation visited on nature overall. Race becomes the distinguishing feature in determining the type of objectification women will encounter. Whiteness as symbolic of both civilization and culture is used to separate objects from animals.

The alleged superiority of men to women is not the only hierarchical relationship that has been linked to the putative superiority of the mind to the body. Certain "races" of people have been defined as being more body-like, more animallike, and less godlike than others (Spelman, 1982, p. 52). Race and gender oppression may both revolve around the same axis of disdain for the body; both portray the sexuality of subordinate groups as animalistic and therefore deviant. Biological notions of race and gender prevalent in the early nineteenth century which fostered the animalistic icon of Black female sexuality were joined by the appearance of a racist biology incorporating the concept of degeneracy (Foucault, 1980). Africans and women were both perceived as embodied entities, and Blacks were seen as degenerate. Fear of and disdain for the body thus formed a key element in both sexist and racist thinking (Spelman, 1982).

While the sexual and racial dimensions of being treated like an animal are important, the economic foundation underlying this treatment is critical. Animals can be economically exploited, worked, sold, killed, and consumed. As "mules," African-American women become susceptible to such treatment. The political economy of pornography also merits careful attention. Pornography is pivotal in mediating contradictions in changing societies (McNall, 1983). It is no accident that racist biology, religious justifications for slavery and women's subordination, and other explanations for nineteenth-century racism and sexism arose during a period of profound political and economic change. Symbolic means of domination become particularly important in mediating contradictions in changing political economies. The exhibition of Sarah Bartmann and Black women on the auction block were not benign intellectual exercises—these practices defended real material and political interests. Current transformations in international capitalism require similar ideological justifications. Where does pornography fit in these current transformations? This question awaits a comprehensive Afrocentric feminist analysis.

Publicly exhibiting Black women may have been central to objectifying Black women as animals and to creating the icon of Black women as animals. Yi-Fu Tuan (1984) offers an innovative argument about similarities in efforts to control nature — especially plant life — the domestication of animals, and the domination of certain groups of humans. Tuan suggests that displaying humans alongside animals implies that such humans are more like monkeys and bears than they are like "normal" people. This same juxtaposition leads spectators to view the captive animals in a special way. Animals require definitions of being like humans, only more openly carnal and sexual, an aspect of animals that forms a major source of attraction for visitors to modern zoos. In discussing the popularity of monkeys in zoos, Tuan notes: "Some visitors are especially attracted by the easy sexual behavior of the monkeys. Voyeurism is forbidden except when applied to subhumans" (1984, p. 82). Tuan's analysis suggests that the public display of Sarah Bartmann and of the countless enslaved African women on the auction blocks of the antebellum American South — especially in proximity to animals — fostered their image as animalistic.

This linking of Black women and animals is evident in nineteenth-century scientific literature. The equation of women, Blacks, and animals is revealed in the following description of an African woman published in an 1878 anthropology text:

> She had a way of pouting her lips exactly like what we have observed in the orangutan. Her movements had something abrupt and fantastical about them, reminding one of those of the ape. Her ear was like that of many apes. . . . These are animal characters. I have never seen a human head more like an ape than that of this woman. (Halpin, 1989, p. 287)

In a climate such as this, it is not surprising that one prominent European physician even stated that Black women's "animallike sexual appetite went so far as to lead black women to copulate with apes" (Gilman, 1985, p. 212).

The treatment of all women in contemporary pornography has strong ties to the portrayal of Black women as animals. In pornography women become nonpeople and are often represented as the sum of their fragmented body parts. Scott McNall observes:

> This fragmentation of women relates to the predominance of rear-entry position photographs. . . . All of these kinds of photographs reduce the woman to her reproductive system, and, furthermore, make her open, willing, and available — not in control. . . . The other thing rear-entry position photographs tell us about women is that they are animals. They are animals because they are the same as dogs — bitches in heat who can't control themselves. (McNall, 1983, pp. 197–98)

This linking of animals and white women within pornography becomes feasible when grounded in the earlier denigration of Black women as animals.

Developing a comprehensive analysis of the race, gender, and class dynamics of pornography offers possibilities for change. Those Black feminist intellectuals investigating sexual politics imply that the situation is much more complicated than that advanced by some prominent white feminists (see, e.g., Dworkin, 1981) in which "men oppress women" because they are men. Such approaches implicitly assume biologically deterministic views of sex, gender, and sexuality and offer few possibilities for change. In contrast, Afrocentric feminist analyses routinely provide for human agency and its corresponding empowerment and for the responsiveness of social structures to human action. In the short story "Coming Apart," Alice Walker describes one Black man's growing realization that his enjoyment of pornography, whether of white women as "objects" or Black women as "animals," degraded him:

> He begins to feel sick. For he realizes that he has bought some of the advertisements about women, black and white. And further, inevitably, he has bought the advertisements about himself. In pornography the black man is portrayed as being capable of fucking anything . . . even a piece of shit. He is defined solely by the size, readiness and unselectivity of his cock. (Walker, 1981, p. 52)

Walker conceptualizes pornography as a race/gender system that entraps everyone. But by exploring an African-American *man's* struggle for a self-defined standpoint on pornography, Walker suggests that a changed consciousness is essential to social change. If a Black man can understand how pornography affects him, then other groups enmeshed in the same system are equally capable of similar shifts in consciousness and action.

Supporters of the waitress at Bette's Diner also protested the *Playboy* read-in that had been organized in opposition to the waitress' action.

Credit: Photographed by Simon Nathan

CHAPTER 11

Pornography and Pride

Van F. White

I'm 59 years old, and I've known something about pornography for many years. When I was younger, I worked in construction. I remember the magazines and the conversations that the men shared. They would look at the pictures and make derogatory remarks: "Boy, what I could do to that bitch." "Look at her—she can't get enough." At one time, I was a part of that, listening and looking and thinking it was a laugh. But now my thoughts have changed. With age has come wisdom.*

I'm a husband, the father of a daughter and a son, and six years ago I became the first person of color elected to the city council of Minneapolis. I've learned a lot about the way pornography affects people. I see the pornography stores in this city; they always seem to be put in the poorest of the neighborhoods—where the poor Blacks, the poor Native Americans, the poor Hispanics, the poor whites, are living. You don't find them in the finer parts of the city, and I resent that. I see the pornography of today showing women in degrading positions, smiling as if to say, "I haven't any intelligence; my body is all there is. . . . " And I see how pornography makes many men believe it.

[In the fall of 1983], as chair of the Minneapolis City Council government-operations committee, I conducted two days of public hearings on pornography. The council members were considering an amendment to the city's human-rights statute that would allow lawsuits against pornographers on the grounds that pornography violates women's civil rights. I was absolutely amazed at what I heard. For over 12 hours, I heard women testify that men had used pornography to coerce them into sex acts; I heard a woman who had been gang-raped by men who had been using pornogra-

---

Reprinted from *Essence*, September 1984, p. 186, by permission of the author.
*On rereading his article Van White commented, "Years have passed since this article, yet my thoughts are still the same."

phy; I heard a woman whose husband used a pornography magazine as a handbook for how to tie her up [with] rope and then sexually assault her.

Those horror stories made me think of the history of slavery in this country—how Black women were at the bottom of the pile, treated like animals instead of human beings. As I listened to these victims of pornography, I heard young women describe how they felt about seeing other women in pornography, how they felt about the way women's genitals and breasts are displayed and women's bodies are shown in compromising postures. I thought about the time of slavery, when Black women had their bodies invaded, their teeth and limbs examined, their bodies checked out for breeding, checked out as you would an animal, and I said to myself, *We've come a long way, haven't we?*

Today we have an industry that grosses $7 billion a year—more than the movie and music businesses combined—showing women in the same kind of submissive and animalistic roles. A lot of housing could be provided for $7 billion, a lot of education, a lot of retraining. As far as I know, the pornography industry reinvests nothing into our society to help upgrade people's self-esteem. Instead, it strips away people's self-esteem by saying, "This is all you really are as a woman—and as a man."

When I was 10 my father died, and after that, like many Black men, I was raised by women. I remember my mother telling me that now I was the man of the family and that being a man didn't mean not having feelings. Dad had taught me a lot of things—to be clean, strong, how to defend myself. But I know that I am endowed with my mother's compassion—and it sustains me. Some people have mistaken my compassion for weakness, but it is my strength. I try to pass on my feelings, my caring about people, to my children. I believe there are a lot of men in our society who are like me; they just never speak out.

So I want to say to men: Take a hard look at what is happening. Understand that there are women and children being degraded daily by pornographers—and that men are degraded too, because by using pornography, by looking at other human beings as a lower form of life, they are perpetuating the same kind of hatred that brings racism to society.

CHAPTER 12

Getting Off on Sexploitation

Martin Dufresne

You start out wanting to know what all the fuss is about. 'Archie' comics and TV shows set you up for The Game: deceit, conflict, stereotypes. And there is sexual curiosity. Adults snicker about achievement and disease, dating and pregnancy but they hide the everyday pleasure. Maybe because it's so often everyday intimidation and anguish. So like most kids I started out leafing through dictionaries, art books, photography magazines, looking for information, finding "nudes."

Jeffrey lived next door and his wealthy non-Catholic father actually subscribed to *Playboy*. Sexploitation ruled the coffee table, maybe a binding agent given the rising divorce rate. Bucking my own religious family, I borrowed piles of back issues, dutifully reading every article and every ad to rationalize my jerking off over those pictures. Such a sucker. . . . Although I was into Sartre and Camus at the time, I really fell for the "Playboy Philosophy": Hefner's endless glorifications of all-out individualism, the Penis as Self and Self as Penis . . . growth at all costs . . .

I was making a bit of cash babysitting evenings around Outremont in ritzy houses and, after sampling the bar, I would hunt for the pornography. Everyone had some. It was usually in the 'master' bedroom: artsy 'testimonials' allegedly written by women on how they enjoyed being tortured or sold. . . . Judges, politicians, lawyers: they all relied on *Histoire d'O* or *Emmanuelle* to keep the wife in line and get it up, stick it in or whatever it was they did. No wonder the system can't seem to curb rapists and child molesters: the men running it *get off* on sexual violence.

And I can testify as to why date rapes are so common. By the time I was ready to date, actually speaking to women, I had been fed thousands of pages of such 'testimonials,' along with jokes and cartoons on how to treat women, what they REALLY liked. I was really dealing with pictures,

---

Reprinted from *The Link*, March 9, 1989, p. 11. Reprinted by permission of the author.

zillions of breasts, buttocks, fantasies of oral sex — very big in the sixties, before the violence became more explicit. I expected long drawn-out multiple orgasms with women babbling deliriously, thanking you as they fainted or died in blissful exhaustion. Primed by this stuff, I actually assaulted the first woman I took to a prom, feeling absolutely entitled to her putting out.

These expectations didn't come from conversations with the guys. Porn taught me everything I 'knew' and taught me how to make it real. The woman I was chatting with had no idea at first she had to measure up to the dozens of pets, playmates, bunnies, pieces of tail I had pored over and fantasized about this past week. They are called 'fantasies' but they sure become real and sink deep when you orgasm to them day in and day out for years. Nobody acknowledges the jerking off.

Hefner, Guccione and Flynt are supposed to be such 'liberators' . . . What a joke! They merely built empires on men's envy and hatred of women, building up these feelings for added profits. They would never dare admit that the Average Playboy Reader spends his evenings choking the chicken, giving up on a love life. Their sexual scenarios pick up on the guilt and envy, offering violence and cynicism as solutions. As in rape, penises become weapons to punish women with, sperm is something filthy to soil their too-perfect bodies. I really believe that porn turns men into fetishists, hooked on overpriced media, with knee-jerk reactions to any woman.

During the seventies, I saw it getting worse with children carefully turned into sex objects, rape made trendy, older women ridiculed, pornography creating a brotherhood of man against women and children. The message is that only men count. The only women you end up 'relating' with are other males' fantasies. What a sick trip! Millions and millions of young men inheriting the warped sex problems of aging, overweight US mafia 'producers.' Kids enticed away from what women want to share, into what 'models' become forced to sell or act out for guys with glazed eyes but extra money. Prostitutes can tell how cruel and dumb 'consumers' can become. Personally, I ended up juggling pseudoaffairs rather than work at solving problems in the relationship with the woman I loved more than anything.

The pornocrats make sex into a ritual, like those stag parties for the groom: they stick you with prostitutes, or with a view of women that makes all of them prostitutes, in order to show you how it's done, how it must be done, which they call freedom. I ended up with fixations on breasts and fellatio, a model of relating where I would mentally lie back and get off on women 'doing' for me, working at my pleasure, even brushing floors by hand, that sort of thing. A regular boss.

Even in the best relationships, with a woman I cared so much about, I found myself unable not to sometimes be swamped by my backlog of rape-and-murder fantasies, straight out of the classiest 'erotica.' I found it almost impossible not to think of her as someone—some thing—to control, like all those "models" Hugh, Bob and Larry had been pimping for me all these years, and went on providing in new high-impact medias: rock videos, cassettes, telephone sex. Owning all that flesh and attention, I didn't have to compromise. The relationship died, as others had.

Still, being in love with a feminist had opened my eyes to the very real rapes, murders, to the real lives of sexploited women such as Linda Marchiano, who wrote this book, *Ordeal*, about the still-famous *Deep Throat*. I read Andrea Dworkin and her passion blew the lid on my secret fantasy garden. It was a fact that women, children I loved weren't safer with me than with any man. I could objectify and use ANYBODY, the feelings were there. And the damage was everywhere. Every woman I have known these last ten years has survived some form of male violence: rape, incest, battering, the criminal negligence of doctors, sexual harassment. To discover the scars of silicone implants on women I respect, knowing this has been done for my viewing and fondling pleasure. . . . And to think that most guys whine that THEY are the ones exploited by the sex 'trade!'

I had kept ONE issue of some porn mag to fall back on. I threw it out, then tried to talk with other men about sexism, showing them the violence. I found out women's lives don't count unless it's a turn-on. They'd only care if I could prove it did something to MEN. And don't we know what it does to men, for men? It still could do it for me.

Yesterday, I saw some pimp on the street carefully slap around, terrorize a woman he was slowly walking somewhere, despite her tears. And the other day, a friend of mine saw a big man throw another woman in a car like a bag of dirty laundry. She called for help, got people to confront him. Turns out he was an off-duty cop, claiming to be 'making an arrest.' Colleagues wouldn't hear of intervening. I didn't even dare walk up to the pimp.

Hurting and scaring women out of their lives is now everyday matter, it has moved from perverse to sexy to normal. A male privilege, a male trait. Why should they keep it from video stores and magazine stands when it is happening all over? Battered women tell of being tortured 'by the book,' the guy coolly acting out video and magazine 'fantasies.' And why should the guy be sanctioned when his convenience store owner goes on renting the same videos to his son? And remember that it's the only sex education the boy is getting, with parents and school boards still playing ostrich about men's current sexuality.

So perversion is normal. What is now perverse is to NOT buy your sex life if you're male, to NOT sell out to male fantasies if you're female. Try convincing friends of either gender to NOT go see a film because of its drawn-out rape and terror scenes, or because it is in other ways full of misogyny. And almost all are. All that 'nouveau porn' in repertory cinemas or those thrillers, feeding our sex fears . . .

There is my ten-year old daughter. Who is going to move on her first, acting out a Guccione/De Palma/Hamilton 'fantasy'? The porn kings are targeting children as the 'last taboo,' calling child molesting a 'lifestyle option.' Someone will get to her. Someone may already have. This makes me sick, afraid, angry. But I see the federal government being bought off by the industry's spokesmen, civil libertarians defending the war against women. I can stay away, they won't. It's not personal, it's social.

So what can you do? Me, I go out with liquid soap in a palm-sized plastic bottle and I squirt it on the porn stands, wetting the magazine covers to freak out buyers. "Gasp! Has this been used already?" . . . Or I nonchalantly tear off a few covers, personally cutting into Benjamin News' profit. I hope that Benjamin's children call him a pimp to his face over some Sunday dinner, out in Westmount. It's time pimps were called pimps. I also write this and try talking to men. Sometimes, it feels like walking out of a time machine in Berlin, 1938 to try and get Germans to feel some compassion for Gypsies and Jews. Is there freedom of speech against a $7 billion-dollar industry? Sometimes, I don't know.

Part III

FEMINIST RESEARCH
ON PORNOGRAPHY

The group "Rampage Against *Penthouse*," holding a demonstration at a B. Dalton bookstore in Durham, NC, expressing outrage against the degradation of women by pornography with violent and coercive content or overtones, such as *Penthouse*.

Credit: Nikki Craft

CHAPTER 13

Pornography and Sexual Abuse of Women

Mimi H. Silbert & Ayala M. Pines

The present study did not attempt to study either the effects of violent pornography on sexual assailants, or the use of juveniles in child pornography. The study was aimed at studying sexual abuse of street prostitutes both prior to and following entrance into prostitution. Yet, as it happens in every large research project, especially an exploratory research, some unexpected information emerged, important information, that unfortunately was not studied in a systematic manner, but which was significant enough to report. Such information is almost always qualitative in nature, and the result of initially unsolicited comments by the subjects. When such comments are repeated often enough, they begin to serve as the basis for a statement that can later be formed into specific hypotheses to be directly studied in future research.

Such was the case in the present study with regard to the relationship between sexual abuse and pornography. From the detailed descriptions the subjects provided to open-ended questions in regard to incidents of juvenile sexual assault in their childhood and to incidents of rape following their entrance into prostitution, it became clear that there is a relationship between violent pornography and sexual abuse in the experience of street prostitutes.

This is an edited version of an article published under the same title in *Sex Roles, 10* (11/12), 1984. Reprinted by permission of the authors.

This research was sponsored through the Delancey Street Foundation by the National Center for the Prevention and Control of Rape, National Institute of Mental Health, Grant Number RO1 MH 32782, Mimi H. Silbert, Principal Investigator. We would like to thank Teri Lynch, Auristela Frias, JoAnn Mancuso, Charlotte Martin, and Alice Watson for their assistance in developing the instrument and in collecting the data.

SUBJECTS

Two hundred juvenile and adult, current and former, women street prostitutes in the San Francisco Bay area participated in the study. The average age was 22. The youngest subject was 10 and the oldest was 46. Seventy percent of the current prostitutes were under 21, almost 60% were 16 or under, and many were 10, 11, 12, and 13 years old. Sixty-nine percent of the subjects were white, 18% were black, 11% were Hispanic, 2% were American Indian, and 1% Asian. Sixty-eight percent were single and never married, 14% divorced, 6% separated, and 2% widowed. Only 10% were either married or living under common law. The average financial situation of the subjects was "just making it," 42% described themselves as very poor, 31% as just making it, 12% as average, 12% as comfortable, and 3% as very wealthy.

INSTRUMENT

A specially designed "Sexual Assault Experiences Questionnaire" written by the authors was used as the survey instrument. The questionnaire had four parts: (1) background information including demographic variables, home background, social support systems, and prostitution history, (2) various forms of assault experienced by the subjects including physical and sexual assault that is job related and sexual assault (in this case completed rape) that is not job related, (3) history of juvenile sexual exploitation prior to becoming a prostitute, and (4) self-concept, plans for the future, and recommendation for an ideal program of intervention for prostitutes who are victims of sexual assault.

PROCEDURE

The "Sexual Assault Experiences Questionnaire" was individually administered to the subjects in sessions that lasted anywhere from 2–4 hr. Questions posed by the interviewers were coded directly onto categories on the questionnaire during the course of the interview, responses were also tape recorded and transcribed. Each interviewer reviewed the questionnaire immediately following the interview for 2 hr. to verify coding and include material there was not time enough to write during the interview.

Interviewers were members of the Delancey Street Foundation, a self-help residential facility well known for its successful treatment of prostitutes, criminals, and drug addicts. The fact that the interviewers reflected the makeup of the sample population maximized their credibility with the subjects (who, in general tend to be distrustful of the "straight world") and their understanding of the jargon terms and lifestyle issues.

RESULTS

The study generated an enormous amount of data, quantitative as well as qualitative documenting stunning amounts of sexual abuse of street prostitutes as part of their job, outside of their work environment, and in their childhood prior to entering prostitution.[1] Many of the open descriptions of these sexual assaults made reference to the role played by pornography. These references were unsolicited by the interviewers. Since the relationship between sexual abuse and pornography was unexpected, no questions addressed it directly. Only after the data collection was completed, was the content from 193 cases of rape (reported by 73% of the women), and from 178 cases of juvenile sexual abuse (reported by 60% of the women), analyzed for any mentioned relationship between these incidents and pornography. Because these data are based on responses from victims rather than research on sex offenders themselves, the results can neither confirm nor reject the "catharsis model" of pornography. The results do, however, lend considerable weight to the "imitation model" of pornography, as reviewed above.

Out of 193 cases of rape, 24% mentioned allusions to pornographic material on the part of the rapist. This figure is even more significant when it is understood that these comments were made by respondents without any solicitation, or reference to the issues of pornography by the interviewer. The comments followed the same pattern: the assailant referred to pornographic materials he had seen or read and then insisted that the victims not only enjoyed the rape but also the extreme violence. For example, the following is a typical comment reported by victims as one in which the assailant made reference to his prior use of pornography.[2] "I know all about you bitches, you're no different; you're like all of them. I seen it in all the movies. You love being beaten." (He then began punching the victim violently.) "I just seen it again in that flick. He beat the shit out of her while he raped her and she told him she loved it; you know you love it; tell me you love it." The assailant continued to beat and slap the woman while raping her, repeating his demand that she say that she loved it, just like the woman he saw in the movies. In the majority of cases, there were no distinctive features about the victims, their situations, or the factors of the rape, which could account for the assailants' mentioning their involvement with pornography. In 12% of the 193 cases of rape, the assailant mentioned his involvement with pornography as a response to the victim's telling the assailant she was a prostitute.

In 19% of the rape cases, the victims tried to stop the violence of the rape by telling the assailant that they were prostitutes. For example, "Calm down. I'm a hooker. Relax, and I'll turn you a free trick without all this fighting." Rather than assuage the violence, this assertion only exacerbated the problem; the assailants *increased* the amount of violence in every single case. They became furious at hearing the woman say she was a prostitute. Most started screaming, demanding that she take back what she had said, insisting on taking her by force. In order to reassert their own control, assailants then became extremely violent. In all 19% of the cases in which the victim told the rapist she was a prostitute, the victim sustained even more serious injuries than those prostitutes who did not disclose their prostitution status. This finding supports the contention that rape is an aggressive act motivated by a desire to establish the rapist's power over his victim, rather than a sexual act. When the victim told the assailant she was a prostitute and offered him sexual gratification, she was trying to assert some control over the situation, which is probably the reason for the excessive violence involved in those rapes, where the rapist insisted on imposing more power and aggression over the victim.

In 12% of the 193 cases, the victims who told the rapists that they were prostitutes not only received more violent abuse than those who didn't tell, but also elicited overt comments from the assailants related to pornography. (In most of the other cases in which victims told the rapists they were prostitutes, indirect references were made to pornography.) An analysis of the 12% of the cases in which victims disclosed they were prostitutes reveals that there is a pattern of response among the assailants to the disclosure. In hearing that their victims were prostitutes, the assailants responded in a manner characterized by the following four elements: (1) their language became more abusive, (2) they became significantly more violent, beating and punching the women excessively, often using weapons they had shown the women, (3) they mentioned having seen prostitutes in pornographic films, the majority of them mentioning specific pornographic literature, and (4) after completing the forced vaginal penetration, they continued to assault the women sexually in ways they claimed they had seen prostitutes enjoy in the pornographic literature they cited. For example,

> "After I told him I'd turn him a free trick if only he'd calm down and stop hurting me, then he just really blew his mind. He started calling me all kinds of names, and then started screaming and shrieking like nothing I'd ever heard. He sounded like a wailing animal. Instead of

just slapping me to keep me quiet, he really went crazy and began punching me all over. Then he told me he had seen whores just like me in [three pornographic films mentioned by name], and told me he knew how to do it to whores like me. He knew what whores like me wanted . . . After he finished raping me, he started beating me with his gun all over. Then he said, "You were in that movie. You were in that movie. You know you wanted to die after you were raped. That's what you want; you want me to kill you after this rape just like [specific pornography film] did."

This particular woman suffered, in addition to forced vaginal penetration, forced anal penetration with a gun, excessive bodily injuries, including several broken bones; and a period of time in which the rapist held a loaded pistol at her vagina, threatening to shoot, insisting this was the way she had died in the film he had seen. He did not, in fact, shoot after all.

Similar results were found in regard to the subjects' experiences of juvenile sexual exploitation. Ten percent of the 200 respondents noted that they had been used as children in pornographic films and magazines. It is significant to note that these comments were made simply in open-ended descriptions of their lives; unfortunately, there were no specific questions on the survey instrument designed to elicit information about the juveniles' relationship to pornography. Therefore, it is assumed that the actual response to this question would be notably higher. All of the respondents who described being used in pornographic films and magazines were under the age of 13 when they were victimized in this way.

Again, in unsolicited comments, 22% of the 178 cases of juvenile sexual exploitation mentioned the use of pornographic materials by the adult prior to the sexual act. The particular manner in which the adult used the pornographic materials varied. For a few, they used the materials to try to persuade the children with comments such as, "Now doesn't that look like something that you and I would have a good time doing together? Come on look at that. Doesn't that make you want to come with me?" Others used pornographic materials to attempt to legitimize their actions. Several victims report that the abuser showed them pictures depicting children involved in sexual acts with adults to convince them that it was acceptable behavior and that it was something they wanted to do. These abusers stated, for example, "See the expression on her face; that's exactly how you look at me." Others used the pornographic materials to arouse themselves prior to abusing the child. For example, one of the subjects in the study described a primitive movie projector her father had set up in the garage. He used to show himself and his friends pornographic movies to get them sexually aroused before they would rape her. (She was 9 at the time.) Her brother would also watch the movies when the father was gone; then he also abused her sexually.

Thirty-eight percent of the 200 women prostitutes interviewed reported that they had been involved in the taking of sexually explicit photographs of themselves when they were children for commercial purposes, and/or the personal gratification of the photographer. The subjects were under the age of 16 years old. It should be noted that while many of the descriptions were open-ended comments included in their stories, some were responses given to questions of how they earned a living once they ran away from home and before they began prostituting.

It is likely, given the numbers who spontaneously described their involvement with pornography, that the cases of pornographic abuse of children would be significantly higher among the prostitute population if studied overtly. Indeed, there is already some evidence indirectly supporting this contention. For example, Baker (1978) mentioned that several authorities have found a close relationship between child pornography and the practice of child prostitution. Rush (1980) mentioned that most runaways can survive only as prostitutes or by posing for pornography. It should be noted that 96% of the juveniles in the present study were runaways and poor, and that all of them were street prostitutes.

SUMMARY AND CONCLUSIONS

It is very difficult to establish conclusively the causal relationship between pornography and sexual abuse of women. Most of the research cited in the introduction is correlational and, thus, only supports an evident relationship between the two variables. In the present study, a detailed content analysis of the responses of 200 street prostitutes, describing sexual abuse in their background, documented a surprising amount of unsolicited references to pornography.

While the results of the data can neither confirm nor reject the "catharsis model" of pornography, because they are based on victims' rather than assailants' responses, nevertheless, the results lend considerable support to the "imitation model" of pornography. Many of the references to pornography noted by the subjects indicated that their abusers were imitating the abusing males in pornographic materials, and believed that, as the victims in pornography, their victims must enjoy the abuse.

The implication of these findings is that further research should replicate the present study, with a direct focus on pornography, and with both prostitute and nonprostitute samples. Further research is urgently needed in order to explore the amount of pornography related to sexual abuse of children, the process of the abuse, and its short and long-term effects. It is also important to study the relationship between pornography and all other forms of sexual abuse of women. Given the high prevalence of juvenile sexual abuse and rape among street prostitutes, which was well documented in the present study (Silbert & Pines, 1982a,b), it is suggested that they be the first group to be studied for a better understanding and documentation of the relationship between pornography and sexual abuse.

CHAPTER 14

Pornography and Rape: A Causal Model

Diana E. H. Russell

> "I don't need studies and statistics to tell me that there is a relation-
> ship between pornography and real violence against women. My
> body remembers."
> —Woman's testimony, 1983[1]

The fact that in many instances the actual *making* of pornography involves or even requires violence and sexual assault was emphasized in the introduction and subsequent chapters. In this chapter I will ignore this aspect of the relationship between pornography and rape to present instead my theoretical model on the causal relationship between the consumption of pornography and rape, as well as some of the research that substantiates this theory. The definition of pornography used here is the same as the one that I discussed at some length in the introduction.

Because it is important to know the proclivities and the state of mind of those who read and view pornography, I will start by discussing some of the data on males' propensity to rape.

MALES' PROPENSITY TO RAPE[2]

"Why do I want to rape women? Because I am basically, as a male, a predator and all women look to men like prey. I fantasize about the expression on a woman's face when I 'capture' her and she realizes she cannot escape. It's like I won, I own her." (Male respondent, Shere Hite, 1981, p. 718)

This chapter is a revised version of an article with the same title originally published in *Political Psychology* 9(1), 1988.

Research indicates that 25 to 30% of male college students in the United States and Canada admit that there is some likelihood they would rape a woman if they could get away with it.[3] In the first study of men's self-reported likelihood to rape that was conducted at the University of California at Los Angeles, the word *rape* was not used; instead, an account of rape was read to the male subjects, of whom 53% said there was some likelihood that they would behave in the same fashion as the man described in the story (quoted below), if they could be sure of getting away with it (Malamuth, Haber, & Feshbach, 1980). Without this assurance, only 17% said they might emulate the rapist's behavior. It is helpful to know exactly what behavior these students said they might enact.

> Bill soon caught up with Susan and offered to escort her to her car. Susan politely refused him. Bill was enraged by the rejection. "Who the hell does this bitch think she is, turning me down," Bill thought to himself as he reached into his pocket and took out a Swiss army knife. With his left hand he placed the knife at her throat. "If you try to get away, I'll cut you," said Bill. Susan nodded her head, her eyes wild with terror. (Malamuth et al., 1980, p. 124)[4]

The story then depicts the rape, describing sexual acts with the victim who is continually portrayed as clearly opposing the assaults.

In another study, 356 male students were asked: "If you could be assured that no one would know and that you could in no way be punished for engaging in the following acts, how likely, if at all, would you be to commit such acts?" (Briere & Malamuth, 1983). Among the sexual acts listed were the two of interest to these researchers: "forcing a female to do something she really didn't want to do" and "rape" (Briere & Malamuth, 1983). *Sixty percent of the sample indicated that under the right circumstances, there was some likelihood that they would rape, use force, or do both.*

In a study of high school males, 50% of those interviewed believed it acceptable "for a guy to hold a girl down and force her to have sexual intercourse in instances such as when 'she gets him sexually excited' or 'she says she's going to have sex with him and then changes her mind'" (Goodchilds & Zellman, 1984).

Some people dismiss the findings from these studies as "merely attitudinal." But this conclusion is incorrect. Malamuth has found that male subjects' self-reported likelihood of raping is correlated with physiological measures of sexual arousal by rape depictions. Clearly, erections cannot be considered attitudes. More specifically, the male students who say they might rape a woman if they could get away with it are significantly more likely than other male students to be sexually aroused by portrayals of rape. Indeed, these men were more sexually aroused by depictions of rape than by mutually consenting depictions. And when asked if they would find committing a rape sexually arousing, they said yes (Donnerstein, 1983, p. 7). They were also more likely than the other male subjects to admit to having used actual physical force to impose sex on a woman. These latter data were self-reported, but because they refer to actual behavior they too cannot be dismissed as merely attitudinal.

Looking at sexual arousal data alone (as measured by penile tumescence), not its correlation with self-reported likelihood to rape, Malamuth reports that:

> About 10% of the population of male students are sexually aroused by "very extreme violence" with "a great deal of blood and gore" that "has very little of the sexual element" (1985, p. 95).
>
> About 20 to 30% show substantial sexual arousal by depictions of rape in which the woman never shows signs of arousal, only abhorrence (1985, p. 95).
>
> About 50 to 60% show some degree of sexual arousal by a rape depiction in which the victim is portrayed as becoming sexually aroused at the end (personal communication, August 18, 1986).

Given these findings, it is hardly surprising that after reviewing a whole series of related experiments, Neil Malamuth concluded that "the overall pattern of the data is . . . consistent with contentions that many men have a proclivity to rape" (1981b, p. 139).

Shere Hite (1981, p. 1123) provides information on the self-reported desire of men to rape women in the general population outside the university laboratory. Distinguishing between those men who answered the question anonymously and those who revealed their identities, Hite reports the following answers by the anonymous group to her question "Have you ever wanted to rape a woman?": 46% answered "yes" or "sometimes," 47% answered "no," and 7% said they had fantasies of rape, but presumably had not acted them out—yet (1981, p. 1123).

For reasons unknown, the non-anonymous group of men reported slightly more interest in rape: 52% answered "yes" or "sometimes," 36% answered "no," and 11% reported having rape fantasies. Although Hite's survey was not based on a random sample, and therefore, like the experimental work cited above, cannot be generalized to the population at large, her finding that roughly half of the more than 7,000 men she surveyed admitted to having wanted to rape a woman one or more times suggests that men's propensity to rape is probably very widespread indeed. It is interesting that Hite's percentages are quite comparable to my finding that 44% of a probability sample of 930 adult women residing in San Francisco reported having been the victim of one or more rapes or attempted rapes over the course of their lives (Russell, 1984).

The studies reviewed here suggest that at this time in the history of our culture, a substantial percentage of the male population has some desire or proclivity to rape females. Indeed, some men in this culture consider themselves deviant for *not* wanting to rape a woman. For example, the answer of one of Hite's male respondents was: "I have never raped a woman, or wanted to. In this I guess *I am somewhat odd*. Many of my friends talk about rape a lot and fantasize about it. The whole idea leaves me cold" (1981, p. 719, emphasis added). Another replied: "I must admit a certain part of me would receive some sort of thrill at ripping the clothes from a woman and ravishing her. But I would probably collapse into tears of pity and weep with my victim, *unlike the traditional man*" (1981, p. 719, emphasis added).

Feminists are among the optimists who believe that males' proclivity to rape is largely a consequence of social and cultural forces, not biological ones. And, of course, having a *desire* to behave in a certain way is not the same as actually *behaving* in that way, particularly in the case of antisocial behavior. Nevertheless, it is helpful to have this kind of baseline information on the desires and predispositions of males, who are, after all, the chief consumers of pornography.

What, then, is the content of the pornography men consume in this country?

THE CONTENT OF PORNOGRAPHY

"I've seen some soft-porn movies, which seem to have the common theme that a great many women would really like to be raped, and after being thus 'awakened to sex' will become lascivious nymphomaniacs. That . . . provides a sort of rationale for rape: 'they want it, and anyway, it's really doing them a favor.'" (Male respondent, Hite, 1981, p. 787)

Don Smith did a content analysis of 428 "adults only" paperbacks published between 1968 and 1974. His sample was limited to books that were readily accessible to the general public in the United States, excluding paperbacks that are usually available only in so-called adult bookstores (1976a). He reported the following findings:

One-fifth of all the sex episodes involved completed rape.

The number of rapes increased with each year's output of newly published books.

Of the sex episodes, 6% involved incestuous rape. The focus in the rape scenes were almost always on the victim's fear and terror, which became transformed by the rape into sexual passion. Over 97% of the rapes portrayed in these books resulted in orgasm for the victims. In three-quarters of these rapes, multiple orgasm occurred.

A few years later, Neil Malamuth and Barry Spinner undertook a content analysis to determine the amount of sexual violence in cartoons and pictorials in *Penthouse* and *Playboy* magazines from June 1973 to December 1977 (1980). They found that:

By 1977, about 5% of the pictorials and 10% of the cartoons were rated as sexually violent.

Sexual violence in pictorials (but not in cartoons) increased significantly over the 5-year period, "both in absolute numbers and as a percentage of the total number of pictorials."

Penthouse contained over twice the percentage of sexually violent cartoons as *Playboy* (13 vs. 6%).

In another study of 1,760 covers of heterosexual magazines published between 1971 and 1980, Park Dietz and Barbara Evans reported that bondage and confinement themes were evident in 17% of them (1982).

Finally, in a more recent content analysis of videos in Vancouver, Canada, T. S. Palys found that 19% of all the scenes coded in a sample of 150 sexually oriented home videos involved aggression, and 13% involved sexual aggression (1986, pp. 26–27).[5] Of all the sexually aggressive scenes in the "adult" videos, 46% involved bondage or confinement; 23%, slapping, hitting, spanking, or pulling hair; 22%, rape; 18%, sexual harassment; 4%, sadomasochism; and 3%, sexual mutilation. In comparison, 38% of all the sexually aggressive scenes in the triple-X videos involved bondage or confinement; 33%, slapping, hitting, spanking, or pulling hair; 31%, rape; 17%, sexual harassment; 14%, sadomasochism; and 3%, sexual mutilation (1986, p. 31).

While Palys's analysis focuses largely on the unexpected finding that "adult" videos "have a significantly greater absolute number of depictions of sexual aggression per movie than [have] triple-X videos," the more relevant point here is that violence against women in both types of pornographic videos is quite common, and that rape is one of the more prevalent forms of sexual violence depicted. Moreover, I would expect a comparable content analysis of videos in the United States to reveal more rape and other sexual violence than was found in this Canadian study, as the Canadian government has played a more active role than the U.S. government in trying to restrict the most abusive categories of pornography.

Palys did not find an increase in the amount of sexual violence portrayed in these videos over time. However, as Palys points out, it was not clear whether this was because some proprietors had become sensitized to issues of sexual violence as a result of protests by Canadian women, or whether they hoped to avoid protests by selecting less violent fare in recent years (1986, p. 34).

In a comparison of the contents of sexual and nonsexual media violence, Malamuth (1986) points out the following important differences between them:

The victim is usually female in pornography and male in nonsexual portrayals of violence on television (p. 5).

"Victims" of nonsexual aggression are usually shown as outraged by their experience and intent on avoiding victimization. They, and at times the perpetrators of the aggression, suffer from the violence" (p. 6). In contrast, "when sexual violence is portrayed, there is frequently the suggestion that, despite initial resistance, the victim secretly desired the abusive treatment and eventually derived pleasure from it" (p. 6).

Unlike nonsexual violence, pornography is designed to arouse men sexually. Such arousal "might result in subliminal conditioning and cognitive changes in the consumer by associating physical pleasure with violence. Therefore, even sexual aggression depicted negatively may have harmful effects because of the sexual arousal induced by the explicitness of the depiction" (pp. 6–7).

In summary: pornography has become increasingly violent over the years — at least in the non-video media — and it presents an extremely distorted view of rape and sexuality.

A THEORY ABOUT THE CAUSATIVE ROLE OF PORNOGRAPHY

Sociologist David Finkelhor (1984) has developed a very useful multicausal theory to explain the occurrence of child sexual abuse. According to Finkelhor's model, in order for child sexual abuse to occur, four conditions have to be met. First, someone has to *want* to abuse a child sexually. Second, this person's internal inhibitions against acting out this desire have to be undermined. Third, this person's social inhibitions against acting out this desire (e.g., fear of being caught and punished) have to be undermined. Fourth, the would-be perpetrator has to undermine or overcome his or her chosen victim's capacity to avoid or resist the sexual abuse.

According to my theory, these conditions also have to be met in order for rape, battery, and other forms of sexual assault on adult women to occur (Russell, 1984). Although my theory can be applied to other forms of sexual abuse and violence against women besides rape, this formulation of it will focus on rape because most of the research relevant to my theory has been on this form of sexual assault.

In *Sexual Exploitation* (1984) I suggest many factors that may predispose a large number of men in the United States to want to rape or assault women sexually. Some examples discussed in this book are (a) biological factors, (b) childhood experiences of sexual abuse, (c) male sex-role socialization, (d) exposure to mass media that encourage rape, and (e) exposure to pornography. Here I will discuss only the role of pornography.

Although women have been known to rape both men and women, males are by far the predominant perpetrators of sexual assault as well as the biggest consumers of pornography (see, e.g., Finkelhor, 1984; Russell, 1984). Hence, my theory will focus on male perpetrators.

A diagrammatic presentation of this theory appears in Figure 14.1. As previously noted, in order for rape to occur, a man not only must be predisposed to rape, but his internal and social inhibitions against acting out his rape desires must be undermined. My theory, in a nutshell, is that pornography (a) predisposes some men to want to rape women and intensifies the predisposition in other men already so predisposed; (b) it undermines some men's internal inhibitions against acting out their desire to rape; and (c) it undermines some men's social inhibitions against acting out their desire to rape.

The Meaning of "Cause"

Given the intense debate about whether or not pornography plays a causal role in rape, it is surprising that so few of those engaged in it ever state what they mean by "cause." A definition of the concept *simple causation* follows:

> An event (or events) that precedes and results in the occurrence of another event. Whenever the first event (the cause) occurs, the second event (the effect) necessarily or inevitably follows. Moreover, in simple causation the second event does not occur unless the first event has occurred. Thus the cause is both the SUFFICIENT CONDITION and the NECESSARY CONDITION for the occurrence of the effect. (Theodorson & Theodorson, 1979)

Figure 14.1 Theoretical Model of Pornography as a Cause of Rape

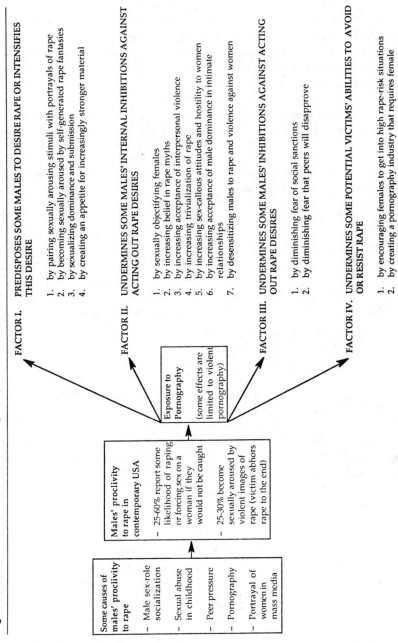

By this definition, pornography clearly does not cause rape, as it seems safe to assume that some unknown percentage of pornography consumers do not rape women, and that many rapes are unrelated to pornography. However, the concept of *multiple causation* is more relevant to this question than simple causation.

> With the conception of MULTIPLE CAUSATION, various possible causes may be seen for a given event, any one of which may be a sufficient but not necessary condition for the occurrence of the effect, or a necessary but not sufficient condition. In the case of multiple causation, then, the given effect may occur in the absence of all but one of the possible sufficient but not necessary causes; and, conversely, the given effect would not follow the occurrence of some but not all of the various necessary but not sufficient causes (Theodorson & Theodorson, 1979).

As I have already presented the research on males' proclivity to rape, I will next discuss some of the evidence that pornography can be a sufficient (though not necessary) condition for men to desire rape (see the list on the far right of Figure 14.1). I will mention when the research findings I describe apply to violent pornography and when to pornography that appears to the viewer to be nonviolent.

As high as is the percentage of male students who report some likelihood of raping women, the percentage who would admit a *desire* to rape women would likely be significantly higher. There must be at least some men who would like to rape a woman, but who would have moral compunctions about doing so. On the other hand, a desire to rape can be assumed to be present in men who disclose some likelihood of raping women. In addition to this desire they must have succeeded in blunting some of their presumed internal or social inhibitions against rape in order to express some likelihood that they would do it.

The Role of Pornography in Predisposing Some Males to Want to Rape

> "I went to a porno bookstore, put a quarter in a slot, and saw this porn movie. It was just a guy coming up from behind a girl and attacking her and raping her. That's when I started having rape fantasies. When I seen that movie, it was like somebody lit a fuse from my childhood on up. . . . I just went for it, went out and raped." (Rapist interviewed by Beneke, 1982, pp. 73–74)

According to Factor I in my theoretical model, pornography can induce a desire to rape women in males who had no such desire previously, and it can increase or intensify the desire to rape in males who have already felt this desire. This section will provide the evidence for the four different ways in which pornography can induce this predisposition that are listed alongside Factor I in Figure 14.1.

(1) Pairing Sexually Arousing/Gratifying Stimuli with Rape. A simple application of the laws of social learning (e.g., classical conditioning, instrumental conditioning, and social modelling), about which there is now considerable consensus among psychologists, suggests that viewers of pornography can develop arousal responses to depictions of rape, murder, child sexual abuse, or other assaultive behavior. Researcher S. Rachman of the Institute of Psychiatry, Maudsley Hospital, London, has demonstrated that male subjects can learn to become sexually aroused by seeing a picture of a woman's boot after repeatedly seeing women's boots in association with sexually arousing slides of nude females (Rachman & Hodgson, 1968). The laws of learning that operated in the acquisition of the boot fetish can also teach men who were not previously aroused by depictions of rape to become so. All it may take is the repeated association of rape with arousing portrayals of female nudity (or clothed females in provocative poses).

Even for men who are not sexually excited during movie portrayals of rape, masturbation subsequent to the movie reinforces the association. This constitutes what R. J. McGuire, J. M. Carlisle, and B. G. Young refer to as "masturbatory conditioning" (Cline, 1974, p. 210). The pleasurable experience of orgasm — an expected and planned-for activity in many pornography parlors — is an exceptionally potent reinforcer.

(2) Increasing Males' Self-Generated Rape Fantasies. Further evidence that exposure to pornography can create in men a predisposition to rape where none existed before is provided by an experiment conducted by Malamuth. Malamuth classified 29 male students as sexually force-oriented or non-force-oriented on the basis of their responses to a questionnaire (1981a). These students were then randomly assigned to view either a rape version or a mutually consenting version of a slide-audio presentation. The account of rape and accompanying pictures were based on a story in a popular pornographic magazine, which Malamuth describes as follows:

> The man in this story finds an attractive woman on a deserted road. When he approaches her, she faints with fear. In the rape version, the man ties her up and forcibly undresses her. The accompanying narrative is as follows: "You take her into the car. Though this experience is new to you, there is a temptation too powerful to resist. When she awakens, you tell her she had better do exactly as you say or she'll be sorry. With terrified eyes she agrees. She is undressed and she is willing to succumb to whatever you want. You kiss her

and she returns the kiss." Portrayal of the man and woman in sexual acts follows; intercourse is implied rather than explicit. (1981a, p. 38)

In the mutually consenting version of the story the victim was not tied up or threatened. Instead, on her awakening in the car, the man told her that "she is safe and that no one will do her any harm. She seems to like you and you begin to kiss." The rest of the story is identical to the rape version (Malamuth, 1981a, p. 38).

All subjects were then exposed to the same audio description of a rape read by a female. This rape involved threats with a knife, beatings, and physical restraint. The victim was portrayed as pleading, crying, screaming, and fighting against the rapist (Abel, Barlow, Blanchard, & Guild, 1977, p. 898). Malamuth reports that measures of penile tumescence as well as self-reported arousal "indicated that relatively high levels of sexual arousal were generated by all the experimental stimuli" (1981a, p. 33).

After the 29 male students had been exposed to the rape audio tape, they were asked to try to reach as high a level of sexual arousal as possible by fantasizing about whatever they wanted but without any direct stimulation of the penis (1981a, p. 40). Self-reported sexual arousal during the fantasy period indicated that those students who had been exposed to the rape version of the first slide-audio presentation, created more violent sexual fantasies than those exposed to the mutually consenting version *irrespective of whether they had been classified as force-oriented or non-force-oriented* (1981a, p. 33).

As the rape version of the slide-audio presentation is typical of what is seen in pornography, the results of this experiment suggest that similar pornographic depictions are likely to generate rape fantasies even in previously non-force-oriented consumers. And, as Edna Einsiedel points out (1986, p. 60):

> Current evidence suggests a high correlation between deviant fantasies and deviant behaviors. . . . Some treatment methods are also predicated on the link between fantasies and behavior by attempting to alter fantasy patterns in order to change the deviant behaviors. (1986, p. 60)

Because so many people resist the idea that a desire to rape may develop as a result of viewing pornography, let us focus for a moment on behavior other than rape. There is abundant testimonial evidence that at least some men decide they would like to perform certain sex acts on women after seeing pornography portraying such acts. For example, one of the men who answered Shere Hite's question on pornography wrote: "It's great for me. *It gives me new ideas to try and see,* and it's always sexually exciting" (1981, p. 780; emphasis added). Of course, there's nothing wrong with getting new ideas from pornography or anywhere else, nor with trying them out, as long as they are not actions that subordinate or violate others. Unfortunately, many of the behaviors modelled in pornography *do* subordinate and violate women, sometimes viciously. For example, a respondent in my probability sample survey, said: "He'd read something in a pornographic book, and then he wanted to live it out. It was too violent for me to do something like that. It was basically getting dressed up and spanking. Him spanking me. I refused to do it." (Many other examples from my survey of men who appear to have imitated pornography are cited in Chapter 15.)

When a man engages in a particularly unusual act that he had previously encountered in pornography, it becomes even more likely that the decision to do so was inspired by the pornography. For example, one woman testified to the Attorney General's Commission on Pornography about the pornography-related death of her son:

> My son, Troy Daniel Dunaway, was murdered on August 6, 1981, by the greed and avarice of the publishers of *Hustler* magazine. My son read the article "Orgasm of Death," set up the sexual experiment depicted therein, followed the explicit instructions of the article, and ended up dead. He would still be alive today were he not enticed and incited into this action by *Hustler* magazine's "How to Do" August 1981 article, an article which was found at his feet and which directly caused his death. (1986, p. 797)

When children do what they see in pornography, it is even more inappropriate than in the case of adults to attribute their behavior entirely to their predispositions.

Psychologist Jennings Bryant testified to the Pornography Commission about a survey he had conducted involving 600 telephone interviews with males and females who were evenly divided into three age groups: students in junior high school, students in high school, and adults aged 19 to 39 years (1985, p. 133). Respondents were asked if "exposure to X-rated materials had made them want to try anything they saw" (1985, p. 140). Two-thirds of the males reported "wanting to try some of the behavior depicted" (1985, p. 140). Bryant reports that the desire to imitate what is seen in pornography "progressively increases as age of respondents *decreases*" (1985, p. 140; emphasis added). Among the junior high school students, 72% of the males reported that "they wanted to try some sexual experiment or sexual behavior that they had seen in their initial exposure to X-rated materials" (1985, p. 140).

In trying to ascertain if imitation had occurred, the respondents were asked: "Did you actually experiment with or try any of the behaviors depicted" within a few days of seeing the materials (1985, p. 140)? A quarter of the males answered that they had. A number of adult men answered no but said that some years later they had experimented with the behaviors portrayed. However, only imitations within a few days of seeing the materials were counted (1985, p. 140). Male high school students were the most likely (31%) to report experimenting with the behaviors portrayed (1985, p. 141).

Unfortunately, no information is available on the behaviors imitated by these males. Imitating pornography is only cause for concern if the behavior imitated is violent or abusive, or if the behavior is not wanted by the recipient. Despite the unavailability of this information, Bryant's study is valuable in showing how common it is for males to *want* to imitate what they see in pornography, and for revealing that many *do* imitate it within a few days of viewing it. Furthermore, given the degrading and often violent content of pornography, as well as the youthfulness and presumable susceptibility of many of the viewers, how likely it is that these males only imitated or wished to imitate the nonsexist, nondegrading, and nonviolent sexual behavior?

Almost all the research on pornography to date has been conducted on men and women who were at least 18 years old. But as Malamuth points out, there is "a research basis for expecting that children would be more susceptible to the influences of mass media, including violent pornography if they are exposed to it" than adults (1985, p. 107). Bryant's telephone interviews show that very large numbers of children now have access to both hard-core and soft-core materials. For example:

The average age at which male respondents saw their first issue of *Playboy* or a similar magazine was 11 years (1985, p. 135).
All of the high school age males surveyed reported having read or looked at *Playboy, Playgirl,* or some other soft-core magazine (1985, p. 134).
High school males reported having seen an average of 16.1 issues, and junior high school males said they had seen an average of 2.5 issues.
In spite of being legally underage, junior high students reported having seen an average of 16.3 "unedited sexy R-rated films" (1985, p. 135). (Although R-rated movies are not usually considered pornographic, many of them meet my definition of pornography.)
The average age of first exposure to sexually oriented R-rated films for all respondents was 12.5 years (1985, p. 135).
Nearly 70% of the junior high students surveyed reported that they had seen their first R-rated film before they were 13 (1985, p. 135).
The vast majority of all the respondents reported exposure to hard-core, X-rated, sexually explicit material (1985, p. 135). Furthermore, "a larg-

er proportion of high school students had seen X-rated films than any other age group, including adults": 84%, with the average age of first exposure being 16 years, 11 months (1985, p. 136).

In a more recent anonymous survey of 247 Canadian junior high school students whose average age was 14 years, James Check and Kirstin Maxwell (1992) report that 87% of the boys and 61% of the girls said they had viewed videopornography. The average age at first exposure was just under 12 years.

> 33% of the boys versus only 2% of the girls reported watching pornography once a month or more often. As well, 29% of the boys versus 1% of the girls reported that pornography was the source that had provided them with the most useful information about sex (i.e., more than parents, school, friends, etc.). Finally, boys who were frequent consumers of pornography and/or reported learning a lot from pornography were also more likely to say that it was "OK" to hold a girl down and force her to have intercourse.

Clearly, more research is needed on the effects of pornography on young male viewers, particularly in view of the fact that recent studies suggest that "over 50% of various categories of paraphiliacs [sex offenders] had developed their deviant arousal patterns prior to age 18" (Einsiedel, 1986, p. 53). Einsiedel goes on to say that "it is clear that the age-of-first-exposure variable and the nature of that exposure needs to be examined more carefully. There is also evidence that the longer the duration of the paraphilia, the more significant the association with use of pornography (Abel, Mittelman, & Becker, 1985)."

The first two items listed under Factor I in my theoretical model both relate to the viewing of *violent* pornography. But sexualizing dominance and submission is a way in which nonviolent pornography can also predispose some males to want to rape women.

(3) Sexualizing Dominance and Submission. Canadian psychologists James Check and Ted Guloien (1989) conducted an experiment in which they distinguished between degrading nonviolent pornography and erotica, and compared their effects. Their experiment is rare not only for making this distinction but also for including non-students as subjects; 436 Toronto residents and college students were exposed to one of three types of sexual material over three viewing sessions, or to no material. The sexual materials were constructed from existing commercially available videos and validated by measuring subjects' perceptions of them. The contents of the sexual materials shown to the three groups of respondents were as follows:

1. The *sexual violence* material portrayed scenes of sexual intercourse involving a woman strapped to a table and being penetrated by a large plastic penis.
2. The *sexually explicit dehumanizing but nonviolent* material portrayed scenes of sexual activity that included a man sitting on top of a woman and masturbating into her face.
3. The *sexually explicit non-degrading* material portrayed sexual activities leading up to heterosexual intercourse (Check & Guloien, 1989).

Check and Guloien's experiment revealed that the viewing of both the nonviolent dehumanizing materials as well as the violent materials resulted in male subjects reporting a significantly greater likelihood of engaging in rape or other coercive sex acts than the control group.

Although self-reported likelihood of raping is not a proper measure of *desire* to rape, as it also indicates that the internal inhibitions against acting out rape desires have been undermined to some extent, Check and Guloien's experiment does offer tentative support for my theoretical model's claim that pornography sexualizes dominance and submission. In addition, it makes theoretical sense that sexualizing dominance and submission would likely be generalized to include eroticizing rape for some men. Further research is needed on this issue, and more researchers need to follow the lead of the Canadian researchers in going beyond the distinction between violent and nonviolent pornography, and distinguishing also between nonviolent degrading pornography and erotica.

(4) Creating an Appetite for Increasingly Stronger Material. Dolf Zillmann and Jennings Bryant have studied the effects of what they refer to as "massive exposure" to pornography (1984). (In fact, it was not that massive: 4 hours and 48 minutes per week over a period of 6 weeks.) These researchers, unlike Malamuth and Donnerstein, focus on trying to ascertain the effects of *nonviolent* pornography and, in the study to be described, they use a sample drawn from a non-student adult population.

Subjects in the *massive exposure* condition saw 36 nonviolent pornographic films, 6 per session per week; subjects in the *intermediate* condition saw 18 such movies, 3 per session per week. Subjects in the control group saw 36 nonpornographic movies. Various measures were taken after 1 week, 2 weeks, and 3 weeks of exposure. In the third week the subjects who were told that they were participating in an American Bar Association study, were asked to recommend the prison term they thought most fair in the case of a rape of a female hitchhiker.

Zillmann and Bryant (1984) found that an appetite for stronger material was fostered in their subjects, presumably, Zillmann suggests, "because familiar material becomes unexciting as a result of habituation" (1984, p.

127). Hence, "consumers graduate from common to less common forms of pornography," that is, to more violent and more degrading materials (1984, p. 127).

According to this research, then, pornography can transform a male who was not previously interested in the more abusive types of pornography, into one who *is* turned on by such material. In turn, Malamuth has shown that males who did not previously find rape sexually arousing, generate such fantasies after being exposed to a typical example of violent pornography, as described in (2) above. And men who have rape fantasies are more likely to act them out than men who do not.

I have argued that the laws of social learning apply to pornography, just as they apply to other media. As Donnerstein testified at the hearings in Minneapolis: "If you assume that your child can learn from Sesame Street how to count one, two, three, four, five, believe me, they can learn how to pick up a gun" (Donnerstein, 1983, p. 11). Presumably, males can learn equally well how to rape, beat, sexually abuse, and degrade females.

The Role of Pornography in Undermining Some Males' Internal Inhibitions Against Acting Out the Desire to Rape

> "The movie was just like a big picture stand with words on it saying "go out and do it, everybody's doin' it, even the movies." (Rapist interviewed by Beneke, 1982, p. 74)

Evidence has been cited showing that many males would like to rape a woman, but for some unknown percentage of these males they have internal inhibitions against doing so. Some males' internal inhibitions are likely to be very weak, others very strong. Presumably, the strength of internal inhibitions also varies in the same individual from time to time. Seven ways in which pornography undermines some males' internal inhibitions against acting out rape desires are listed in Figure 14.1. Research evidence about these processes will be presented in this section.

(1) Objectifying Women. The first way in which pornography undermines some males' internal inhibitions against acting out their desires to rape is by objectifying women. Feminists have been emphasizing the role of objectification in the occurrence of rape for years (e.g., Medea & Thompson, 1974; Russell, 1975). Some men in this culture literally do not see women as human beings but as body parts. They are tits, cunts, and asses. This makes it easier to rape them. "It was difficult for me to admit that I was dealing with a human being when I was talking to a woman," one rapist reported, "because, if you read men's magazines, you hear about

your stereo, your car, your chick" (Russell, 1975, pp. 249–250). After this rapist had hit his victim several times in her face, she stopped resisting and begged, "All right, just don't hurt me." "When she said that," he reported, "all of a sudden it came into my head, 'My God, this is a human being!' I came to my senses and saw that I was hurting this person." Another rapist said of his victim, "I wanted this beautiful fine *thing* and I got it" (Russell, 1975, p. 245, emphasis added).

Dehumanizing oppressed groups or enemy nations in times of war is an important mechanism for facilitating brutal behavior toward members of those groups. However, the dehumanization of women that occurs in pornography is often not recognized because of its sexual guise and its pervasiveness. And it is important to note that the objectification of women is as common in nonviolent pornography as it is in violent pornography.

Doug McKenzie-Mohr and Mark Zanna conducted an experiment to test whether certain types of males would be more likely to sexually objectify a woman after viewing 15 minutes of nonviolent pornography. They selected 60 male students who they classified into one of two categories: masculine sex-typed or gender schematic — individuals who "encode all cross-sex interactions in sexual terms and all members of the opposite sex in terms of sexual attractiveness" (Bem, 1981, p. 361); and androgenous or gender aschematic — men who do not encode cross-sex interactions and women in these ways (McKenzie-Mohr and Zanna, 1990, pp. 297, 299).

McKenzie-Mohr and Zanna found that after exposure to nonviolent pornography, the masculine sex-typed males "treated our female experimenter who was interacting with them in a professional setting, in a manner that was both cognitively and behaviorally sexist" (1990, p. 305). For example, in comparison with the androgynous males, the masculine sex-typed males positioned themselves closer to the female experimenter, and had "greater recall for information about her physical appearance" and less about the survey she was conducting (1990, p. 305). The experimenter also rated these men as more sexually motivated based on her answers to questions such as, "How much did you feel he was looking at your body?" "How sexually motivated did you find the subject?" (1990, p. 301).

This experiment confirmed McKenzie-Mohr and Zanna's hypothesis that exposure to nonviolent pornography causes masculine sex-typed men, in contrast to androgynous men, to view and treat a woman as a sex object.

(2) Rape Myths. If males believe that women enjoy rape and find it sexually exciting, this belief is likely to undermine the inhibitions of some of them who would like to rape women. Sociologists Diana Scully and Martha Burt have reported that rapists are particularly apt to believe rape

myths (Burt, 1980; Scully, 1985). For example, Scully found that 65% of the rapists in her study believed that "women cause their own rape by the way they act and the clothes they wear"; and 69% agreed that "most men accused of rape are really innocent." However, as Scully points out, it is not possible to know if their beliefs preceded their behavior or constitute an attempt to rationalize it. Hence, findings from the experimental data are more telling for our purposes than these interviews with rapists.

As the myth that women enjoy rape is widely held, the argument that consumers of pornography realize that such portrayals are false is totally unconvincing (Brownmiller, 1975; Burt, 1980; Russell, 1975). Indeed, several studies have shown that portrayals of women enjoying rape and other kinds of sexual violence can lead to increased acceptance of rape myths in both men and women. For example, in an experiment conducted by Neil Malamuth and James Check, one group of college students saw a pornographic depiction in which a woman was portrayed as sexually aroused by sexual violence, and a second group was exposed to control materials. Subsequently, all subjects were shown a second rape portrayal. The students who had been exposed to the pornographic depiction of rape were significantly more likely than the students in the control group (a) to perceive the second rape victim as suffering less trauma; (b) to believe that she actually enjoyed it; and (c) to believe that women in general enjoy rape and forced sexual acts (Check & Malamuth, 1985, p. 419).

Other examples of the rape myths that male subjects in these studies are more apt to believe after viewing pornography are as follows: "A woman who goes to the home or the apartment of a man on their first date implies that she is willing to have sex;" "Any healthy woman can successfully resist a rapist if she really wants to;" "Many women have an unconscious wish to be raped, and may then unconsciously set up a situation in which they are likely to be attacked;" "If a girl engages in necking or petting and she lets things get out of hand, it is her own fault if her partner forces sex on her" (Briere, Malamuth, & Check, 1985, p. 400).

In Maxwell and Check's 1992 study of 247 high school students described above, they found very high rates of rape supportive beliefs. The boys who were the most frequent consumers of pornography and/or who reported learning a lot from it, were more accepting of rape myths and violence against women than their peers, who were less frequent consumers and/or who said they had not learned as much from it.

A full 25% of girls and 57% of boys indicated belief that in one or more situations, it was at least "maybe okay" for a boy to hold a girl down and force her to have intercourse. Further, only 21% of the boys and 57% of the girls believed that forced intercourse was "definitely not okay" in any of the situations. The situation in which forced intercourse was most accepted, was that in which the girl had sexually excited her date. In this case 43% of the boys and 16% of the girls stated that it was at least "maybe okay" for the boy to force intercourse. (1992)

According to Donnerstein, "After only 10 minutes of exposure to aggressive pornography, particularly material in which women are shown being aggressed against, you find male subjects are much more willing to accept these particular myths" (1983, p. 6). These men are also more inclined to believe that 25% of the women they know would enjoy being raped (1983, p. 6).

(3) Acceptance of Interpersonal Violence. Males' internal inhibitions against acting out their desire to rape can also be undermined if they consider male violence against women to be acceptable behavior. Studies have shown that viewing portrayals of sexual violence as having positive consequences increases male subjects' acceptance of violence against women. Examples of some of these items include "Being roughed up is sexually stimulating to many women;" "Sometimes the only way a man can get a cold woman turned on is to use force;" "Many times a woman will pretend she doesn't want to have intercourse because she doesn't want to seem loose, but she's really hoping the man will force her" (Briere, Malamuth, & Check, 1985, p. 401).

Malamuth and Check (1981) conducted an experiment of particular interest because the movies shown were part of the regular campus film program. Students were randomly assigned to view either a feature-length film that portrayed violence against women as being justifiable and having positive consequences (*Swept Away* or *The Getaway*) or a film without sexual violence. The experiment showed that exposure to the sexually violent movies increased the male subjects' acceptance of interpersonal violence against women. (This outcome did not occur with the female subjects.) These effects were measured several days after the films had been seen.

Malamuth suggests several processes by which sexual violence in the media "might lead to attitudes that are more accepting of violence against women" (1986, p. 4). Some of these processes also probably facilitate the undermining of pornography consumers' internal inhibitions against acting out rape desires.

1. Labeling sexual violence more as a sexual rather than a violent act.
2. Adding to perceptions that sexual aggression is normative and culturally acceptable.
3. Changing attributions of responsibility to place more blame on the victim.

4. Elevating the positive value of sexual aggression by associating it with sexual pleasure and a sense of conquest.
5. Reducing negative emotional reactions to sexually aggressive acts (1986, p. 5).

(4) Trivializing Rape; (5) Sex-Callous Attitudes; (6) Acceptance of Male Dominance in Intimate Relationships. According to Donnerstein, in most studies "subjects have been exposed to only a few minutes of pornographic material" (1985, p. 34I). In contrast, Zillmann and Bryant examined the effects of "massive exposure" to pornography (this experiment was described on pp. 134–135). As well as creating an appetite for increasingly stronger material, Zillmann and Bryant found that:

- "Heavy exposure to common nonviolent pornography trivialized rape as a criminal offense" (1984, p. 117). In addition, sexual aggression and abuse was perceived as causing less suffering for the victims, for example, an adult male having sexual intercourse with a 12-year-old girl (1984, p. 132).
- "Males' sexual callousness toward women was significantly enhanced" (1984, p. 117). For example, there was an increased acceptance of statements such as "A woman doesn't mean 'no' until she slaps you"; "A man should find them, fool them, fuck them, and forget them"; and "If they are old enough to bleed, they are old enough to butcher." Judging by these items, it is difficult to distinguish sexual callousness from a general hostility to women.
- The acceptance of male dominance in intimate relationships was greatly increased (1984, p. 121), and the notion that women are or ought to be equal in intimate relationships was more likely to be abandoned (1984, p. 122). Support of the women's liberation movement also sharply declined (1984, p. 134).

All these effects — both separately and together — are likely to contribute to undermining some males' inhibitions against acting out their desires to rape.

(7) Desensitizing Males to Rape. In an experiment specifically designed to study desensitization, Linz, Donnerstein, and Penrod showed 10 hours of R-rated or X-rated movies over a period of 5 days to male subjects (Donnerstein & Linz, 1985, p. 34A). Some students saw X-rated movies depicting sexual assault; others saw X-rated movies depicting only consenting sex; and a third group saw R-rated sexually violent movies — for example, *I Spit on Your Grave, Toolbox Murders, Texas Chainsaw Massacre.* Donnerstein (1983) describes *Toolbox Murders* as follows: There is an erot-

ic bathtub scene in which a woman massages herself. A beautiful song is played. Then a psychotic killer enters with a nail gun. The music stops. He chases the woman around the room, then shoots her through the stomach with the nail gun. She falls across a chair. The song comes back on as he puts the nail gun to her forehead and blows her brains out. According to Donnerstein, many young males become sexually aroused by this movie (1983, p. 10).

Donnerstein and Linz point out that, "It has always been suggested by critics of media violence research that only those who are *already* predisposed toward violence are influenced by exposure to media violence" (1985, p. 34F). But these experimenters had actually preselected their subjects to ensure that they were not psychotic, hostile, or anxious.

Donnerstein and Linz described the impact of the R-rated movies on their subjects as follows:

> Initially, after the first day of viewing, the men rated themselves as significantly above the norm for depression, anxiety, and annoyance on a mood adjective checklist. After each subsequent day of viewing, these scores dropped until, on the fourth day of viewing, the males' levels of anxiety, depression, and annoyance were indistinguishable from baseline norms. (1985, p. 34F)

By the fifth day, the subjects rated the movies as less graphic and less gory and estimated fewer violent or offensive scenes than after the first day of viewing. They also rated the films as significantly less debasing and degrading to women, more humorous, and more enjoyable, and reported a greater willingness to see this type of film again (1985, p. 34F). However, their sexual arousal by this material did *not* decrease over this 5-day period (Donnerstein, 1983, p. 10).

On the last day, the subjects went to a law school where they saw a documentary reenactment of a real rape trial. A control group of subjects who had never seen the films also participated in this part of the experiment. Subjects who had seen the R-rated movies: (a) rated the rape victim as significantly more worthless, (b) rated her injury as significantly less severe, and (c) assigned greater blame to her for being raped than did the subjects who had not seen the film. In contrast, these effects were not observed for the X-rated nonviolent films.[6] However, the results were much the same for the violent X-rated films, despite the fact that the R-rated material was "much more graphically violent" (Donnerstein, 1985, pp. 12–13).

In summary: I have presented only a fraction of the research evidence for seven different effects of pornography, all of which likely contribute to the undermining of some males' internal inhibitions against acting out rape desires. This list is not intended to be comprehensive. Indeed, I now have several additions to make, but space precludes my including them here.

The Role of Pornography in Undermining Some Males' Social Inhibitions Against Acting Out Their Desire to Rape

> I have often thought about it [rape], fantasized about it. I might like it because of having a feeling of power over a woman. But I never actually wanted to through *fear of being caught and publicly ruined.* (Hite, 1981, p. 715, emphasis added)

A man may want to rape a woman *and* his internal inhibitions against rape may be undermined by his hostility to women or by his belief in the myths that women really enjoy being raped and/or that they deserve it, but he may still not act out his desire to rape because of his *social* inhibitions. Fear of being caught and convicted for the crime is the most obvious example of a social inhibition. In addition to Hite's respondent quoted above, a second man's answer to her question on whether he had ever wanted to rape a woman illustrates this form of inhibition:

> I have never raped a woman, but have at times felt a desire to—for the struggle and final victory. I'm a person, though, who always thinks before he acts, and *the consequences wouldn't be worth it. Besides, I don't want to be known as a pervert.* (1981, p. 715, emphasis added)

(1) Diminishing Fear of Social Sanctions. In one of his early experiments, Malamuth, along with his colleagues Haber and Feshbach (1980), reported that after reading the account of a violent stranger rape, 17% of their male student subjects admitted that there was some likelihood that they might behave in a similar fashion in the same circumstances. However, 53% of the same male students said there was some likelihood that they might act as the rapist did *if they could be sure of getting away with it.* This higher percentage reveals the significant role that can be played by social inhibitions against acting out rape desires. My hypothesis is that pornography also plays a role in undermining some males' social inhibitions against acting out their desire to rape.

In his content analysis of 150 pornographic home videos, Palys investigated "whether aggressive perpetrators ever received any negative consequences for their aggressive activity—if charges were laid, or the person felt personal trauma, or had some form of 'just deserts'" (1986, p. 32). The answer was no in 73% of the cases in which a clear-cut answer was ascertainable. Similarly, Don Smith (1976a) found that fewer than 3% of the rapists portrayed in the 428 pornographic books he analyzed were depicted as experiencing any negative consequences as a result of their behavior. Indeed, many of them were rewarded. The common portrayal in pornography of rape as easy to get away with likely contributes to the undermining of some males' social inhibitions against the acting out of their rape desires.

(2) Diminishing Fear of Disapproval by Peers. Fear of disapproval by one's peers is another social inhibition that may be undermined by pornography. For example, Zillmann found that "massive" exposure to nonviolent pornography produced overestimates by the subjects of uncommon sexual practices, such as anal intercourse, group sexual activities, sadomasochism, and bestiality (1985, p. 118). Rape is portrayed as a very common male practice in much violent pornography, and the actors themselves may serve as a kind of pseudo-peer group and/or role models for consumers. Further research is needed to evaluate these hypotheses.

In general, I hypothesize the following disinhibiting effects of viewing violent pornography — particularly in "massive" amounts: (a) viewers' estimates of the percentage of men who have raped women would likely increase; (b) viewers would be likely to consider rape a much easier crime to commit than they had previously believed; (c) viewers would be less likely to believe that rape victims would report their rapes to the police; (d) viewers would be more likely to expect that rapists would avoid arrest, prosecution, and conviction in those cases that are reported; (e) viewers would become less disapproving of rapists, and less likely to expect disapproval from others if they decide to rape.

The Role of Pornography in Undermining Potential Victims' Abilities to Avoid or Resist Rape

"He . . . told me it was not wrong because they were doing it in the magazines and that made it O.K." (*Attorney General's Commission*, 1986, p. 786).

Obviously, this fourth factor (the role of pornography in undermining potential victims' abilities to avoid or resist rape) is not necessary for rape to occur. Nevertheless, once the first three factors in my causal model have been met — a male not only wants to rape a woman but is willing to do so because his inhibitions, both internal and social, have been undermined — a would-be rapist may use pornography to try to undermine a woman's resistance (consider the testimony by prostitutes and ex-prostitutes in Part I, for example). Pornography is more likely to be used for this purpose when men attack their intimates (as opposed to strangers).

(1) Encouraging Females to Get into High Rape-Risk Situations. Most adult rape victims are not shown pornography in the course of being raped, although the testimony in Part I of this book reveals that this is quite a common experience for many prostitutes who are raped. Pornography is more often used to try to persuade a woman or child to engage in certain acts, to legitimize the acts, and to undermine their resistance, refusal, or disclosure of these acts. For example, Donald Mosher reported in his 1971 study that 16% of the "sex calloused" male students had attempted to obtain intercourse by showing pornography to a woman, or by taking her to a "sexy" movie. To the extent that this strategy succeeds in manipulating some women into sexual engagements that do not include intercourse, it can result in women being very vulnerable to date rape.

In a more recent study conducted in Canada, Charlene Senn found that "the more pornography women were exposed to, the more likely they were to have been forced or coerced into sexual activity they did not want" (1992). In addition, a male was present in most of the cases in which women were exposed to pornography. This means that most women who consume pornography are doing it because a man wants them to (1992). This is a particularly important finding because the media have made much of the alleged fact that increasing numbers of women are renting pornographic videos.

The positive correlation between the quantity of pornography to which women are exposed and their experiences of forced or coerced sex suggests that women who cooperate with men's requests for them to see it are more likely to be sexually assaulted. This in turn implies that viewing pornography somehow undermines their ability to avoid being sexually assaulted.

Following are two examples of men who used pornography to undermine their victims' resistance. Although these examples do not include rape, the first two cases make it easy to see how being shown pornography can increase a child's vulnerability to rape.

> I was sexually abused by my foster father from the time I was seven until I was thirteen. He had stacks and stacks of *Playboys*. He would take me to his bedroom or his workshop, show me the pictures, and say, "This is what big girls do. If you want to be a big girl, you have to do this, but you can never tell anybody." Then I would have to pose like the woman in the pictures. I also remember being shown a *Playboy* cartoon of a man having sex with a child. (*Attorney General's Commission*, 1986, p. 783)

> He encouraged me by showing me pornographic magazines which they kept in the bathroom and told me it was not wrong because they were doing it in the magazines and that made it O.K. He told me all fathers do it to their

daughters and said even pastors do it to their daughters. The magazines were to help me learn more about sex. (*Attorney General's Commission*, 1986, p. 786)

When women are shown such materials, they probably feel more obliged to engage in unwanted sex acts that they mistakenly believe are normative. Evidence for this hypothesis is provided by Zillmann and Bryant's previously quoted finding that massive exposure to pornography distorts the viewers' perceptions of sexuality by producing the lasting impression that relatively uncommon sexual practices are more common than they actually are, for example, "intercourse with more than one partner at a time, sadomasochistic actions, and animal contacts" (1984, pp. 132–133).

Following is a statement by a woman about how her husband used pornography for this purpose.

> Once we saw an X-rated film that showed anal intercourse. After that he insisted that I try anal intercourse. I agreed to do so, trying to be the available, willing creature that I thought I was supposed to be. I found the experience very painful, and I told him so. But he kept insisting that we try it again and again. (*Attorney General's Commission*, 1986, p. 778)

Women in this situation who try to stop unwanted sex acts are at risk of being raped. (Other more detailed examples of pornography-related sexual abuse and rape of women by their husbands were cited in Part I.)

More systematic research is needed to establish how frequently males use pornography to try to undermine the ability of potential victims to avoid or resist rape and other sexual abuse, and how effective this strategy is. Even if pornography could not predispose men to want to rape women, and it could not intensify the desires of men who are already so predisposed, and it could not undermine men's internal and external inhibitions against acting out their desires to rape, the use of pornography to undermine potential victims' abilities to avoid rape would be cause enough to be deeply concerned about its harmfulness.

(2) A Pornography Industry that Requires Female Participation. Because the portrayal of rape is one of the favorite themes of pornography, a large and ever changing supply of girls and women have to be found to provide it. Clearly, some women are voluntary participants in simulated acts of rape. But many of the rapes that are photographed are real (see Part I of this book for examples).

In summary: A significant amount of research supports my theory that pornography can, and does, cause rape. Nevertheless, much of the research undertaken to date does not adequately examine the four key variables in my theory. For example, Malamuth's self-reported likelihood-of-raping construct merges the desire to rape with the undermining of internal inhibitions against acting out this desire. I hope that more research will be guided in the future by the theoretical distinctions required by my model.

FURTHER EMPIRICAL FINDINGS ON THE CAUSATIVE ROLE OF PORNOGRAPHY IN RAPE

As Donnerstein points out, "One cannot, for obvious reasons, experimentally examine the relationship between pornography and *actual* sexual aggression" (1984, p. 53). However, he has conducted experiments that have shown that the level of aggression of male subjects toward females increased after they had been exposed to violent pornography in which a female rape victim was portrayed as becoming aroused by the end of the movie (aggression was measured by the intensity of electric shock subjects were willing to administer; Donnerstein, 1984). Violent films that were nonpornographic (depicting, for example, a man hitting a woman) also increased male subjects' levels of aggression toward women, but not to the same extent as violent pornographic films. When Donnerstein used violent pornography in which the victim was portrayed as being distressed by the sexual assault throughout the movie, the levels of aggression of male subjects toward females became increased only when they had first been angered by a confederate of the experimenter before seeing the movie.

To explain these findings, Malamuth suggested that: "positive victim reactions . . . may act to justify aggression and to reduce general inhibitions against aggression" (1984, p. 36). This interpretation is consistent with my causal model's emphasis on the important role pornographic depictions play in undermining males' inhibitions against acting out hostile behavior toward women.

Malamuth also undertook an experiment to test whether men's attitudes and sexual arousal to depictions of rape could predict aggression in the laboratory. A week after measuring male subjects' attitudes and sexual arousal to rape, they were angered by a female confederate of the experimenter. When the subjects were given an opportunity to behave aggressively toward her by administering an unpleasant noise as punishment for errors she made in an alleged extrasensory perception experiment, men who had higher levels of sexual arousal to rape and who had attitudes that condoned aggression, "were more aggressive against the woman and wanted to hurt her to a greater extent" (Malamuth, 1986, p. 16).

On the basis of this experiment, as well as two others, Malamuth concluded that "attitudes condoning aggression against women related to objectively observable behavior—laboratory aggression against women" (1986, p. 16).

Both Donnerstein and Malamuth emphasize that their findings on the relationship between pornography and aggression toward women relate to aggressive or violent, not to nonviolent, pornography. For example, Donnerstein maintains that "nonaggressive materials only affect aggression when inhibitions to aggress are quite low, or with long-term and massive exposure. With a single exposure and normal aggressing conditions, there is little evidence that nonviolent pornography has any negative effects" (1984, pp. 78–79). In the real world, however, inhibitions to aggress are often very low, and long-term and massive exposure to nonviolent material is also quite common. Furthermore, there is a lot of evidence of harm from nonaggressive pornography, aside from its impact on aggressive behavior (for example, see my earlier discussion of some of Zillmann's findings).

Finally, given how saturated U.S. culture is with pornographic images and how much exposure many of the male subjects being tested have already had, the task of trying to design experiments that can show effects on the basis of one more exposure is challenging indeed. Because of this methodological problem, when no measurable effects result, it would be wrong to interpret the experiment as proving that there are no effects in general. We should therefore focus on the effects that *do* show up, rather than being overly impressed by the effects that do not.

Some people are critical of the fact that most of the experimental research on pornography has been conducted on college students who are not representative of men in the general population. Hence, the research of Richard Frost and John Stauffer (1987) comparing the responses to filmed violence of college students and residents of an inner-city housing project is of particular interest.

In 5 of the 10 violent films shown to these two groups the violence was directed at females. Frost and Stauffer evaluated these men's sexual arousal to these films by applying both self-report and physiological measures. They found that "there was no single form of violence for which the responses of the college sample exceeded those of the inner city sample on either measure" (1987, p. 36). Four of the five most physiologically arousing categories of violence were the same for both groups: a female killing another female; a male killing a female; rape/murder; and a female killing a male (1987, p. 37). Interestingly, depictions of male–female assault were the least exciting of all ten types of violence measured to all subjects (1987, p. 39). Have men become bored by such a mundane form of violence in movies?

The greatest disparity between the two groups in both physiological and self-reported sexual arousal was to depictions of rape, which "caused the highest response by inner-city subjects but only the fifth highest by the college sample" (1987, p. 38). Although it is not acceptable to infer action from arousal, nevertheless men who are aroused by depictions of violence toward women are more likely to act violently toward them than men who are not aroused by such depictions.

Hence, Frost and Stauffer's study suggests that college students are less prone to sexual violence than some other groups of men. While this is hardly surprising for many people, as inner-city environments are more violent than colleges or than the places in which most college students grew up, it does invalidate attempts to discount the pornography researchers' high figures for self-reported likelihood to rape reported by college males.

⌈The 25 to 30% of male students who admit that there is some likelihood that they would rape a woman if they could be assured of getting away with it, increases to 57% after exposure to sexually violent images, particularly sexually violent images depicting women enjoying rape (Donnerstein, 1983, p. 7). This means that *as a result of one brief exposure to pornography, the number of men who are willing to consider rape as a plausible act for them to commit actually doubles.*⌉

One such brief exposure to pornography also increases male subjects' acceptance of rape myths and interpersonal violence against women. Given the hypothesis that such increased acceptance would serve to lower viewers' inhibitions against acting out violent desires, one would expect pornography consumption to be related to rape rates. This is what one ingenious study found.

Larry Baron and Murray Straus (1984) undertook a 50-state correlational analysis of reported rape rates and the circulation rates of eight pornographic magazines: *Chic, Club, Forum, Gallery, Genesis, Hustler, Oui,* and *Playboy.* A highly significant correlation (+0.64) was found between reported rape rates and circulation rates. Baron and Straus attempted to ascertain what other factors might possibly explain this correlation. Their statistical analysis revealed that the proliferation of pornographic magazines and the level of urbanization explained more of the variance in rape rates than the other variables investigated (for example, social disorganization, economic inequality, unemployment, sexual inequality).

In another important study, Mary Koss conducted a large national survey of over 6,000 college students selected by a probability sample of institutions of higher education (Koss, Gidycz, & Wisniewski, 1987). She found that college men who reported behavior that meets common legal definitions of rape were significantly more likely than college men who denied such behavior to be frequent readers of at least one of the following magazines: *Playboy, Penthouse, Chic, Club, Forum, Gallery, Genesis, Oui,* or *Hustler* (Koss & Dinero, 1989).

Several other studies have assessed the correlation between the degree of men's exposure to pornography and attitudes supportive of violence against women. Malamuth reports that in three out of four of these studies "higher levels of reported exposure to sexually explicit media correlated with higher levels of attitudes supportive of violence against women" (1986, p. 8).

> "In a sample of college men, Malamuth and Check (1985) found that higher readership of sexually explicit magazines was correlated with more beliefs that women enjoy forced sex."
>
> "Similarly, Check (1985) found that the more exposure to pornography a diverse sample of Canadian men had, the higher their acceptance of rape myths, violence against women, and general sexual callousness."
>
> "Briere, Corne, Runtz, and Malamuth (1984) reported similar correlations in a sample of college males."

In her study of male sexuality, Shere Hite found that 67% of the men who admitted that they had wanted to rape a woman reported reading men's magazines, compared to only 19% of those who said that they had never wanted to rape a woman (1981, p. 1123). With regard to the frequency of exposure to pornography, of the 7,000 men she surveyed, Hite reports that only 11% said that they did not look at pornography, and never had. Thirty-six percent said they viewed it regularly, 21%, sometimes, 26%, infrequently, and 6% simply acknowledged that they used to look at it (1981, p. 1123). While correlation does not prove causation, and it therefore cannot be concluded from these studies that it was the consumption of the pornography that was responsible for the men's higher acceptance of violence against women, their findings are consistent with a theory that a causal connection exists.

If the rape rate was very low in the United States, or if it had declined over the past few decades, such findings would likely be cited to support the view that pornography does not play a causative role in rape. While drawing such a conclusion would not be warranted, it is nevertheless of interest to note that my probability sample survey in San Francisco shows that a dramatic increase in the rape rate has occurred in the United States over the last several decades during which there has also been a great proliferation of pornography (Russell, 1984). Unlike the rapes studied by Straus and Baron, 90% of the rapes and attempted rapes described in my survey were never reported to the police.

Finally, it is significant that many sex offenders claim that viewing pornography affects their criminal behavior. Ted Bundy is perhaps the most notorious of these men. For example, in one study of 89 non-incarcerated sex offenders conducted by William Marshall, "slightly more than one-third of the child molesters and rapists reported at least occasionally being incited to commit an offense by exposure to forced or consenting pornography" (Einsiedel, 1986, p. 62). Exactly one third of the rapists who reported being incited by pornography to commit an offense said that they deliberately used pornography in their preparation for committing the rape. The comparable figure for child molesters was much higher—53 versus 33% (Einsiedel, 1986, p. 62).

However, as these sex offenders appear to have used the pornography to arouse themselves after they had already decided to commit an offense, it could be argued that it was not the pornography that incited them. To what extent they actually required the pornography in order to commit their offenses, like some perpetrators require alcohol, we do not know. But even if these perpetrators were eliminated from the data analysis, that still leaves 66% of the rapists and 47% of the child molesters who claimed that they were at least sometimes incited by pornography to commit an offense.

Gene Abel, Mary Mittelman, and Judith Becker (1985) evaluated the use of pornography by 256 perpetrators of sexual offenses, all of whom were undergoing assessment and treatment. Like Marshall's sample, these men were outpatients, not incarcerated offenders. This is important because there is evidence that the data provided by incarcerated and non-incarcerated offenders differ (Einsiedel, 1986, p. 47). It is also likely that incarcerated offenders might be substantially less willing to be entirely frank about their antisocial histories than non-incarcerated offenders, for fear that such information might be used against them.

Abel and his colleagues reported that 56% of the rapists and 42% of the child molesters implicated pornography in the commission of their offenses. Edna Einsiedel, in her review of the social science research for the 1985 Attorney General's Commission on Pornography, concluded that these studies "are suggestive of the implication of pornography in the commission of sex crimes among *some* rapists and child molesters" (1986, p. 63).

In another study, Michael Goldstein and Harold Kant found that incarcerated rapists had been exposed to hard-core pornography at an earlier age than men presumed to be non-rapists. Specifically, 30% of the rapists in their sexual offender sample said that they had encountered hard-core pornographic photos in their preadolescence (i.e., before the age of 11; 1973, p. 55). This 30% figure compares with only 2% of the control group subjects exposed to hard-core pornography as preadolescents. (The control group was obtained by a random household sample that was matched with the offender group for age, race, religion, and educational level; 1973, p. 50.) Could it be that this early exposure of the offenders to hard-core pornography played a role in their becoming rapists? Hopefully, future research will address this question.

CONCLUSION

This chapter describes my theory about how pornography — both violent and nonviolent — can cause rape. I have drawn on the findings of recent research to support my theory. I believe that my theory can be adapted to apply to other forms of sexual assault and abuse, as well as woman battering and femicide (the misogyny-motivated killing of women). I have done the preliminary work on such an adaptation to the causal relationship between pornography and child sexual abuse and plan to publish this work in the future.

Just as smoking is not the only cause of lung cancer, neither is pornography the only cause of rape. I believe there are many factors that play a causal role in this crime (see Russell, 1984, for a multicausal theory of rape). I have not attempted here to evaluate the relative importance of these different causal factors, but merely to show the overwhelming evidence that pornography is a major one of them.

CHAPTER 15

The Experts Cop Out

Diana E. H. Russell

"We have now seen that there is a direct causal relationship between exposure to aggressive pornography and violence against women."
—Edward Donnerstein, 1984, p. 78

"If one were to raise the question of whether or not pornography influences behaviors and attitudes toward women the answer would be difficult."
—Edward Donnerstein and Daniel Linz, 1985, p. 34J

In a pioneer article, Seymour Feshbach and Neil Malamuth (1978) reported on the effects on men's sexual arousal of viewing pornography depicting a female enjoying being raped. They chose this myth-perpetuating material for their experiment because it is one of the more popular scenarios in contemporary pornography. They concluded that exposure to either pornographic or violent materials could induce males to behave aggressively toward women.

This provocative article heralded a new era in research on pornography, most of which had previously reported it to be harmless, and practically all of which had been conducted by men motivated by the desire to prove it so (Bart & Jozsa, 1980; Cline, 1974; Diamond, 1980; Russell, 1980; *Technical Report*, 1970). A small sample of Malamuth and his colleagues' subsequent research on the effects of viewing pornography is described in Chapter 14 of this book.* Their cumulative work has strengthened the evidence for the violence-promoting effects on male subjects of viewing material commonly portrayed in pornography.

Members of the 1985 Attorney General's Commission on Pornography,

---

*Chapter 14 should be read first to fully appreciate the significance of this chapter.

whose mandate was to evaluate the effects of pornography on individuals and on the nation, invited Neil Malamuth, Edward Donnerstein, Daniel Linz, Dolf Zillmann, and Jennings Bryant, among others, to testify about their research. Some of the Commissioners were clearly astonished when these experts insisted that no direct causal link had been established between rape and pornography — including violent pornography — outside of the laboratory.

I was bewildered and dismayed that these researchers had so drastically downplayed the significance of their own research. It was disconcerting too, as I have frequently cited their research to substantiate the opposite conclusion. I decided to try to explain this anomaly. I studied the transcripts of these men's testimonies and their responses to the Commissioners' questions to see if these would provide clues to the switch in their views. (Excerpts of these transcripts will be cited later in this chapter.) I examined Donnerstein's testimony at the Minneapolis Hearings on Pornography organized by Catharine MacKinnon and Andrea Dworkin in 1983, just 2 years before the Government Commission. The two epigraphs at the beginning of this chapter demonstrate his extreme turnabout on this issue before and after he testified to the Government Commission.

During Donnerstein's testimony at the Minneapolis Hearings he was asked: "What type of an effect does this type of material [violent pornography] have on aggressive behavior against women?" Donnerstein replied, "There is a lot of research that shows *if you expose male subjects to specifically violent erotica* [sic], you will find increases in violent behavior" (1983, p. 7, emphasis added). Donnerstein stressed how unusual this finding is:

> Let me point out, I have been in the area of [research on] aggression for years. Those of us who have worked in media violence or television will say one thing: it is almost impossible to find individuals becoming aggressive when they see violent films unless they have been [previously] angered or predisposed [to act violently]. Here [with violent pornography] we have a group of subjects who are not angered or predisposed. Yet *after seeing several types of sexually violent material, particularly the common scenario in which women enjoyed being brutalized, enjoyed being raped, you get increases in aggressive behavior.* Keep in mind throughout all of this . . . we are not dealing with hostile people; we are not dealing with a prison population of sex offenders. We are dealing with normal, healthy males. (1983, p. 8, emphasis added)

Donnerstein went on to claim that:

> This shows if you can measure sexual arousal to sexual images and measure people's attitudes about rape *you can predict aggressive behavior with women weeks and even months later. . . . We are not talking about correlations*

where we get into chicken and egg problems of which came first. We are talking about causality. [We are talking about] the ability . . . to take certain types of images, expose people to those images and make a prediction independent of their background, independent of their past viewing habits, independent of their initial hostility, and make quite accurate predictions of potential aggressive behavior. . . . I think *it suggests quite strongly there are strong relationships between the material and subsequent aggression.* (1983, p. 8, emphasis added)

Further emphasizing his opinion that a causal relationship exists between violent images and aggressive behavior, Donnerstein observed that:

In fact, good colleagues of mine would argue that *the relationship between particularly sexually violent images in the media and subsequent aggression and changes in or toward callous attitudes toward women, is much stronger statistically than the relationship between smoking and cancer,* mainly because most of that research is correlational. This is not. (1983, p. 8, emphasis added)

In addition, Donnerstein reported that "standard hard-core pornography" — which presumably includes nonviolent as well as violent portrayals — had been found to have harmful effects.

If you expose male subjects to six weeks' worth of standard hard-core pornography which does not contain overtly physical violence in it, you find changes in attitudes towards women. They become more calloused towards women. You find a trivialization towards rape, which means after six weeks of exposure, male subjects [in the role of jurors] are less likely to convict for a rape, less likely to give a harsh sentence to a rapist if in fact convicted. (1983, p. 9, emphasis added)

Two years later, Donnerstein's assessment of the impact of pornography appears to have undergone a radical change. In striking contrast to his testimony at the 1983 Minneapolis hearings, here are some excerpts of his testimony to the Attorney General's Commission on Pornography in 1985.

Commissioner Judith Becker, a sex offender researcher, asked Donnerstein: "Were there any causative effects when individuals were exposed to X-rated nonviolent stimulus material?"

Donnerstein: "For X [-rated movies], for both males and females, *you basically get no changes in anything that we can ascertain, except finding the material a little more boring with the passage of time.*" (1985, p. 22, emphasis added)
Becker: "Can you draw from your research any plausible inferences from

the lab to the outside world regarding the impact that nonviolent sexual material, as well as violent sexual material, has on our society?"
Donnerstein: I think we can say at least from the laboratory studies, that
certain types of materials do affect at least perceptions of violence and
attitudes about violence. I think there is no question about that. Now,
I think one has to ask, is less sensitivity to a rape victim in a mock jury
trial a negative effect? My answer would be yes.

Now, that does not imply that these subjects are going to go out and
commit violent acts like rape, not at all. We have never said that, nor
has the research said that. But I think at least with the type of film I
just saw [a clip from an R-rated movie called "Toolbox Murders"], I
think our research does indicate that it can make people less sensitive
to rape, a little more callous about rape; *how that manifests itself into
behavior is an issue we cannot really address from our research.*
(1985, p. 23, emphasis added)

Note that Donnerstein evaded answering Becker's question about the impact of nonviolent pornography.

Aside from the striking contrasts between Donnerstein's two testimonies about largely the same body of research, he also ignores the fact that
his research is not confined to attitudes. As MacKinnon has pointed out,
acquitting a rapist in a jury trial — even a mock one — is not an attitude.
Nor is giving him a light sentence.

It seems hardly credible that Donnerstein really believes that conditioning men to have erections to depictions of rape (also not an attitude!)
only occurs in the laboratory, or that conditioned erections would not
continue to occur after subjects leave the laboratory, unless there were
effective debriefing sessions.

In the paper Donnerstein and his former student, Linz, prepared for
the Commission on Pornography, they concluded:

> *If one were to raise the question of whether or not pornography influences
> behaviors and attitudes toward women the answer would be difficult.* The
> problem we believe centers on what we mean by pornography. . . . Are we
> talking about aggressive materials? In this case the research might be more
> supportive of a potential "harm" effect conclusion. The problem, however, is
> that the aggressive images are the issue, not the sexual, in this type of materi-
> al. In fact, more important here is the message about violence and the sexual-
> ized nature of violence which is crucial. The problem . . . is that while these
> types of messages may be part of some forms of pornography, they are also the
> very pervasive message of media in general . . . from prime time TV to popu-
> lar films. Do males in our society have callous attitudes about rape? Research
> would suggest that some do possess such attitudes. But where do they come

from? Is the media and, in particular, pornography the cause? We would be hard pressed to place the blame on the media. If anything, the media acts as a reinforcer for already existing attitudes and values regarding women and violence. In that sense they are a contributor . . . but only one of many contributors. Furthermore, it is all types of media, from violent pornography to daytime soap operas. (1985, pp. 34J–34K, emphasis added)

Donnerstein and Linz appear to believe that when sexuality and aggression are fused — as in rape — it makes sense to say that only the aggressive part of this combination "might be" harmful. They also argue that because sexualized violence is not confined to violent pornography, but is common in many other types of media, this undermines the significance of violent pornography. This is like arguing that because smoking is not the only cause of lung cancer, it has little significance. Finally, they ignore Zillmann and Bryant's research showing that males become more callous about women and rape after viewing pornography, along with many other attitude and behavior changes that have been substantiated by these researchers and many others, including Donnerstein himself (1984).

Donnerstein's most recent research is on R-rated woman-slashing[1] movies, which he considers nonpornographic, presumably because he accepts the U.S. film industry's distinction between X-rated and R-rated movies (Donnerstein, Linz, & Penrod, 1987). Despite an R-rating, the most frequent scenario in woman-slashing movies involves nude or partially nude victims in seductive poses or sexual acts (for example, masturbating in a bath tub, with breasts exposed) being murdered by male heroes in long drawn-out orgies of sexual violence. Only in a misogynist intercourse-obsessed society could this kind of material be seen as nonpornographic.

Donnerstein testified to the Commissioners that R-rated woman-slashing movies have more harmful effects on male viewers than violent pornographic movies. If this is true, it may be because R-rated movies that combine sexual arousal with the murder of females portray more severe forms of abuse than X-rated movies that eroticize less serious forms of violence against women, such as rape. Few would dispute the view that murder is more serious than rape.

And if more extreme R-rated films are more harmful than less extreme pornographic ones, it does not follow — as Donnerstein seems to imply — that pornographic films are therefore harmless. His argument seems to be: Woman-slashing films and some prime-time TV shows are more violence-promoting than violent pornography; therefore people should not be concerned about pornography.

Despite Donnerstein's fancy footwork to try to use his research on woman-slashing movies to minimize the harmfulness of violent pornography, the R-rated movies that he has studied fit many feminists' definition of pornography, including mine (see Chapter 1). And his admission that woman-slashing movies have harmful effects provides yet more evidence that eroticized violence is harmful to women. Donnerstein's implicit opinion that eroticized violence with an R-rating is more damaging than the equivalent degree of eroticized violence with an X-rating is ludicrous. It is more likely that the more extreme the eroticized violence, the more extreme the harmful effects will be.

Donnerstein's claim that woman-slashing movies are more harmful than violent pornography is also totally inconsistent with his testimony at the Minneapolis Hearings where he noted that, "In the media violence area we have some ambiguity and the relationships are statistically not as strong as they are here [in pornography]" (1983, p. 12).

When the Commissioners quoted Donnerstein's statement affirming a causal link between violent pornography and violence against women [see first epigraph at the beginning of this chapter], he accused them of having "engaged in a 'bizarre' leap of logic" ("Defeated by pornography," 1986, p. 116). But in July 1986, I witnessed feminist rape researcher Pauline Bart remind Donnerstein about his statement at the Minneapolis Hearings that there is a much stronger relationship between sexually violent images in the media and subsequent aggression against women than there is between smoking and lung cancer. Donnerstein again endorsed this statement.

While Neil Malamuth does not appear to be as flagrantly inconsistent as Donnerstein in his statements about a causal link between violent pornography and violence against women, he nevertheless greatly downplayed this link in his testimony before the Commission. This is how he ended his formal presentation to them:

> Clearly, the mass media is certainly not just a matter of fantasy, and it can affect responses relevant to aggression against women such as attitudes. Such attitudes, finally, *may* in combination with other factors affect actual behavior such as aggression against women. (1985, p. 86, emphasis added)

Understandably, Commissioner Judith Becker asked Malamuth why he had changed the conclusions he had previously drawn from his research. He denied having done so. In his answers to the Commissioners' questions, Malamuth kept emphasizing how small and indirect the effects of sexually violent media are, and how there is insufficient research to answer this or that question. For example, Malamuth stated:

> Certainly, one could conjecture that in the equation, mass media [forget pornography!] could be one of those factors that may break the camel's back, that may be some sort of triggering effect, but at this point, that has to remain conjecture because it has not been directly addressed. (1985, p. 92)

On being asked if the sexual arousal that commonly occurs in the viewers of violent sexual materials causes pornography to have more of an impact on viewers than other media violence, Malamuth hedged:

> I think at this point that is an empirical question that needs to be researched. It's very difficult to say degree of effect. So I would want to be very cautious on it. I would say that there appears to be some reason to suspect a possibility of more powerful effects when you have a combination of high arousal and these images; and the arousal may interfere, sort of, with critical cognitive processing and so forth. But again [it is] something that has not empirically been weighed, and I think it would be a little difficult to do that. (1985, pp. 102–103)

In answer to a blunter question by a Commissioner: "Do you consider violent pornography harmful to the average citizen?" Malamuth replied: "I really feel more comfortable in terms of answering questions on a research basis and what the data show." After a reformulation of the question, Malamuth, with what appeared to be great reluctance, answered: "I think that, yes, violent pornography is, to look at it in and of itself, harmful. There are many other elements in the society I find harmful as well" (1985, p. 106). He then described these other harmful elements.

Malamuth was willing to concede that, "It's clear that if a person is sexually aroused by violence against women, they have some motivation to commit actual aggressive acts" (1985, p. 93); and that, "exposure to violent pornography does increase aggression against women if aggression is measured immediately after exposure" (1985, p. 107). But he also maintained that, "If you measure the aggression after a delay, a week, a month, then we do not find any significant increase" (1985, pp. 107–108).

A Commissioner responded to Malamuth's admission: "Then I suppose you would agree that someone who may be predisposed to commit a violent sexual act may very well as a result of reading pornography, be incited into the actual commission of that act?" (1985, p. 108). Malamuth replied:

> I would have to say that at this point I don't think there is sufficient data to answer that question one way or the other, *because the laboratory is a situation where we create sanction for aggression, where aggression to some degree is justified or at least given a context where it is acceptable.* (1985, p. 108, emphasis added)

What, one wonders, does Malamuth think the situation for women is like *outside* the laboratory? For example, what happens to some of the women who are asleep when their husbands or lovers go to bed after having become aroused by watching portrayals of women enjoying rape on their VCRs — not 1 week or 1 month after exposure, but *immediately* afterwards? And what is it like for a woman who is without a ride home after a frat party where "Linda Lovelace" was shown? What is it like for a prostitute at a stag party after the men have viewed a violent pornographic movie? What is it like for a woman who has to walk past a porn store in the red light district on her way to the bus at night? These are but a few of the situations in which aggression is considered justifiable by some/many men.

Malamuth went on to reluctantly concede that:

> You could certainly *speculate* that there are many other settings in nonlaboratory situations where aggression *may* also be sanctioned, and where violent pornography *may* be one of the factors that could trigger the aggressive response. But at this point I would say it's a hypothesis that needs to be more directly addressed in research. (1985, pp. 108–109, emphasis added)

Does Malamuth really believe that all the studies and statistics on rape, battery, and child abuse are of so little scientific merit that he has to *speculate* that there *may* be settings outside the laboratory where aggression is also sanctioned? I trust that rape and battery rarely occur in the laboratory. I *know* that they frequently occur in many homes, on the streets, at places of work, in student dormitories, at frat parties, in cars, in parks, and just about anywhere.

"You do have to agree," said a Commissioner — trying once more to pin Malamuth down on this crucial issue — that the idea that someone already predisposed to commit a violent sexual act may be incited by pornography to commit such an act "would be consistent with your findings, would it not?" (1985, p. 109). Malamuth replied: "I would say at this point it is still premature to judge that one way or the other. That it's a possibility on the basis of the findings; but as a scientist, I really can't answer that question" (1985, p. 109).

Dolf Zillmann and Jennings Bryant were also extremely evasive in their answers to the Commissioner's questions:

Commissioner: Dr. Zillmann, based upon your research and your readings in the field, do you feel that certain forms of violent pornography may well trigger individuals to commit violent crime? (Zillmann, 1985, p. 143).

Zillmann: Maybe I should disqualify myself. I am not an authority on this. You did query Professor Malamuth who did most of the research in this area, and maybe you should look again at the answers that he has given. Because of our research, if I limit myself to our research, I should not answer this question. (1985, pp. 143–144; Zillmann and Bryant's research focuses on nonviolent pornography.)

Commissioner: Dr. Bryant, do you have a viewpoint?

Bryant: We would go beyond our research findings if we did so and I
   would feel very uncomfortable. (1985, p. 144).

In my opinion, the research of Zillmann and Bryant provides strong
empirical evidence in support of a causal link between pornography and
rape, as does the research of Donnerstein and Malamuth. And pornography demonstrably does *considerably* more than trigger a few highly predisposed individuals to commit violent acts against women (see Chapter 14).

EXPLANATIONS FOR COPPING OUT

What might explain why *I* am willing to recognize a causal relationship between pornography and rape, while some of the major experts are
not?

The difference in our academic disciplines may be one reason. The
fact that I am a sociologist and they are psychologists is significant because
psychologists tend to focus on the individual while sociologists more often
focus on groups or larger units of analysis. On the individual level, all
viewers of pornography are not affected in the same way. The effects of
viewing pornography are mediated by individual and/or social variables.
Hence it becomes a little more comprehensible why Malamuth (1986)
would maintain that even violent pornography has only indirect effects.

Instead of trying to explain why Mr. X is affected by viewing violent
pornography while Mr. Y is not, sociologists typically investigate whether
the average aggression scores (or whatever is being measured) of those
exposed to violent pornography are significantly higher than the aggression
scores of those exposed to erotica or to nonsexual, nonaggressive material.
Nor would we describe as "indirect" any significant differences in the
aggression scores of men in these two or three groups.

Whereas the individual level of analysis is more relevant for clinicians,
the group level of analysis is more relevant to social policy makers. Had
researchers insisted on being able to understand why Mr. X died from lung
cancer after 20 years of smoking whereas Mr. Y did not, before warning
the public that smoking causes lung cancer, there would have been a lot
more deaths from lung cancer. Similarly, if we refused to see the causal
relationship between excessive alcohol consumption by drivers and traffic
accidents because not all drivers who are drunk have traffic accidents, no
law would have been enacted to impose stiffer penalties on drunk drivers,
and consequently there would have been even more deaths on the road.
Although it can be important for researchers to try to explain individual

differences, we do not need this information before recognizing group effects.

But I do not believe the difference in our disciplines fully accounts for our different conclusions regarding the causal link between pornography and rape. Nor does this difference explain why Malamuth and Donnerstein changed their views when they testified to the Attorney General's Commission on Pornography. What might explain their turnabout?

Obviously, scientists sometimes change the conclusions they draw from their own, or others', research. It seems appropriate in such cases that they explain the change. To my knowledge, neither Donnerstein nor Malamuth have acknowledged a change.

Because the Commission on Pornography was appointed by former President Ronald Reagan to evaluate the effects of pornography and to make recommendations about it, perhaps Donnerstein, Linz, Malamuth, Zillmann, and Bryant downplayed the causal link because they were afraid that the Commission would use their research as a rationale to further restrict pornography. There are probably many who share his fear, and who would have been enraged with them had they not contradicted their earlier statements about the damaging effects of pornography. While I personally empathize with the discomfort scientists feel when they believe their research may be used to promote policies to which they are adamantly opposed, distorting the implications of one's research is not an ethical way to handle this dilemma. If they were concerned that their research might result in greater censorship, they could have explained why they were adamantly opposed to this policy. If explaining their views seemed a futile strategy, they could have refused to testify. But downplaying the harm of pornography is not only unethical, unscientific, and unprofessional; it is also dangerous for women.

For Donnerstein, at least, there must be more than fear of how conservative Republican administrations might have used his research to ban pornography because his inconsistent statements about the causal relationship between pornography and rape predated the Commission. For example, in a chapter that was published a year before the Commission Hearings, Donnerstein ended the summary of his research as follows: "We have now seen that *there is a direct causal relationship between exposure to aggressive pornography and violence against women*" (Donnerstein, 1984, p. 78, emphasis added). One and a half pages later, he writes: "But more importantly, we need to be more certain as to what the causal factor is, *if there is one*, in the relationship between pornography and violence against women" (1984, p. 80, emphasis added).

As for Malamuth, I asked him if his fear of what the conservatives would do with his research had caused him to downplay it. He steadfastly denied that he had changed his views or that he had downplayed the causal relationship when testifying to the Commission (personal communication, June, 1988).

Were Malamuth, Donnerstein, Linz, Zillmann, and Bryant just being scrupulously cautious scientists, unwilling to exaggerate the significance of their work? Donnerstein's many inconsistent, and sometimes wild, statements make him the picture of *in*cautiousness. In contrast, Malamuth appeared to be playing the role of cautious scientist to the hilt (although I personally found it unconvincing). Why would Malamuth suddenly start to argue that it is impossible to conjecture that the results of his large body of research have any implications outside the laboratory? As Stewart Page has observed:

> The limitations of laboratory research have been known and acknowledged for many years. Still, psychologists have chosen to conduct a plethora of studies on pornography, on the assumption that they have relevance to the real world (Malamuth, 1984). However, in the present case, it may be that the most serious drawback of the cumulative evidence is that it could be taken as support for perspectives and positions advocated by unpopular political groups within the social science and academic communities. (1989, p. 580)

Indeed, the view that pornography is harmful has become significantly more unpopular in academia, in the scientific community, in the publishing industry, and among liberals in general. The consequences for Malamuth, Donnerstein, and their colleagues, had they testified to the Commission that their research substantiates the harmfulness of violent pornography, would probably have included unpopularity with their university colleagues and students as well as other members of their professions and the larger liberal community, including most publishers. (It is significant that the Commission had a very difficult time finding a commercial publisher for their two-volume report.)

Malamuth's apparent reluctance to generalize from the laboratory to real life because of his principles is also suspect as at other less politically charged times he has argued that his laboratory experiments have important implications for the understanding of violence against women in the real world. Following is but one example of how far Malamuth and his colleague Seymour Feshback were willing to go after but one experiment in 1978:

> We see, then, how one exposure to violence in pornography can significantly influence erotic reactions to the portrayal of rape. . . . There was also evidence that the men were identifying with the rapist — and even considered rape as conceivably within their own range of behavior. . . . We share the belief that the depiction of violence in erotica and pornography could be

harmful. Unlike the typical violent episodes on television, pornographic violence is, typically, not an integral part of a larger dramatic theme. Rather, the
erotic violence itself is the theme. The erotic presentation sometimes even
approximates a how-to-do-it instructional film. Further, the juxtaposition of
violence with sexual excitement and satisfaction provides an unusual opportunity for conditioning of violent responses to erotic stimuli. The message that
pain and humiliation can be "fun" encourages the relaxation of inhibitions
against rape. . . .

Psychologists, in our judgment, ought not to support, implicitly or explicitly, the use and dissemination of violent erotical [sic] materials. (Feshbach
& Malamuth, 1978, pp. 116–17)

Perhaps Malamuth, Donnerstein, and Linz are willing to forfeit their
scientific integrity to prevent being outcasts in their communities.

Of course, many researchers subscribe to the notion that scientists are
not supposed to take a stand on moral issues as scientists. Doing so jeopard-
izes their claim — false though it is — to objectivity. When Donnerstein was
asked by a Commissioner about his interview for a feature in *Penthouse*
magazine, including whether he had been paid for the interview and
whether the pornography industry had ever tried to influence him, he
replied: "I have never taken sides on this issue, and have tried to stay as
objective as possible" (1985, p. 33).

If Donnerstein was doing research on racism rather than on aggression
against women, and if he had found that media portrayals of African-
Americans seriously desensitized people to violence against them, would he
be so proud to announce that he has never taken sides on *this* issue? Are
researchers on the Holocaust supposed to not take sides? Are scholars supposed to not take sides on the damaging effects of poverty? Or nuclear
war? Or rape?

I personally take sides on all these issues. I do not believe scientists
should be expected to be morally indifferent to human suffering and
abuse. Yes, we need to be very clear about which of our statements are
based on data and how good the data are, which are based on theory, and
which are based on hunch. But once there is sound evidence that harm is
being caused — by pornography, for example — surely it is the duty of scientists — and others — to say so. And surely these scientists should be able to
exercise their freedom of speech by feeling able to say that they deplore the
harm done. Moral bankruptcy should not be the norm or ideal for scientists or anyone else!

These men made their research appear so inconsequential that it is
difficult to understand why anyone would want to continue funding it. It
would usually be a death knell to future funding for researchers to argue
that there is little to be learned from their years of research despite the

mountains of data they have accumulated at great cost; that their basic methodology — laboratory research — makes it impossible to learn anything about the real world; and that the question the researchers are trying to answer is unanswerable. For example, in a recent televised interview, Donnerstein expressed the view that finding a causal link between pornography and aggression against women was probably impossible: "I think we're never going to truly be able to get there," he said (Donnerstein, 1990).

MacKinnon hypothesizes that as long as the causal connection between pornography and harm was just an academic question for researchers to debate, it was tolerated. The turning point came when she and Dworkin organized the Minneapolis Hearings on Pornography as a prelude to launching their proposal for legislation that would actually *do* something about this industry (personal communication, January 27, 1992). This became a turning point because it was very nearly successful, not just in Minneapolis, but in several other communities in the United States.

And then there's the Mafia. Had the testimonies of the experts supported the causal link between pornography and harm to women, they may have been in danger of retaliation by the Mafia or other groups or individuals who are deeply invested in the continuation of a flourishing pornography industry. (Rumor has it that one expert's life was threatened by the Mafia before he testified to the Commission.)

I do not wish to imply that these researchers are equally culpable for misleading the public, nor to deny the value of their work. For example, although Zillmann and Bryant were unwilling to speak up in front of the Commission, they have continued to do groundbreaking research, particularly on the destructive effects of nonviolent pornography. Their failure to take a stand when testifying was an unfortunate aberration, not a reflection of an ongoing minimization of the harmful effects of pornography.

My greatest criticism is reserved for Donnerstein for his irresponsible inconsistencies, distortions, bizarre responses (e.g., in denouncing the Commission for correctly quoting him as saying that pornography is harmful to women), and, most seriously, the radical switch in his position on this issue despite the lack of any research basis for it. This does not mean his research is without value. But it does mean that one has to be very wary about the interpretations and conclusions he draws from it.

It is significant to note that Donnerstein is the only one of these researchers (to my knowledge) to sell out to the pornography industry. Bob Guccione published an interview with Donnerstein in *Penthouse* in 1985, thereby contributing to *Penthouse*'s image as different from, and more respectable than, "real" pornography. Donnerstein apparently believes this action does not constitute taking sides! I doubt that he would have been equally willing to grant an interview to an anti-Semitic Nazi publication.

It will probably take many years to correct the message that there is no evidence for the existence of a causal relationship between pornography and harm to women. For this, Donnerstein, Linz, Malamuth, Zillmann, and Bryant all bear some responsibility, but Donnerstein and Malamuth bear most of it. Their cop out on this issue totally undermined the Commission's conclusion that pornography causes harm to women, despite the accuracy of this conclusion. As with the 1970 Commission on Pornography and Obscenity, male researchers have once again downplayed the harmfulness of material that victimizes women.

A PERSONAL POSTSCRIPT

A draft of this chapter has been hidden in my files since 1986. After writing it, I decided I could not publish it. This was not an easy decision. On the one hand, I felt it was vital that someone publish the kind of critique that I had written. On the other hand, I was reluctant to publicly criticize colleagues whom I believed would be angry with me for so doing. Most particularly, I anticipated losing a friendly and professional relationship with Malamuth, despite my high regard for his research (although not his recent conclusions).

I vacillated about this decision many times. After a male friend and colleague told me that publishing this critique would be perceived as a stab in the back to researchers who are basically "good guys," my resolution to suppress it prevailed for several years. My friend advised me to discuss my criticisms directly with the researchers instead. I followed his advice in the case of Malamuth (I wouldn't waste my breath on Donnerstein). I asked him why he had minimized the causal relationship between pornography and violence against women when he testified to the Commission in 1985. He denied that he had.

So here I am, 7 years later, still feeling ambivalent about publishing this chapter. The scholarly community is supposed to be searching for truth, open to new ideas, open to criticism. Despite the extraordinary contribution of feminists to the field of violence against women, we rarely get credit for this, but instead are frequently penalized for challenging misogynist theories and research. The threat of ostracism is but one of the many mechanisms used to keep us in line. I eventually decided I must publish this chapter, whatever the personal consequences may be.

One of the things that has made it easier for me to publish this chapter is my discovery that other scholars have published excellent critiques of Donnerstein's extreme reversal on the issue of pornography and harm to women. For example, Canadian psychologist Stewart Page notes that, "Although Linz et al. felt that the Commission must abandon the notion of a 'causal relationship' between pornography and antisocial effects, one can find numerous statements in *Pornography and Sexual Aggression* supporting this relationship (Malamuth & Donnerstein, 1989, p. 579).

Page also observes that Linz, Donnerstein, and Penrod (1987) fault the Pornography Commissioners for failing to recognize "that much available research has confounded sexual explicitness and violence." Linz et al. maintain that violence is the harmful factor, not explicitness. But, as Page points out, "The materials of concern *intentionally* combine violence and explicitness, and a substantial market for them exists" (1989, p. 579, emphasis added). Hence their point "is not necessarily germane to the Commission's mandate or to the essential validity of its conclusions, *any more than is asking which parts of a revolver are more important in a murder*" (1989, p. 579, emphasis added). Page then cites Donnerstein's observation in 1983, "that in some studies, the effects of nonpornographic violent material alone have not in fact been as strong as those elicited by violently pornographic depictions." Page notes that Donnerstein, Linz, and Penrod themselves reported two such studies in their article critiquing the Commissioner's conclusions (1989, p. 579; see also Page, 1990a and b).

Another catalyst for my decision to publish this chapter was my recent discovery that Donnerstein has flip-flopped yet again on the causal relationship between pornography and harm to women. Early in 1992 he testified as an expert witness for Thomas Schiro, who raped a woman acquaintance, Laura Luebbehusen, three times, then shattered a vodka bottle on her head, beat her with an iron, and strangled her to death (Schiro v. Clark, 1992, p. 966). Schiro then "performed vaginal and anal intercourse on the corpse and chewed on several parts of her body" (1992, p. 966).

Schiro argued at his trial that he was a sexual sadist whose "extensive viewing of rape pornography and snuff films rendered him unable to distinguish right from wrong" (1992, p. 971). Donnerstein supported Schiro's claim. He testified "that after a short exposure to aggressive pornography 'nonrapist populations . . . begin to say that women enjoy being raped and they begin to say that using force in sexual encounters is okay. Sixty percent of the subjects will also indicate that if not caught they would commit the rape themselves'" (1992, p. 972). The account of this case in the *Federal Reporter* (a legal publication) characterizes Donnerstein's testimony as supporting the conclusion that "pornography generally encourages men to commit acts of violence against women" (1992, p. 972). At closing argument, Schiro's attorney relied on the testimony of Donnerstein and another expert witness, Frank Osanka, to support his claim that "premature exposure to pornography and continual use with more violent forms . . . created a person who no longer distinguishes between violence and rape, or violence and sex" (1992, p. 972).

Edward Donnerstein owes the scholarly community and other concerned people an explanation for the repeated reversals in his allegedly research-based conclusions regarding the causal link between pornography and sexual violence. He is making a mockery of the notion of scholarly integrity, and revealing a callous disregard for the immense significance of this issue for the safety and well being of women.

In a personal letter feminist activist Nikki Craft wrote to Donnerstein about how betrayed she felt when he allowed *Penthouse* to publish an interview with him. She wrote: "I do hope that some good comes from the money you got from *Penthouse*, because you know better than anyone that it drips with our blood" (personal communication, August 15, 1985). The same can be said for researchers who choose to downplay the causal connection between pornography, misogyny, and violence against women.

Women and children will continue to be abused, pressured into unwanted sex acts, beaten, raped, tortured, and killed in the making of pornography, and as a consequence of men viewing it. Pornography will continue to fuel hate crimes against women until men are willing to face the consequences of their desire for this vicious hate propaganda, and voluntarily forgo it.

CHAPTER 16

Racism in Pornography

Alice Mayall & Diana E. H. Russell

"The pornography industry's exploitation of the Black woman's body is qualitatively different from that of the white woman. While white women are pictured as pillow-soft pussy willows, the stereotype of the Black 'dominatrix' portrays the Black woman as ugly, sadistic, and animalistic, undeserving of human affection."
—Luisah Teish, 1980

"In pornography, all of the culture's racist myths become just another turn-on. Thus, Asian women are portrayed as pliant dolls; Latin women as sexually voracious yet utterly submissive; and black women as dangerous and contemptible sexual animals."
—Dorchen Leidholdt, 1981

I visited seven largely heterosexual pornography stores in the San Francisco Bay area to investigate the kinds of racist pornography being sold. I also wanted to find out which ethnic groups are most often portrayed in pornography, and in what manner. Once in the store I looked at every accessible piece of pornography on every shelf. I noted all the titles and covers that displayed people of color.

I divided the pornography into the following categories: magazines, books, films, videos, and for one store, games and cards. I recorded the total number of items found in each category as well as the number containing people of color in each category.

Once I had identified the pornography as containing a person of color, I listed the title, a description of the cover picture, as well as the type of pornography it represented. My observations of magazines were limited to

The original research for this chapter was conducted by Alice Mayall in 1985 when she was an undergraduate at Mills College in Oakland, California. Diana Russell, a professor of sociology at Mills College at that time, supervised Mayall's research. Russell excerpted a section of Mayall's much longer unpublished report on racism in pornography, and radically revised it for this anthology. The "I" in the rest of the chapter refers to Mayall, the "we" refers to both authors.

their covers because most of them were encased in plastic. I also selected eight pornography books about people of color and Jews in order to make more detailed analyses of their contents.

The salience of skin color is evident in most of the materials displayed in pornography stores. White women were featured in most pornography (92% of total) presumably because they fulfill the prevailing racist equation of beauty with whiteness and Caucasian features. People of color fall into the special interest category, other examples of which are rape, bondage and sado-masochism, anal sex, sex with children, large breasted women, and sex between women. Some pornographic covers also focus on particular body parts or different methods of penetrating bodies.

A large majority of the magazine covers that portrayed people of color in sexual poses (N = 109), but not engaged in sexual contact, used African-American women: 73 covers exhibited African-American women, 18 Asian or Asian-American women, and 4 Hispanic women. Of the covers displaying men of color, 9 were African-American transvestites or transsexuals, while 2 others were portrayed as "normal," 3 were Asian transvestites, and only 1 was Hispanic.

My analysis of book titles revealed the same disproportionate numbers of portrayals of African-Americans compared with other people of color. Anti-Semitic pornography is another special interest evident in the book titles examined, along with a smaller amount of anti-Arab pornography. We can think of no explanation for the relatively small amount of pornography using Hispanics, nor why African-Americans are so overrepresented among people of color.

The breakdown of the ethnicity of the 131 cover pictures in which a person of color was displayed in a state of sexual contact is too complex to describe completely as there are so many possible interethnic and intraethnic permutations. The largest number of these covers portrayed African-American women with white men (28), followed by white women with African-American men (20), Asian women with white men (17), and Asian women with men of unknown ethnicity (12).

Significantly, as judged by these covers, interest in intraethnic heterosexual relations was minimal. For example, there were only six covers portraying sex between African-American women and men, and two portraying intra-Asian sex. Homosexual themes were also uncommon: There were six covers depicting sex between African-American and white men, four depicting African-American and white women, three depicting Asian women together, two African-American women together, and two African-American and Asian women together. Obviously there are some porn stores that cater specifically to the gay male community. The representation of gay men engaged in interethnic sex may well be very different in such stores.

When people of color are used in books, magazines, or videos, the titles usually conveyed this information for consumers. For example, an average of 77% of the magazines on display in six different stores identified the ethnicity of the person in the title. This presumably means that skin color is very salient to most consumers. It comes as no surprise in a racist culture like the United States, that people of color are a specialty item in pornography.

It was sometimes difficult to determine the ethnicity of the people on magazine covers portraying explicit sexual contact, especially in some of the bondage photographs. For example, I compiled a long list of "Asian Woman and Unknown Man" for which it was impossible to determine the ethnic identity of the penis photographed. With regard to magazines that portrayed explicit sexual-genital contact, there were *very* few in which African-Americans were present without whites. By and large, African-American men who consume pornography have a choice of buying magazines in which only whites are portrayed, or in which white men use African-American women or African-American men use white women. Whether these disproportionate portrayals of the ethnicity of pornographic covers reflect the interest of the consumers or the makers of pornography, we do not know. However, these findings are consistent with Alice Walker's (1984) observation that pornography serves to drive African-American men and women away from each other.

A majority of the men depicted in pornography as transvestites and transsexuals are people of color. Perhaps it is more acceptable to portray people of color as "social deviants." Some of the pornography titles listed in Figure 16.1 provide examples of blatant racist stereotypes, for example, "Animal Sex Among Black Women," "Black Bitch," "Black Girl's Animal Love," "Bitch's Black Stud," "Gang Banged by Blacks," "Geisha's Girls," "Oriental Sadist's Pet," "Raped by Arab Terrorists," "Bound Harem Girl."

Note that the term "bitch" is exclusively used for African-American women in the list of titles recorded in Figure 16.1. The word bitch means female dog. In contrast with other women of color, several titles in Figure 16.1 associate animals with African-American women. As Alice Walker has pointed out, "where white women are depicted in pornography as 'objects,' Black women are depicted as animals. Where white women are at least depicted as human bodies if not beings, Black women are depicted as shit" (Walker, 1984, p. 103). Luisah Teish makes a similar point in the epigraph that opens this chapter (1980, p. 117).

Tracey Gardner makes an interesting observation about male preferences: "I have noticed that while white men like Black women 'looking baaad' in leather with whips, Black men like Black women in bondage, helpless and submissive" (1980, p. 113).

Asian women tend to be depicted either as sweet young lotus blossoms

Figure 16.1 Pornographic Book Titles Using People of Color*

African-Americans

Animal Sex Among Black Women
Animals and Black Women
Bisexual Teacher
Bitch's Black Stud
Black Beauty
Black Bitch
Black Fashion Model
Black Ghetto Teens
Black Girl's Animal Love
Black Head Nurse
Black Lady's Lust for Girls
Black Leather Doll
Black Passion
Black Stepfather
Black Teacher
Black Woman's Hunger
Boy for Black Mama
By Sex Possessed
Candy's Black Lover
Dark Detective
Diner Doll
Demon Dictator
Gang Banged by Blacks
Garment Center Black Sex
The Heiress' Black Slave Boy
Her New White Master
Hot for Black Studs
Man-Hungry Black Bitch
Mother's Black Lovers
Seductive Black Bitch
Spread Black Thighs
Teacher's Black Passion
Young Intern's Surprise

Nazi–Jewish

Gestapo Bondage Brothel
Gestapo Lust Slave
Gestapo Sex Crimes
Gestapo Stud Farm
Gestapo Training School
Nazi Dungeon Slave
Nazi Sex Captives
Nazi Whip Mistress
Sadist's Prisoner
Sluts of the S.S.
Swastika She Devil

Asian

Bawdy Tales of Wu Wu Wang
Bloody Encounters
Geisha's Girls
Geisha's Torment
Japanese Sadist's Dungeon
May Ling's Master
Oriental Sadist's Pet
Samurai Slave Girl
Teen Slaves of Saigon
Vietcong Rape Compound
Whips of Chinatown

Asian/Indian

The Talking Pussy

Arab

Bound Haren Girl
Harem Hell
Raped by Arab Terrorists
Sheik's Hand Maiden

*This is a complete list of the pornography book titles that portrayed people of color on their covers from six stores.

or objects of bondage. The notorious December 1984 issue of *Penthouse* contained a nine-picture-spread of Asian women, some of whom were

> bound tightly with ropes cutting into their ankles, wrists, labias and buttocks. Two of the images showed women bound and hanging from trees, heads lolling forward, apparently dead. . . . Throughout these murderous images are sprinkled 'artsy' haiku quotes which exude dominance and subordination. (Farley, 1992)

These femicidal photographs eroticizing the murder of Asian women prompted Nikki Craft and Melissa Farley to organize a 2-year feminist rampage against *Penthouse* in nine states. More than 100 women participants in the rampage were arrested for their civil disobedience activities (Farley, 1992).

Some of the book titles presented historical periods of abuse as if they were sexually stimulating, for example, the enslavement of African-Americans—"The Heiress' Black Slave Boy," "Her Non-White Master"—and the genocide of Jews—"Gestapo Lust Slave," "Nazi Sex Captives."

The magazine titles are much the same as those used on books. A few examples of particularly racist titles include "Jungle Babies," "Wet, Wild and Black," "Black Mother Fucker," "Geisha Twat," "Hot Asian Asses," "Oriental Pussy," and "Oriental Bondage."

Dorchen Leidholdt points out that "pornography contains a racial hierarchy in which women are rated as prized objects or despised objects according to their color" (1981, p. 20). Nevertheless, Hugh Hefner ignorantly boasted "that portraying women of color as sex objects to a predominantly white male readership is a radical development that shows *Playboy*'s social conscience" (Leidholdt, 1981, p. 20). Gardner perceives *Playboy*'s inclusion of African-American women as follows:

> So, Black women have been elevated from the status of whore to "Playmate." Now white boys can put them in *Playboy* without damaging the magazine's respectability too much (though after the first appearance of Black women in *Playboy*, there were some angry letters to the editor saying "get them niggers out") (1980, p. 113).

The following section presents a content analysis of eight books that exemplify the racism and violence against women prevalent in such "literature." These eight books represent literally thousands of books that are presumably read regularly by thousands of men in the United States, and of course, by men in other countries as well.

Soul Slave (Anonymous, 1981b) is one of a series of "Punishment Books" that presents violent sexual attacks as pleasurable for the women. A 16-year-old African-American woman is portrayed in *Soul Slave* as the willing victim of her white master. The following passages are typical examples of the contents of this book.

> Rance Godwin leaned over and drove his fist right into my lower stomach. I jerked and sighed when he gave me that blow, and I listened to the words that he had to say to me. "I told you to get naked, you nigger slut," he said. And I knew then that, no matter how much I loved the pain, I would have to get naked. (p. 22)

Soul Slave is filled with examples of this kind of masochism. The "hero" commands his "soul slave":

> "Say that you like it. I know that you do. There is nothing that a nigger girl likes more than being hit by a white man." And I did not know if the feelings that I had would be like the feelings that all nigger girls had, but I did know that I did like it. (p. 71)

The author implies that the woman's pain is special because it is inflicted on an African-American woman by a white man. The derogatory term "nigger" is used approximately 245 times in the 180-page book. This word is frequently put in the mouth of the young woman to describe herself and other African-Americans, and she is always depicted as enjoying it. For example, "Rance looked down at me and said, 'Get naked, Nigger!' And these words were like the greatest poetry in the world to me" (1981, p. 20).

A second book entitled *Black Head Nurse* (Dakin, 1977), is a compilation of sexual encounters between patients, nurses, and doctors in a Harlem hospital. Interracial sex is presumed to constitute evidence that racial or sexual discrimination is not a problem. "In this hospital there is no discrimination. . . . Black nurses, white doctors, black doctors, white patients. It's all the same when the great equalizer Sex comes into play" (p. 34). Absurd as this statement is, it is widely believed that sexual unions nullify sexism and racism.

For example, "It just blew their minds to see this white chick on her knees begging that black dude to give her a little" (p. 142). One of the messages here is that it is extraordinary for a white woman to beg an African-American man for sex. On the other hand, African-American women are frequently portrayed in pornographic literature as begging white men for sex. For example, "Sucking on this fancy white doctor's cock was certainly living the good life. No one could talk her out of that" (p. 178).

The stereotypically tough, powerful, African-American woman is played out in *Black Head Nurse*: "Up in the Harlem hospitals black nurses rule" (p. 34). The most powerful African-American women are portrayed as physically aggressive dykes. For example, the sadistic head nurse is depicted as whipping her nurses and as seducing another young woman.

Black Head Nurse presents other stereotypes about African-American life. For example, this is how the author describes the success story of an African-American doctor:

> He had worked his way through one of the toughest medical schools in the East and his mother hadn't even scrubbed floors! Of course, she had to push a lot of drugs and fuck a lot, but even Scott knew that some sacrifice was in order. After all, he had forfeited a lot of good times himself by studying.

The author also normalizes notions of sexually promiscuous African-American children. For example, a 13-year-old African-American female patient, the leader of a gang of girls who thrive on sex, is portrayed as propositioning an African-American doctor for a blow job. He eventually satisfies her wishes. In another case an African-American madam recalls her childhood: "She remembered her first sexual experiences as a small child in a crowded bedroom where all her brothers and sisters slept together. Already at the age of ten she was an expert at blowing her brothers off and eating out her sisters" (p. 175).

Abuse: Black and Battered (Anonymous, 1981a) is described as a collection of "true" case studies based on "Dr. Lamb's" interviews with eight African-American women. Violent sexual attacks are vividly described in coarse and racist language in all of these stories. They begin with a description of the woman's skin color, so important in this racist country. For example, one woman is depicted as a mulatto, whose "skin is an incredible light cream color." And, "Ellie is a short, attractive black woman, whose skin is a lovely cream shade" (p. 5). "Shari is a very dark-skinned black girl . . . " (p. 22). Some descriptions focus on other ethnicity-related features of physical appearance. For example, "Her nose is flat and her nostrils are large, yet her lips are thin and sleek looking."

The first woman portrayed in these fake case studies observed after her alcoholic African-American husband raped her, "I thought he was letting me go, but you can bet no drunk nigger was gonna do that." In the second case, the woman gives a lengthy, gory description of watching her African-American father raping her mother. He and his friends later rape her when she is 16 years old. Four other cases also depict young girls observing their fathers raping their mothers.

In one particularly racist story, a young girl watches her white father having a positive sexual encounter with her mother. After his death, her mother remarries an African-American man who forces her into violent sexual acts. The mulatto daughter is later gang raped in school by a group of African-American girls and, at another time, by a gang of African-American boys, because she is a "half-nigger." When she gets out of the ghetto by going to college, she has a wonderful sexual relationship with a blonde college man.

The fourth story portrays a girl who is repeatedly raped and gang raped by her father and three brothers. In three other stories, the women have been raped as children or as young teenagers by their African-American fathers, other African-American male family members, or male friends of their fathers. In one case a man is described as watching his father rape his mother. His mother then rapes him after his father dies.

The last interview depicts a woman who becomes a prostitute after she was raped by her father and by a gang of African-American men. She blames the ghetto, not the racist social structure, for all this violence: "So blow it up. . . . Just get it off the fucking face of the earth and save other ghetto girls from the shit we're put through" (Anonymous, 1981, p. 177). As is typical in pornography, all the perpetrators of sexual violence in these "case studies" escape punishment.

In *Black Ghetto Teens* (Marr, 1977), teenage African-American girls are depicted as thriving on "stealing, lying, and fucking those rich white dudes who come to the city looking for some nice Black meat" (p. 4). An African-American woman in *Soul Food* is raped by three white men. "He got to his feet and grabbed the black girl by her hair. He forced his thick, white cock into her mouth" (Berry, 1978, p. 21). As the pornography industry keeps broadcasting to the world, the victim ends up enjoying the rape: "She had gained some confidence from having sex [sic] with the three men." The woman tells her rapists, "'You really have taught me something,' Pearl laughed. . . . 'It can be fun. My ex asked me to do things like this and I always told Bruce 'no way.'" Rape as a liberating experience for women is a popular male fantasy in pornography.

Another common racist and sexist myth about African-American women is articulated in *Soul Food*. One of the white rapists explains:

> I was curious to know what it would be like to screw a black girl," he told her. "I've heard some black women are more lewd and animalistic." "Were they right?" Pearl asked anxiously. Throwing his arms around her, Mike assured her that she was all he had hoped for and more.

After another man's first "screw" with an African-American woman, he compliments her on her "animal lustiness." In several other encounters with white men, African-American women's "animalistic lust," sexual prowess, and desire for pain are stressed.

In *Animal Sex Among Black Women* (Washington, 1983), the case study fabrication is used again, even including a bibliography listing other pornography books about sex with animals. This particular book presents five stories of African-American women having voluntary or coerced sexual encounters with animals. In one fantasy, a go-go dancer is coerced by two

African-American men into having sex with a dog. In another, an African-American woman finds comfort in sex with a German shepherd after being dumped by a white man. "All of a sudden I felt a sense of belonging. I had found someone who needed me," she said of her new pet (p. 74). Later, she sees her need for the dog as punishment: "I guess it serves me right for fucking around with a white guy. . . . If I was going to fuck with a guy, it should have been a black guy, not some white stud like Gary" (pp. 80–81).

In a third fantasy, a 31-year-old twice-divorced dental assistant has sex with an African-American ex-fighter, and then has sex with her male cat. Another go-go dancer is paid by an African-American man to have sex with him and his Doberman. And finally, after a 34-year-old divorcee meets a white woman at a bar, she goes home to have sex with her and her Dalmatian.

In the 160-page *Black Fashion Model* (Wilson, 1978), the word "black" is used 155 times to describe people, "white" 50 times, and "Negress" eight times. As usual, the African-American rape victims end up loving the abuse. One victim's thoughts as she is forced to have oral sex with a man are described as follows: "I must be the worst little nigger girl in the entire city. . . . Here I am sucking this man's cock like a tramp . . . and worst of all, I'm enjoying it."

And again, the fact that the woman was African-American is portrayed as rendering the rape all the more gratifying for her white rapist: "It was twice as exciting to him because she was black and he was white." As consumers of pornography often do not know what is true and what is false about female sexuality, particularly the sexuality of women of color, myths like this one probably encourage some white men to rape African-American women in search of the heightened gratification described (for example, see Russell, 1975, pp. 129–140).

One blatantly anti-Semitic book, *Sluts of the S.S.* (Anonymous, 1979), uses the torture of Jewish women as its source of excitement. This book starts with a description of Rachel's first experience of intercourse with her Jewish boyfriend. The author emphasizes the relationship between sex and ethnicity: "Fuck me," Rachel whispered. "Fuck me, Aaron. I want to feel your hard Jewish cock inside me. Take me. Take me now" (p. 8).

Throughout the book there are rapes, killings, as well as non-violent sex. In the rapes by Nazis, Jewish women are referred to as "Jewish dog," "Jewish whore," "Yiddish swine," "Jewish slut," and so forth, while the Nazis refer to themselves as members of the master race. "'Whore,' he yelled. 'You will love the cock of your master.'"

There are especially violent scenes of Jewish women being kicked to death, raped anally, forced to eat human excrement, and being killed by dogs. "Filthy Jewish slut," he barked. "Drink my Nazi piss, you little pig" (p. 106). And:

She sucked off the cum and blood and shit from his dick as he pounded it into her throat. She gagged at the taste and at the force with which he was fucking her face. He let go with a stream of hot piss and nearly drowned her as he filled her mouth with his hot yellow piss stream choking her as she tried to swallow it. "Human toilet," he sneered . . . (p. 107).

A relationship between a Nazi man and a Jewish woman is portrayed in the midst of all this violence. It begins when she is imprisoned as a prostitute for Nazis and he pays to have sex with her. She likes him and becomes the classic willing victim, no longer "enslaved." But their relationship turns violent when he sees her being forced to eat shit by another Nazi. In reaction to her "inherent dirtiness," he sets out to kill and rape Jews: "Hans could not wait to turn his dogs loose on a pack of helpless, cowering, filthy Jews" (p. 123). For her part, she goes out at night to lure Nazi men into dark corners for sex — then slits their throats instead.

Sluts of the S.S. is a series of explicit descriptions of sexual interactions — warped, violent, and sometimes "loving." It is written to excite the reader with the violence, which is portrayed as being highly pleasurable. The Jewish woman ends up needing and wanting the Nazi man despite the fact that he treated her perversely and physically assaulted her. According to this tale, she was as much at "fault" as he was, and in the end they were *both* able to forgive and forget.

CONCLUSION

This study's main purpose was to document the way different ethnic groups are portrayed in pornography. No comparable studies have been undertaken, to our knowledge.

The content analysis of seven pornography books about African-Americans shows that they were depicted in a variety of derogatory and stereotypic ways — as animalistic, incapable of self-control, sexually depraved, impulsive, unclean, and so forth. This kind of pornography is likely to foster racist–sexist stereotypes as well as racist–sexist behavior, including sexual abuse and sexual violence against African-American girls and women. Similarly, anti-Semitic pornography is likely to foster anti-Semitic sexism as well as sexual violence against Jewish girls and women. Future studies should include books portraying a greater variety of people of color, as well as whites.

An important unanswered question is why the liberal and radical community, as well as people of color who are not part of this community, appear to be totally unconcerned about the racism in pornographic materials in contrast to their concern about other manifestations of racism, such as those in ads, literature, media, verbal statements, and so on. If it is due to ignorance, then bringing the virulent racism in pornography to people's attention, as we have done in this chapter, will hopefully shock them into action.

Unfortunately, we think there is a more consequential explanation for this apathy about racist pornography. The combination of sex and racism appears to blunt people's response to pornographic racism just as the combination of sex and violence appears to dull concern about the consequences of violent pornography.

Teish explains the lack of reaction by African-American women as follows: "Pornography is a branch of the media that Black-activist feminists have considered a 'white market'" (1980, p. 117). Many others have shared the perception that pornography has little relevance for people of color ever since the President's Commission on Obscenity and Pornography reported that the buyers of pornography were "predominantly white, middle-class, middle-aged males" (1970). While not necessarily contradicting this view, Gardner nevertheless maintains that:

> The Black man, like the white man, is buying pornography. He is beating, raping, and murdering all kinds of women. Black women are going to have to deal with him on this. But when we do, we must deal with the Black man as a Black man, not as a white man. In this country it is the *white* man who is producing pornography, and it is the *white* man who is profiting from it. (1980, p. 113)

Dorchen Leidholdt offers two other reasons why the liberal left has been, and continues to be, indifferent to racism in pornography.

> First, in liberal ideology there is an invisible boundary separating the public and political from the personal and sexual. Whereas liberals readily deplore inequality and injustice in the public sector, the private sphere — and sexual relationships in particular — are sacrosanct. Radical feminists' insistence that the personal is political and that public life grows out of private, sexual interactions has been ignored or denied. Second, some "progressive" men have not simply ignored pornography's racism, they have incorporated it into their personal sexual repertoires. (1981, p. 20)

Whatever the best explanations turn out to be, it is vital that people start to question their old assumptions about pornography, including racist pornography. Addressing African-American activists in particular, Teish recommended in 1980 that the "clearly ignored" area of pornography deserves further investigation (p. 117). The liberal, radical, and feminist communities must recognize the glaring contradiction in being concerned about the destructive effects of racism and outraged by all manifestations of it — except when it appears in pornography.

Thousands of women march to protest pornography and violence against women, Times Square, NYC.

Photo: © Bettye-Lane

CHAPTER 17

The Research on Women and Pornography: The Many Faces of Harm

Charlene Y. Senn

I started reading the radical feminist literature on pornography in 1981 while working at a women's shelter.[1] My work with assaulted women led me to explore the relationship between pornography and the physical and sexual assaults on women within heterosexual relationships. I enrolled in graduate school in 1983 and began conducting research into the effects of pornography on women. My first step as a graduate student was to read what had been written about the issue in the psychological literature. While I found hundreds of studies on the issue of pornography, few spoke to the kinds of issues that I had concerns about or that the feminists I was reading had written about. I began to design my own research asking the questions to which I was interested in finding answers. At the same time, I started to gain an understanding of the reasons for the limitations in the psychological literature. In this chapter I will point out some of the problems in the existing research and show how I attempted to deal with these issues in my research. I will present the main findings of my research investigating how women perceive pornography and how it harms them. I will then summarize the harms of pornography to women as I now see them.

When I searched the "scientific" literature for information on the effects of pornography I found that the conclusions were difficult to decipher. There were studies suggesting that pornographic materials were harmful and other studies suggesting that they were not. How could these differences in findings be understood?

Printed by permission of the author.

179

One of the major problems in the published research was the ambiguous language employed to identify the images used in the studies. Researchers and theorists (feminist and non-feminist) believed that different content in sexual images would have different effects on people. For example, it was expected that viewing an image of a naked women would have a different effect on a person than viewing a bestiality scene. Therefore it was important that research make distinctions between various kinds of sexually explicit materials.

There was no agreement in the field about the terminology that should be used to make these distinctions. Radical feminists were using terminology in a highly specific way based on the origins of the words "erotic" and "pornographic" (see Dworkin, 1981). Accordingly, it became a common distinction in radical feminist writings (e.g., Lederer, 1980) to use "erotic" to refer to positive sexual imagery (no sexism or violence) and "pornographic" to refer to negative sexual imagery with sexist and violent content. In contrast, the words "pornography," "erotica," and "obscenity" were used interchangeably within psychological research to refer to images as diverse as nude females, sexual activity between consenting adults, and mutilation scenes. The primary reason for this confusion in terminology was that researchers believed that if they used terms that had negative connotations to describe sexual materials, they would lose their scientific objectivity. Evidence for my assertion is found in the work of Malamuth (one of the primary researchers in the field) who footnoted the first occurrence of the word "pornography" in several articles to assure the reader that these words were not intended to imply a "pejorative [negative] meaning" (e.g., Ceniti & Malamuth, 1984, p. 535).

Researchers described the materials they were using in research but there was often not enough detail to make the kinds of distinctions that feminists suggested were necessary. Many researchers chose to use only mildly sexually explicit materials (e.g., nude females) in their research. Problems arise with assessing the effects of exposure to these mildly sexually explicit materials as the context of the materials and the positioning of the models generally were not described. The materials used in these studies may have been "erotic" or could have had sexist connotations. There is no way of knowing.

Alternatively, some researchers chose the most blatantly violent depictions to use in their research. These included "sadomasochistic themes" (e.g., Zillmann, Bryant, Comisky, & Medoff, 1981), depictions of "bestiality" (e.g., Zillmann, Bryant, & Carveth, 1981), and "rape depictions" (e.g., Donnerstein & Berkowitz, 1981). While these were examples of blatantly violent pornography (and it is difficult to know how one couldn't apply the label "negative" to them), they represented only a small sample of the types of violent pornography that were available. It is difficult to know whether the results obtained with such specialized materials can be generalized to violent pornography as a whole, or whether they apply only to the specific type, for example, "rape depictions."

As mentioned earlier, both non-feminist researchers and feminist theorists hypothesized different types of effects for different types of sexually explicit materials. The policy of many researchers to maintain objectivity by keeping their terminology neutral has meant that it has been nearly impossible to establish whether pornography as a whole is harmful or not. In fact, several people attempted reviews of the literature and each arrived at somewhat different conclusions due in part to these definitional problems (e.g., Donnerstein & Linz, 1985; Einsiedel, 1986; Malamuth & Donnerstein, 1984; Zillmann & Bryant, 1988).

CATEGORIES OF SEXUAL MATERIAL

One of the first things I addressed in my own research was to define the categories of sexual materials I was using so the conclusions I came to would be unambiguous. Based on the work of various feminist theorists (Dworkin, 1981; Longino, 1980; Lorde, 1980; Parker & Pollock, 1981; Riddington, 1983; Steinem, 1980), I derived the following definitions for sexual materials:

Erotica—Nonsexist and Nonviolent. These images have as their focus the depiction of "mutually pleasurable, sexual expression between people who have enough power to be [involved] by positive choice" (Steinem, 1980, p. 37). They have no sexist or violent connotations and are hinged on equal power dynamics between individuals as well as between the model(s) and the camera/photographer (Sontag, 1977).

Nonviolent Pornography—Sexist and Dehumanizing. These images have no explicitly violent content but may imply acts of submission or violence by the positioning of the models (e.g., male standing, female prone or kneeling) or the use of props (e.g., guns, whips, chains in the background). They may also imply unequal power relationships by different dress (e.g., male fully dressed, female naked), costuming (e.g., dressing adult models to look like children, model dressed in clothing that implies violence), positioning (e.g., behind bars, in position of vulnerability); (Steinem, 1980) or by setting up the viewer as a voyeur[2] (the model is engaged in some solitary activity, such as bathing, and seems totally unaware or very surprised to find someone looking at her; Parker & Pollock, 1981).

Violent Pornography—Sexist and Dehumanizing. These images portray explicit violence of varying degrees perpetrated against one individual by another (e.g., hair pulling, slapping, whipping, etc.). This category also includes images that portrays self-abuse or self-mutilation (Longino, 1980). Also included are images in which no actual violence is occurring, however the model appears to be suffering from the aftermath of abuse (bruises, black eyes, welts, etc.).[3]

These groupings and their corresponding definitions are only useful if the categories are meaningful in a broader sense, that is, if other women also find them meaningful. I tested whether other women would agree with or be able to use these categories in two ways. First, I wanted to make sure that other women could use the definitions to classify images. I made 310 slides from sexual images in *Penthouse, Playboy*, and *Hustler* magazines, and from two books *Rising Goddess* and *Women's Experience of Sex*. I gave my definitions to five female graduate students[4] and asked them to use my definitions to classify the slides into the categories erotica, nonviolent pornography, or violent pornography. It was a forced choice task as it did not allow them to say that a slide did not belong in any of the three categories. The agreement between the raters was very high (effective reliability = .93).

My results showed that women could discriminate between types of sexually explicit materials on the basis of nonsexual content such as sexism and violence. A group of women (unknown to each other) could do this kind of task independently with a high degree of consensus.

The second stage of testing my definitions explored whether my divisions of the materials represented more than untested theoretical distinctions. If these categories of sexual materials were meaningful then each group must contain images with content that is unique in a psychological sense. For example, women viewing erotic images should perceive them in a different way than women viewing nonviolent pornography even if they are unaware of my written definitions.

I selected the 75 slides from each category (violent pornography, nonviolent pornography, and erotica) that had the highest interrater agreement. None had less than three raters agreeing. These were the images I used in the remainder of my study.

Ninety-six women were recruited from the University of Calgary undergraduate subject pool for the next phase of the research. The women were randomly assigned to one of four groups (erotic, nonviolent pornography, violent pornography, or a neutral condition, i.e., nature scenery). The decision to allow each woman to see only one category was made so comparisons of the categories would not lead women to think differently about the images. The participants came to the laboratory four times. In the first session, women filled out questionnaires on their background and attitudes. In the second and third sessions they saw the slides, and in the fourth session they completed the attitude questionnaires again and were debriefed. In all of these sessions, the participants were alone in the room or with one other woman.

In the slide sessions, the participants viewed 50 randomly chosen slides from the pool of 75 slides. The slides were displayed one at a time for a period of 25 seconds. In order to assess women's perceptions of the slides (without my written definitions), I asked the participants to evaluate each of the slides that they viewed. The women rated the slides on the following seven adjective pairs (Osgood, Suci, & Tannenbaum, 1957):

good	— — — — — — —	bad
cruel	— — — — — — —	kind
dirty	— — — — — — —	clean
beautiful	— — — — — — —	ugly
painful	— — — — — — —	pleasurable
healthy	— — — — — — —	sick
positive	— — — — — — —	negative

These ratings were then scored from −3 (most negative) to +3 (most positive) for each of the pairs of words, and the seven scores added to get a score for each slide of somewhere between −21 and +21. Each session's ratings were averaged for each woman and the groups (erotic, nonviolent pornography, violent pornography, and control) were compared statistically. The women's perceptions, as measured by ratings of the slides, were significantly different in each group. This was the case even though each woman only saw one type of image and was not aware of the content of the slides in the other groups. Violent pornography was rated most negatively by the women with an average score of −10.60. The nonviolent pornography was rated negatively (−1.62) but not as negatively as the violent pornography. The erotica was rated positively (5.34) and the control slides were rated the most positively (12.09).

Women's perceptions of the images reliably differentiated between erotica and pornography, and between nonviolent and violent pornography and these were consistent across two viewings. This finding suggests that development of meaningful definitions is possible[5] and that general agreement with those definitions (at least by women) is also feasible. This is in direct contradiction to the suggestion made by some people that *any* restrictions on *any* sexual materials would necessarily put *all* sexual materials at risk. It also reveals that women can feel positively toward some types of sexually explicit materials and react negatively (selectively) to images that contain sexism and/or violence. This counters the view that women simply don't like pornography because they don't like sexual content. It also supports the notion that definitional distinctions are crucial to an understanding of women's responses to sexual materials. An understanding of women's responses to pornography must focus on the content that pornography adds to the sexual explicitness, that is, sexism, coercion, and violence.

WOMEN'S EXPOSURE TO PORNOGRAPHY

Research investigating the effects of exposure to pornography on women increases in importance if a large number of women would see it during their lives. The pervasiveness of pornography virtually ensures that most women will view it at some point in their lifetimes, whether or not they seek it out. Few studies, however, have actually measured the amount of exposure to pornography that women experience.

I designed a questionnaire to measure women's previous exposure to sexually explicit materials. On this questionnaire, women indicated how often they had seen specified sexually explicit materials (*Playboy*, *Penthouse*, *Hustler*, other men's magazines, sexually explicit films or videos [intended as entertainment], and sex education materials). "Encountered" was defined as: "includ[ing] reading them, flipping through them, or simply being shown them." Ninety-nine percent of the women reported that they had encountered *Playboy*, 71 percent *Penthouse*, and 43 percent *Hustler*. (These were the materials used in the study.) Fifty-four percent reported having encountered other men's magazines and 85 percent had viewed films and videos in which "sex is the most important feature." Most of the women had seen these materials more than once. By contrast, very few of the women had encountered "sexually explicit materials used for educational purposes (e.g., sex education courses, human sexuality, etc.")" even once or twice. Certainly this suggests that studies investigating the direct effects of pornography on women are needed. It also makes a sad comment on the state of sexuality education when most sexually explicit materials women see are pornographic rather than educational.

EFFECTS OF PORNOGRAPHY ON WOMEN

Pornography has been hypothesized to affect women in various ways. The most straightforward effects possible are the effects produced when women view pornography directly. Although researchers have begun to pay attention to feminist demands for studies on women, they have tended simply to include female subjects in their samples or replicate research done on males with females.

Using both male and female subjects in research does allow comparison of reactions and effects and therefore is a somewhat positive step. For example, studies of sexual arousal using both men and women have shown that sex differences in arousal to sexually explicit materials (no violent content) do not exist (Byrne & Lamberth, 1971; Fisher & Byrne, 1978; Schmidt, 1975). This has helped to dispel the myth that women are not sexually aroused by sexual images.[6] This kind of research does assume however that the same theories can interpret the behaviour of men and women within any particular context. We know within certain situations, for example, in a screening of the movie "Not a Love Story," that women and men are not thinking about or responding to the film in the same way (Bart, Freeman, & Kimball, 1985). Therefore, the assumption of similarity between women and men in this field may be incorrect.

Males are predominantly the perpetrators of violent crimes in the United States and Canada (Russell, 1984) and within pornographic portrayals females are predominantly the victims of these crimes (Malamuth & Check, 1981; Smith, 1977; Stock, 1983). Therefore, the psychological effects of exposure to pornography on women are likely to be qualitatively different from the effects on men. Moreover, even when a similar effect is produced in men and women, the psychological meaning of that event may be quite different. Nowhere is this more clear than in the research on sexual arousal to sexually explicit materials.

Sexual Arousal Effects

As mentioned earlier, no sex differences exist in levels of arousal to sexually explicit materials without violent content. Contrary to prevailing myths, women are as aroused as men to pictures and written depictions of sex (Byrne & Lamberth, 1971) whether the content is affectional and romantic or not (Fisher & Byrne, 1978; Schmidt, 1975). Women are therefore equally capable of experiencing sexual arousal to sexual materials. There is some evidence however, that even when sex differences in physical levels of arousal do not exist, men and women may not experience the event the same way psychologically.

For example, in 1974, Byrne, Fisher, Lamberth, and Mitchell tried to examine how emotional reactions predicted evaluations of nonviolent sexually explicit materials. They assumed that evaluation was mediated in some way by positive and negative affect (feelings). Male and female participants rated each image on a six-point scale with the endpoints "nonpornographic" and "pornographic," where "pornography" was defined by a common dictionary definition as being "lewd, obscene," etc. This was the evaluation measure. The affect measure was an 11-dimension Feelings Scale, measuring responses to the items: sexually aroused, disgusted, entertained, anxious, bored, angry, afraid, curious, nauseated, depressed, and excited. Factor analysis of the Feelings Scale resulted in the identification of two independent dimensions, positive affects (items scored in positive direction: excited, entertained, sexually aroused, anxious, and curious; item scored in reverse direction: bored) and negative affect (items scored in positive direction: disgusted, nauseated, angry, and depressed).

Byrne and colleagues (1974) found that feelings were related to evaluation in a different way for women and men. Males rated materials as pornographic only if they had high levels of negative feelings *and* low levels of positive feelings. They labelled something as pornographic (obscene, lewd, negative) only if they experienced disgust, anger, fear, nausea, and so forth *and* they were *not* sexually aroused, entertained, curious, or excited. Women on the other hand, rated images as pornographic if they experienced negative emotions *whether or not* they were sexually aroused, curious, and the like. Women were not using their sexual arousal to make judgments about the materials whereas this was a part of men's evaluations. Women were thinking about and/or experiencing their arousal in a different way than men were.

These differences in perception are increased when the images show sexual activity mixed with violence and domination. Arousal levels of men and women do differ when the sexually explicit materials contain overt violence. Women consistently respond with little or no arousal to violent sexual depictions. For example, females have been found to show considerably less arousal to gang rape films than males (Schmidt, 1975). Moreover manipulating the violence cues in written rape depictions appears to have differential effects on men and women. Malamuth, Heim, and Feshbach (1980) found that females were most aroused to a rape story when the victim suffers no pain and experiences an orgasm, while males were aroused most when the victim experienced both pain and orgasm.

Some researchers have explored women's reactions to the specific content of pornographic and erotic depictions. Stock (1983) investigated women's sexual arousal to tape recorded depictions of rape. She compared women's reactions to a portrayal of mutually consenting sex, a realistic rape portrayal (in which the victim was described as experiencing fear and pain in response to the attack), and a "rape myth" portrayal (a common pornographic portrayal in which the victim's negative reactions are minimized and the narration focuses on the sexual cues of the situation, for example, the victim's body is eroticized). Women were sexually aroused to mutually consenting sex and to "rape myth" depictions. Women were not at all aroused to realistic rape depictions. The difference in arousal between the two rape depictions shows that women are not aroused by rape. They experience arousal to eroticized descriptions of sex where harm to women is not present (or does not appear to be present).

Arousal differences are also present when the violence is less overt. Garcia, Brennan, DeCarlo, McGlennon, and Tait (1984) found that women reported more sexual arousal *and* fewer negative feelings when the female character was "dominant" than when the male character was dominant. While this study did not use violent pornographic portrayals, it used subtle dominance implied by who was active and in control. This aspect (i.e., dominance implied by who is in control) is important in understanding women's reactions to rape portrayals and other dominance interactions, and in explaining the apparent contradictions (equivalent arousal in some but not all circumstances, negative affect accompanying arousal, etc.) in much of the female arousal literature. More assistance in understanding the female arousal literature comes from new radical feminist theory.

In the views of Jeffreys (1990), Stoltenberg (1989) and others (e.g., Kitzinger, 1987) sexual arousal is socially constructed, meaning that it is not experienced or perceived outside of other socialization, historical, and cultural effects. Stoltenberg has discussed in detail what this means for men's sexual identity and experience in sexual relationships. Jeffreys (1990) tackled the meaning of sexual arousal for women in a society in which women are abused on a regular basis and images of women in subordinate and demeaned positions are common place. She points out that "[i]t is not unusual for abused girls to experience sexual response during episodes of abuse. The implications for women's learning of sexuality in this way are several. If a girl responds sexually to her own degradation, when she is being used as a 'thing,' sexual arousal is unlikely to be a positive experience for her. Sex and self-loathing are linked. A distrust of sexual response is likely to develop from an unwillingness to experience the feelings which are associated with shame" (p. 243). Other abused women may experience a lack of all sexual feelings to later consensual sexual experiences (Jeffreys, 1990). While not all women have experienced overt sexual abuse as children, the culture produces many messages and images that eroticize women's submission and/or violation. It is not so surprising then that women may experience their own arousal as a betrayal.

"There is a cultural assumption in a post-sexual-revolution society that sexual arousal is 'pleasure.' This makes it particularly painful to experience pornography, which clearly shows the humiliation of women, as sexually arousing.

We feel guilt at having taken pleasure in or 'enjoyed' the oppression of women. The literature of libertarians[7] has no word or category for sexual response that is not positive, no word that would allow us to describe the complexity of our feelings in such a situation. . . . A feminist approach to the question of desire requires the invention of a new language. We need to be able to describe sexual response which is incontrovertibly negative." (Jeffreys, 1990, pp. 303–304)

Valuable research on sexual arousal of women to pornography must take these complex social constructions into account if they are to represent women's experiences accurately. It is my view that sexual arousal should not be measured in isolation and that women participants must be given an opportunity to express how they experience their arousal or lack of arousal in any research context.

Emotional Effects

Judging from my own and other women's experiences of exposure to pornography, I believed that the most profound effects of pornography would be on how it makes women feel. Thus, the research that I conducted examined the effects of viewing pornography using women's moods as a measure of emotional state. Another feminist researcher, Wendy Stock (1983), had found that women's moods were affected by listening to various rape depictions. I wanted to research the effects of what I felt would be a more common experience for women, viewing still images (e.g., in magazines).

The 96 women who participated filled in a questionnaire called the *Profile of Mood States* (POMS; McNair, Lorr, & Droppleman, 1971) before and after they viewed the slides in both sessions. The POMS measures six different aspects of a person's mood: tension/anxiety, hostility/anger, confusion/bewilderment, fatigue/inertia, vigor/activity, and depression/rejection. A total "mood disturbance" (negative effects) score was created by adding across all of the negative mood states (anxiety, anger, confusion, fatigue, and depression) and subtracting the positive mood state (vigor). Mood disturbance scores were compared across the four groups of women (erotica, nonviolent pornography, violent pornography, and control). Counter to common beliefs suggesting that violent pornography is the most harmful type of pornography, no difference was found between the pornography groups on the amount of emotional disturbance caused. Exposure to both violent pornography *and* nonviolent pornography was found to cause significant mood disturbance in women. When the negative emotional reactions were examined separately, viewing nonviolent and violent pornography were found to make women more tense and anxious, more angry and hostile, and more confused. Viewing violent pornography also increased women's levels of depression. By contrast, viewing erotica did not cause any mood changes (negative or positive).

These results show that pornography need not be violent to have negative effects on women; the unequal power and the implicit coercion and force can in some cases affect women as much as the more blatant images. These negative effects in women's emotional state were found following even 20 minutes of exposure to images from mainstream magazines.

Desensitization was detected across the two exposures to violent and nonviolent pornography. While the women were still angry, confused, and tense after viewing the slides in the second session, their levels of anger were considerably lower than they had been after the first viewing. This lowered the overall disturbance score significantly. This decrease in anger occurred even though women's evaluations of the slides were consistent across the two sessions. This is an example of "affective desensitization" caused by repeated exposure to pornography. Even though women perceived the materials to be as negative, they did not (or could not) respond as strongly (emotionally) against them.

The emotional effects of pornography may be even more harmful than they appear on the surface. I tried to create a supportive, non-pressured atmosphere by treating the women who participated with respect, providing a private or semi-private protected setting in which to view the images, and remaining unobtrusive while they were viewing the slides. Thus, it is likely that the women felt free to express their views without fear of judgment. In a natural environment, women may be more likely to experience pornography in settings that include some pressure to hide negative feelings, for example, in the home of a male subscriber or at a party (Senn, 1991). This could result in internalization (or stuffing) of the feelings created by the materials. According to Miller (1976), suppression of anger is a common response for women, which causes emotional difficulties in many areas of their lives. In relationships with men, women may suppress anger to lessen the risk of destroying the relationship. My study showed that pornography could be one factor in a relationship that could cause anger in women. If women are exposed to pornography within relationships that encourage suppression of anger, emotional difficulties could arise.

This decrease in anger following repeated exposure to pornography could also affect the political struggles of women. Assuming that emotional arousal produces some of the impetus for social action (such as Take Back the Night Marches, picketing theatres, etc.), lessened anger might reduce the chance of social responses. As Vivar (1982) stated: "Violent pornography extols male dominance and female submission in a world where many women are trying to overcome these erroneous beliefs and practices. Brutal depictions, if allowed to flourish, may finally lead women to accept the idea that male–female relationships are premised on terror, violence, and cruelty" (p. 63) and thereby accept that powerlessness is inevitable.

Even if women's response to the desensitization is not acceptance, the effects are nonetheless severe. Even the most experienced activists against pornography are not immune to this desensitization effect. Andrea Dworkin touched on this problem in a speech she gave in 1978. She said, "I wanted to come here militant and proud and angry as hell. But more and more, I find that anger is a pale shadow next to the grief I feel. If a woman has any sense of her own intrinsic worth, seeing pornography in small bits and pieces can bring her to a useful rage. Studying pornography in quantity and depth, as I have been doing for more months than I care to remember, will turn that same woman into a mourner" (Dworkin, 1988, p. 19).

Effects of Pornography on Women's Experiences

The previous discussion of the effects of pornography was primarily restricted to studies of direct exposure to pornography, that is, what we think and feel when we see it ourselves. Pornography can have an impact on women's lives even if they never see it.

Silbert and Pines (1984) investigated sexual abuse experiences in the backgrounds of 200 street prostitutes. They were surprised when pornography was mentioned spontaneously by many of the women as part of the sexual abuse they experienced. Of 193 rapes reported by the women, "25% [of the rape victims] mentioned allusions to pornographic material on the part of the rapist" (p. 863). In 22% of the cases involving juvenile sexual abuse the use of pornography was mentioned. These findings are particularly noteworthy as experience with pornography was not directly asked about in any of the interviews.

Russell (1980) explored sexual coercion in the lives of 930 women in the San Francisco Bay area. She asked women whether they had "ever been upset by someone trying to get you to do something which they had seen in pornographic magazines, movies, or books?" Ten percent of the women answered "yes." When the results were separated by marital status and coercion, certain women were at even higher risk. For example, of the married women who had been raped by their husbands, 24% answered "yes" to the question.

In my own research I tried to replicate Russell's finding by asking the same question "Have you ever been upset by someone trying to get you to do something which they had seen in pornographic magazines, movies, or books?" Twenty-three of the 96 women (24%) said that they had experienced this. This is considerably higher than the 10% figure obtained by Russell. Her study was based on a random sample of women in the San Francisco Bay area so differences could be due to the sample of university undergraduates used in my study. Nonetheless, there is no reason to expect that university students should be at higher risk for this particular type of coercion. Alternatively, as the trend appears to have been toward increasing violence in pornographic materials (Malamuth & Spinner, 1980) or in mainstream images (Palys, 1986) there may be a greater likelihood of men asking their partners to perform offensive acts today than when Russell conducted her study. It is also important to note that these figures are probably underestimations as women are not likely to know if pornography was involved in attacks by unknown assailants.

I also tried to test the relationship between pornography and sexual coercion in another way. I assessed the amount of sexual coercion and violence a woman had experienced and then correlated that with the amount of exposure to pornography she had. I was looking for a pattern that would indicate that women's viewing of pornography may have been in a coercive context.

I asked the 96 women in the study to complete a questionnaire designed by Koss and Oros (1982) that measured unreported sexual victimization and general sexual experience. Two questions asked about voluntary heterosexual activity and ten questions asked about various types of coercive sexual experiences. Women reported whether they have had the specified experience and how frequently since the age of 14.

Consistent with the findings of others that coercion in sexual relationships is commonplace (e.g., Clark & Lewis, 1977), over half of the women had been coerced by a male in a sexual context. These experiences ranged from continual arguments and pressure to participate in sexual acts to severe sexual harassment, the use of drugs and alcohol to induce compliance, attempted rape, and violent sexual assaults of various descriptions. Most of the women who had experienced the "continual arguments and pressure" type of coercion had experienced more than one such incident. In addition, over half of the women who had been assaulted had been assaulted more than once. This finding is consistent with other studies. Kanin and Parcell's (1977) study found that women who had experienced violent sexual acts had experienced an average of 5.1 incidents. Russell (1984) found that 50% of the rape victims in her sample had been raped more than once.

My purpose in gathering these experience data was to answer the question, "Was exposure to pornography related to sexual experiences in women's lives?" To do this I correlated the two measures of coercion I got from Koss and Oros (1982) *Sexual Experiences Survey* (the frequency of coercion in a woman's background that was not explicitly violent, and the frequency of violent coercion), and the measure of coercive use of pornography (had the woman experienced upset as a result of someone trying to get her to do something they had seen in pornography) with the amount of prior exposure to pornography the woman had. These correlations were all statistically significant. The higher a woman's prior exposure to pornography, the more likely she was to have been upset by the coercive use of pornography, to have been coerced through psychological pressure into sexual activity, and to have been the victim of at least one violent (threats or use of physical violence) sexual attack. This pattern of relationships replicated the findings of my preliminary study (Senn & Radtke, 1985) and suggests that exposure to pornography is tied to women's coercive sexual histories. One possible interpretation of these findings is that some women's exposure to pornography has taken place within a coercive sexual context.

Although care must be taken in interpreting these findings (as I did not ask the women how they had been exposed to pornography), other evidence does support these interpretations. First, men are the primary consumers of pornography. Second, the women (in my study) rated the pornography negatively, suggesting that they would not be likely to seek it out themselves. Third, Mosher (1971) reported that as many as 16% of men try to obtain intercourse by showing a woman pornography or taking her to a "sexy" movie. Finally, research has found increased aggression by male subjects toward a female after exposure to sexually violent stimuli in a laboratory setting (Donnerstein & Berkowitz, 1981). It is likely then that many women have been exposed to pornography by male partners either as part of sex-related coercion or as a precursor to sex-related coercion.

SUMMARY

Having reviewed the findings of research (my own and others) investigating the effects of pornography on women, I draw the following conclusions.

Theoretical divisions that have been made by radical feminists between various types of sexual materials are meaningful to the study of pornography's effects on women. Detailed definitions of types of sexual materials can be written in ways that can then be used by other women in a consistent manner. In addition, divisions made between sexist pornography, sexist and violent pornography, and erotica are psychologically meaningful to women. Women's perceptions of different types of sexual materials differ even if the women are unaware of the definitions that have been used to divide them.

Women are harmed directly when they view pornography. The portrayals of coercion and violence that are commonplace in mainstream pornography are realities in many women's lives. It is not surprising then that when women view these materials the result is emotional distress including tension, depression, anger, and confusion. These harms are specific to sexual materials that include sexism and/or violence. Erotica does not have these harmful effects.

Women are harmed indirectly by pornography when they come in contact with men who view and consume pornography. Pornography has been used in overtly harmful ways, with as many as one out of four women having been upset by being asked to imitate pornographic images. Moreover, exposure to pornography is related to the amount of sexual coercion in a woman's life, suggesting a link between the situation in which women view pornography and their sexual abuse. This link is likely to be the presence of a male consumer.

While exploration of these links in research is important (e.g., Russell, 1988), the impact of pornography on the lives of women is already clear. As a Canadian feminist has recently stated, "As women, we are directly affected by pornography, regardless of whether or not some men copy what they see in it and then affect us in turn; and we have every right to speak up and say what we see, how we feel about it, and what we want" (Valverde, 1985, p. 134). My hope is that the research being done by women for women on pornography will ultimately help us to prove to the world that the harms done to women by pornography are harms so great that no society could defend them.

CHAPTER 18

Evidence of Harm

Diana E. H. Russell & Karen Trocki

"He [husband] forced me to go down on him. He said he'd been going to porno movies. He'd seen this and wanted me to do it. He also wanted to pour champagne in my vagina. I got beat up because I didn't want to do it. He pulled my hair and slapped me around. After that I went ahead and did it, but there was no feeling in it."

—Respondent in Russell's study, 1980

"I was upset by how much the pictures revealed hatred of women. It was hard not to feel disgusted by my own body, and hard not to be frightened by most men because it felt that was all they would want from me."

—Respondent in Russell's study, 1980

In 1978 I conducted a survey funded by the National Institute of Mental Health to try to ascertain the prevalence of rape, incest, and other kinds of sexual assault.[1] I subcontracted with Field Research Corporation, a highly respected public opinion polling firm located in San Francisco, to draw a probability sample that yielded 930 women respondents 18 years of age and older. Face-to-face interviews were conducted with each of these women by a team of interviewers trained under my auspices.[2] This survey is particularly valuable because it was based on a large probability sample of community women, whereas most studies have been based on unrepresentative samples of college students. The 930 respondents were also asked a few questions on pornography. Their answers will be the focus of this chapter. These questions include the following:

This chapter is an edited version of Diana Russell and Karen Trocki's testimony to the U.S. Attorney General's Commission on Pornography in Houston, Texas, in 1985. Reprinted by permission of the authors.

194

1. "Have you ever been upset by seeing pornographic pictures?" If yes, "What exactly upset you about them?"
2. "Has anyone ever tried to get you to pose for pornographic pictures?"
3. "Have you ever been upset by anyone trying to get you to do what they'd seen in pornographic pictures, movies, or books?" If, yes, "How many different people can you think of, right now, that that's happened with?" The interviewers were instructed to probe for the exact number of such experiences. Then they asked, "Could you tell me briefly about the experience that upset you the most."

Interviewers were required to record the respondents' answers verbatim. No definition of pornography was provided. If they asked for a definition, they were told, "It's whatever it means to you."

FINDINGS

Fourteen percent of the 930 women — or almost one in every seven women — reported that they had been asked to pose for pornographic pictures. Ten percent said they had been upset by someone trying to get them to enact what he or she had seen in pornographic pictures, movies, or books.

Before providing illustrative examples of women's replies to the two questions that elicited the above results, the limitations of these data should be pointed out. First, the question on requests to enact pornography did not ask for the gender of the person who made the requests, so this information was sometimes missing. All of the answers in which the requestors' gender was ascertainable referred to males. Second, in some cases it was not clear why the respondents' believed their unwanted experiences were related to pornography.

Third, some of the women who described experiences they believed were inspired by pornography may have been wrong. For example, some men may have mentioned pornography in an attempt to validate their desires or to persuade the women to accommodate them. Of course, these are not mutually exclusive possibilities; some men may have sought to imitate certain behaviors portrayed in pornography *and* used it to legitimize their requests. Viewing pornography might also have served to delude some of the men into believing that their desires were normal and acceptable. However, women's underestimation of pornography's impact may have been an even greater problem. Many of the women are likely to not have known when requests were inspired by pornography.

Following are some of the respondents' answers to the question on whether they had ever been upset by anyone trying to get them to do something they had seen in pornographic pictures, movies, or books. These respondents mentioned movies as the stimulus for the requests that upset them more often than pictures, magazines, or books. Videos were never mentioned as the survey was undertaken before they were generally available for private viewing. The following quotations illustrate the imitation hypothesis, where men are reported to have mimicked sexual acts they have seen in pornography. Some of the interviewers' questions appear paraphrased in brackets.

"We went to a movie and then he wanted everything to be like the movie."

"My lover would go to porno movies, then he'd come home and say, 'I saw this in a movie. Let's try it.'"

"This couple who had just read a porno book wanted to try the groupie number with four people. They tried to persuade my boyfriend to persuade me. They were running around naked, and I felt really uncomfortable. I lied and said I had to go out on a flight, so they left."

"This guy had seen a movie where a woman was being made love to by dogs. He suggested that some of his friends had a dog and we should have a party and set the dog loose on the women. He wanted me to put a muzzle on the dog and put some sort of stuff on my vagina so that the dog would lick there."

"I was staying at this guy's house. He tried to make me have oral sex with him. He said he'd seen far-out stuff in movies, and it would be fun to mentally and physically torture a woman. [Did he use force?] No, he didn't succeed."

"This guy wanted me and this other girl to do things he had seen in a movie. He wanted both of us to go down on one another."

"Somebody suggested an anal approach to sex on a date. He mentioned a magazine where he'd seen this 'fantastic thing,' but it turned me off."

"We went together to see movies. But he couldn't sit through them without asking me if I would do the same thing the lady was doing to the man in the movies. I refused."

"A friend had learned many different sex tricks from seeing movies, and he wanted to teach them to me. I told him no. He said I was crazy. I asked him why he wanted to do those things, and he said that a lot of people do them."

Of course, there is nothing wrong with imitating pornography if the imitated acts are nonabusive. Nevertheless, those who view pornography as a release of desires already present, often deny that imitation occurs, particularly imitation of sexual acts not previously desired. The cases above clearly do not provide support for the theory that viewing pornography is cathartic; instead they provide support for the imitation theory.

THE VICTIMS OF PORNOGRAPHY

Social Class, Ethnicity, and Pornography

Women victimized by requests to enact pornography came from all social classes in our study. We found no significant relationship between this form of victimization and social class.[3] However, women who were asked to pose for pornography came from families in which the fathers and mothers were significantly more educated than women not subject to this request ($p = <0.05$). Yet the women who were asked to pose were also significantly poorer at the time of the interview than other women in the sample ($p = <0.01$).

There were also significant relationships between race and ethnicity, requests to pose and requests to enact pornographic depictions. Pornography-induced victimization of Native American women was by far the highest in both situations, but as only 11 women from this group were represented in the sample, this finding is only suggestive (see Figure 18.1).

African-American, Jewish, and white non-Jewish women were more likely to be asked to pose for pornographic pictures than the women from other ethnic groups. And African-American, Jewish, Latina, and Filipina women were more likely to be asked to enact pornographic scenes than Asian and white non-Jewish women.

Further research is needed to confirm these associations and to explain them.

Age and Pornography-related Victimization

The younger women in our sample were significantly more likely than the older women to report requests to pose for pornographic pictures (with the exception of the 18- and 19-year-old women, of whom only 4% had been asked to pose; see Figure 18.2).

Because older women have been at risk of posing requests longer than younger women, why would they have reported fewer requests? One plau-

Figure 18.1 Percent of Women* in Each Race or Ethnic Group Who Were Victimized by Pornography

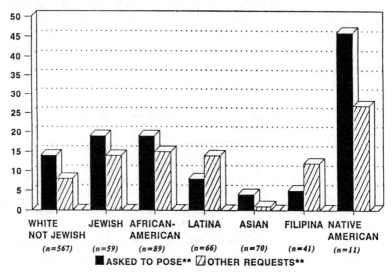

*SAMPLE SIZE ADDS TO 903 BECAUSE 27 MEMBERS OF "OTHER" RACES OMITTED
**EACH DISTRIBUTION SIGNIFICANT AT P<.02

Figure 18.2 Percent of Women of Different Age Groups Who Were Asked to Pose for Pornographic Pictures Sometime in Life

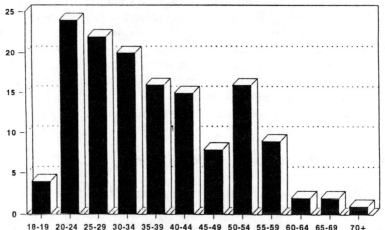

NOTE: AGE DISTRIBUTION DIFFERENCES IN REQUESTS TO POSE ARE SIGNIFICANT AT <0.01 LEVEL

198

sible explanation is that such requests have become more common in recent years. The so-called sexual revolution that began in the early 1960s may be responsible for the greater frequency of requests to pose reported by the younger women. And the proliferation and mainstreaming of pornography in the United States since 1970 may also help account for these findings. Another factor may be the longer time spent in the dating market by women in this century due to the rising age at marriage and the decrease in age when dating starts.

What might explain the sizable discrepancy between the very low percentage (4%) of the 18- and 19-year-olds who were asked to pose, compared with nearly a quarter (23%) of the 20- to 24-year-olds, 22% of the 25- to 29-year-olds, 20% of the 30- to 34-year-olds, 16% of the 35- to 39-year-olds, and so on (see Figure 18.2)? (The discrepancy cannot be explained by the fact that the 18- to 19-year-olds are the only age group that covers only 2 years, because the percentages are based on the total number in each age group.) Perhaps the men who asked women to pose avoided the 18- and 19-year-olds because they were afraid of being punished for propositioning minors (women under 18 years of age).

Similarly, there was also a statistically significant relationship between women's ages at the time of the interview and how often they were upset by requests to engage in acts seen in pornography. Women aged 18 to 49 were almost equally vulnerable to requests to enact pornography, while the three older age groups reported significantly fewer such experiences (see Figure 18.3).

Once again, remember that the younger women had been at risk of unwanted requests to enact pornography for fewer years than the older women. Thus the fact that the 18- to 19-year-olds reported the same percentage of requests as the 30- to 39-year-olds suggest that this form of victimization may actually be significantly more common in the younger women. This suggests that increasing numbers of men in recent years may be trying to persuade or force women to engage in acts that they have seen in pornography.

Incest Survivors and Pornography

Incestuous abuse was defined in my survey as any kind of exploitative sexual contact or attempt at contact that occurred between relatives, no matter how distant the relationship, before the victim turned 18 years old. Experiences involving sexual contact or attempted contact with a relative that were wanted and with a peer were regarded as nonexploitative—for example, sex play between cousins or siblings of approximately the same

Figure 18.3 Percent of Women of Different Age Groups Who Were Upset by
Requests to Enact Pornography

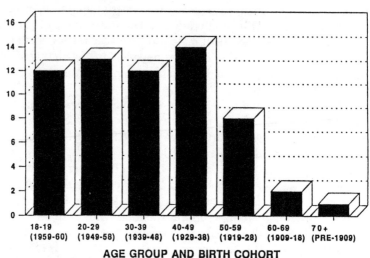

NOTE: AGE GROUP DISTRIBUTION SIGNIFICANT AT <0.01 LEVEL

ages. An age difference of less than 5 years was the criterion for a peer
relationship.

Of the 152 respondents who were survivors of incest, 18% reported
being upset by someone trying to get them to enact sexual scenes seen in
pornographic pictures, movies, or books. This is 10% more than the wom-
en who reported no history of incestuous abuse (significant at $p <$
0.0001). There was also a significant relationship between incestuous
abuse and being asked to pose for pornography ($p < 0.05$). However,
women with a history of incestuous abuse were no more likely than the
other women to report being upset by seeing pornography (see Table 18.1).

Almost a third (31%) of the survivors of father–daughter incest reported being upset by requests to enact pornography. This is about four times
higher than the percentage of non-incest survivors who were upset by such
requests. Similarly, 43% of father–daughter incest survivors reported being
asked to pose for pornography — about four times higher than the percentage reported by non-incest survivors (see Table 18.2).

Table 18.2 also shows that over a third (35%) of the women who had
been sexually abused by more than one relative reported being upset by
requests to enact pornography, and just under a third (30%) reported being
asked to pose for pornography. As was the case for the survivors of father–

Table 18.1 Incest Victimization Before 18 Years and Experiences with Pornography

Experiences with Pornography	Incest Victimization N = 151		No Incest Victimization N = 778	
	%	N	%	N
Upset by requests to enact pornography[a]	18	27	8	62
Asked to pose for pornography[a]	27	40	11	88
Upset by seeing pornography[b]	43	33	44	137

[a]Significant at <0.001 level.

[b]Based only on women who had <u>seen</u> pornography. Not significant at <0.05 level.

Missing observation: 1

Table 18.2 Father–Daughter Incest and Victimization by More Than One Relative Before 18 Years and Experiences with Pornography

Experiences with Pornography	Victims of Father-Daughter Incest N = 42		Victims of More Than One Relative N = 23[b]		No Incest Victimization N = 778	
	%	N	%	N	%	N
Upset by requests to enact pornography[a]	31	13	35	8	8	62
Asked to pose for pornography[b]	43	18	30	7	11	88

[a]Significant at <0.001 level

[b]Missing observation: 1

201

daughter incest, these percentages are significantly different from those obtained for non-incest survivors (p < 0.001).

One possible explanation for these findings may be that incest perpetrators — particularly fathers — were more likely than other men to ask their victims to pose for pornographic pictures and to enact sexual behavior they had seen in pornography. However, it is also possible that incest survivors were more aware of the influence of pornography on their perpetrators' sexual behavior because they are usually on more familiar terms with their perpetrators than other survivors of sexual abuse.

Another plausible explanation is that childhood incest victimization may increase a woman's vulnerability to these forms of revictimization. Because incest victims are frequently powerless to stop their abuse and often threatened with dire consequences if they reveal it to anyone, the resulting trauma often leads to a significantly greater probability of their being raped and battered at some time in their lives.[4]

Although the questions we asked on pornography relate to verbal propositions some of which were never acted out, it could be that some men perceive a greater vulnerability in these women, and/or that knowing about the women's earlier victimization, some may feel freer to make such proposals. Further research is needed to elucidate the relationship between incestuous abuse and victimization by pornography. If these findings are replicated, it will be important to investigate explanations for this relationship.

Pornography and Rape

For the purposes of this analysis, rape and attempted rape will be defined as forced and attempted vaginal, oral, or anal intercourse; completed or attempted intercourse because of physical threat or when the woman was unable to consent because she was completely physically helpless; and forcible penetration with a foreign object.[5]

There were at least 15 cases of rape or attempted rape that women in the survey attributed to pornography. Because the interviewers often failed to probe the exact nature of the unwanted pornography-related sexual experiences reported by the respondents, this is likely to be an underestimate of the actual incidence. Nevertheless, 15 cases represents 1.6% of the sample of 930 women.

For example, one woman described several different experiences with the same man, the last of which was forced oral rape.

> I was intimidated. But I also did the intercourse somewhat willingly because of his baiting me. He said he's send me to Hollywood for a screen test, a Lil' Abner take-off. He said he had to try all his starlets

just once. So I did it, almost like a prostitute. After the intercourse, he tried to force me to suck him off, but I wouldn't. He also suggested I get a friend and have a lesbian experience in front of him. [Declined?] Yes. He had already pushed me too far. Then he tricked me. He put me in front of a mirror, saying, "I want you to do something." Then he took my hair and forced my head down onto his penis. He made me suck him off while he watched in the mirror. [He used physical force?] Yes. A strong arm.

Several other examples of these rapes or attempted rapes appear in the section on wife rape below.

Pornography and Wife Rape

Almost one third (32%) of the 87 women who reported experiences of wife rape in our survey said that they had been asked to pose for pornography.[6] This is over double the 14% of women in the entire sample of 930 women who reported being asked to pose.

Similarly, almost a quarter (24%) of the survivors of wife rape said that they had been upset by requests to enact pornography. This compares with 10% of the 930 women who reported being upset by such requests. Hence, almost two-and-a-half times more of the survivors of wife rape reported being upset by such requests than those who said they had never been raped by their husbands.

Although women were not specifically asked what their relationship was to the person who asked them to enact pornography, out of the 21 survivors of wife rape who reported being upset by requests to enact pornography, eight volunteered that the person involved was a husband or ex-husband. This reveals that *well over 38% of the survivors of wife rape reported being upset by their husbands' requests to enact pornography.*

Although it is difficult to draw any definitive conclusion from eight cases, these findings signify that there may be a causative relationship between husband–rapists' use of pornography and their sexual abuse of their wives.

Following are some examples of the experiences mentioned by these women in answer to the question on whether or not they had ever been upset by someone trying to get them to do what they had seen in pornographic pictures, movies, or books. Any mention of age in the following quotations refers to the respondent's age when interviewed.

The respondents' statements reveal that many were able to avoid doing what their husbands asked or demanded of them. Despite this, they often ended up feeling used, insulted, harassed, or humiliated.

A 22-year-old woman: "My husband showed me a book of naked women. I don't like seeing it and I hate for him to show it to me. He tried to get me to stand and dance naked. I don't like for him to push me to do things like that. It's just not me."

A 27-year-old woman: "It was oral sex. I didn't want to do it with him, but I was made to do it. I'd ask him 'why are you making me do something I feel uncomfortable with?'"

A 28-year-old woman: "He'd go to a porno movie, come home, and then want to try out what he'd seen. He'd put his penis in my rectum. I reminded him that my rectum was not for his penis. After I went to sleep on my stomach I felt a throbbing in my butt. He was trying to insert his penis. I tried to get up so that I could slap him, but I couldn't move."

A 31-year-old woman: "My third husband tied me up against my will."

A 31-year-old woman: "It was S and M stuff — being asked if I would participate in being beaten up. It was a proposition. It never happened. I turned it off. I didn't like the idea. [Anything else?] Anal intercourse. I have been asked to do that, but I don't enjoy it at all. I have had to do it very occasionally."

This respondent mentioned that the anal intercourse is no longer forced by her husband because she uses a drug to dull the pain.

A 45-year-old woman: "He started bringing home shit. Dirty, kinky stories. He tells me to read them. I make a mockery of him. I tear them up. He's come up with a few dillies he'd like to do but he never forces me. It's more mental torment than physical torment."

A 62-year-old woman: "My husband enjoys pornographic movies. He tries to get me to do things he finds exciting in these movies. They include two-somes and three-somes. I always refuse. Also, I was always upset with his ideas about putting objects in my vagina, until I learned this is not as deviant as I used to think. He used to force or put whatever he enjoyed into me."

Some women whose husbands had not raped them, also described their husbands' requests to enact pornography. For example, a 48-year-old woman said: "It was my second husband. He'd see some weird picture and say, 'We'll try that.' I'd say, 'Oh no we don't!'" A 33-year-old woman said:

"Pretty often my husband likes to use paraphernalia to accompany sex, like movies, books, tapes, and magazines. He gets wrapped up in the movie, making love on a fantasy level during intercourse. I make love on an emotional level. It upsets me when his attention is diverted by the technical side of sex instead of the emotional side."

We have shown the evidence provided by our survey that women who have been raped by their husbands are more likely to report unwanted requests to enact pornography than other women. But why? It could be a reflection of the causal relationship between pornography and men's rape behavior. It could also be that the type of men who rape their wives are also the kind who consume pornography. More specifically, both wife rape and trying to get women to enact pornography could be manifestations of a particularly sexist and violence-prone man. Yet another possible explanation is that the kind of men who rape their wives are more willing than other men to reveal to their wives that they want to act out scenes viewed in pornography. I hope that future research will explore these and other possible explanations.

Pornography and Child Sexual Abuse

Although respondents were not asked what their ages were when they were asked to enact pornography, a few of the women disclosed that they were under 18 years of age at the time. One 21-year-old woman said: "I was really young—like 14. It was a three girls-and-him situation. We had sex." An 18-year-old woman disclosed the following experience:

> "He hypnotized me and got me to do something sexual when I was 16. I came out of the spell and knew [what had happened]. I was lying there naked and he just used me. [What did he do?] Oral sex, and stimulating me with his hand. [Why do you attribute this to pornography?] He explained that he had seen it in a movie."
>
> A 27-year-old woman said: "My first exposure was in fifth grade to 8 × 10 glossy photos of people having sex. The babysitter showed my brother and me pornographic pictures. After we refused to do it [have sex] he would barricade us in the bathroom and make us watch him jerk off. He also made us touch him. [Where?] On his genitals. He'd show us pictures and he'd demonstrate a hard-on for us so we'd know what it was. He made fun of my brother because he was so little. [What did you feel about the pornographic pictures?] I felt repulsed and that it was ugly and wrong. I didn't want to grow up and have to do it. I thought about becoming a nun and got more religious. I didn't feel good about my body. [Effects?] It took me a long time to feel comfortable with certain sexual positions and sex."

Another woman was propositioned by a man who took her to be a child although she was 21 years old at the time.

> In my drawing class a guy asked me to be in nude pictures. It was scary because he thought I was younger than I was, and I'm against child porn. It was upsetting to know he was for it. When I said no, he said nothing else to me. These guys have to be careful not to get caught. I wanted to call the police but I didn't.

One woman explained her reaction when she first saw pornographic pictures: "When I was 7 or 8, I saw pictures of orgies. They were really weird. I didn't understand them, but I felt confused and scared. They were so unusual."

WHY SOME WOMEN WERE UPSET BY PORNOGRAPHY

Upset by Seeing Pornography

The respondents were asked *"Have you ever been upset by seeing pornographic pictures?"* Unfortunately, only a minority of the women who said they were upset were asked to explain why.[7] Some objected to the separation of sex from love, tenderness, and respect. For example, one respondent said, "Sex is beautiful with love. The pictures I see are disrespectful to love and sex." Another woman said, "My husband was a virgin when I met him. His only experience of sex was very pornographic. He related to sex as separate from love, like sex was pornography." Along the same lines, other women found pornography very impersonal: "I saw the movie *The Constant Sex*. The woman in it has sex with about 25 different people. I feel that sex is tied into one's emotional well-being and to just show sex without focusing on the person at all is very misleading." Another woman stated, "They were too graphic. Sex between two people is personal. It was like open heart surgery rather than anything romantic."

Several women objected to the distorted portrayal of women's sexuality conveyed in pornography. For example, one woman said, "They were violent, frightening experiences and *made to look like pleasure*. Sex should be mutual, not cause a woman harm." Another woman stated: "I saw a movie in a motel in which one man was sucking on another man and one man had a nude woman tied up and he was beating her. It upset me because I couldn't see getting any pleasure from being beaten. *She was supposed to like it.*"

One of the most common objections to pornography from our respondents was the opinion that pornography demeans, exploits, and/or subordinates women. One woman, who mentioned that she had never seen violent pornography, said: "Women seem to be demeaned in it. They are treated like pieces of flesh and not much else. It's generally women doing the work for men's sexual gratification and not vice-versa." Another woman replied, "I saw a film which was so debasing to women I couldn't watch it. The whole film was about the many different ways they can debase and humiliate women. It was a horrible experience for me." Another reported, "In a sex and crime course in college I saw a four-hour [pornographic] movie. I felt a general anger at how they exploit women on the screen. In pornography women are always passive." And yet another woman said, "In one movie I saw, women were treated as objects that were thrown around. It was really humiliating."

One woman could not articulate why she was so upset by viewing pornography, except to say that she became "hysterical" when she saw one particular movie, and that "I can't understand why people would go to see that sort of thing." Another woman described herself as "nauseated after seeing a [pornographic] movie." She added that, "it affected my sex life for a month afterwards." One woman described her distress on seeing pornography as follows: "My boyfriend was into these movies. I saw one that was so gross, I broke down and cried one time. A woman was masturbating with a snake."

Two women discussed their distress with the use of children in pornography. "In the featurette [I saw] a teenager was rubbing a man's penis and making him come. She looked 12 or 13 years old." And the second woman noted: "Pornography abuses sex. It makes it seem cheap and dirty, especially when it involves children. The use of children in pictures showing them in sexual acts affects them sexually for the rest of their lives."

One woman mentioned her shock at encountering pornography when she was a child: "At 15 years of age I found my brother's book on sadomasochism. God! It scared me. It also almost excited me, and this reaction scared me too. Is this what sex is about, I wondered."

Several women objected to the violence in pornography. "I don't like the brutality and people having to perform sex against their wishes," one woman explained. Anther woman was disturbed by — among other things — the vulnerability of the models to violence: "[I'm upset by] the presentation of women as sexual objects and in the implied violent situations where they're vulnerable to that sort of treatment, for example, by being chained to a chair."

One woman was upset by the impact that she saw a pornographic movie have on men:

"They exploited women in the film. I didn't like the effect it had on the male members of our group. They acted like those women were really great stuff. I got up and walked out. Women were put in a position where they should cater to men. The man's word was it. Women were being forced to do what men wanted without men returning any such privileges."

Some respondents' answers to the question as to why they were upset by seeing pornography suggest that they felt personally pressured just by viewing it. For example, one woman said, "It used to depress me to think I might have to do those things." Another woman disclosed, "Seeing pictures and reading about oral sex makes you feel your marriage may be shaky if you don't do it."

Two women talked about their distress about requests to pose for pornography: "One person encouraged me to have my picture taken. [Pornographic pictures?] Yes. He was someone I trusted and cared about. The coercion was really damaging. I ended up feeling really negative about myself." Another woman said: "I get upset when a friend asks me to pose. It upsets me because they know me and yet they ask me to do it."

Other women were upset when men expected them to be interested in pornography. "A man brought a dirty magazine to my home. He wanted me to go to see dirty movies with him. I threw his magazine into the garbage." Some were distressed by being forced to see pornography. One woman said, "I had an employer who forced me to view pornography when I didn't want to. It made me furious. I was made to feel very helpless because had I objected, I would have been fired. I couldn't afford to lose my job at the time."

Another woman said she was distressed by pornography because, "I felt really exploited, like I was being put in a mold." Two women refused to describe what had upset them, one pleading that it was "so repulsive" to her, and the other that it was too "sickening."

These respondents' explanations as to why pornography upsets them have a consistent underlying theme. Their responses show their disgust with how women are portrayed in such material, and the depiction of women as passive objects of torture, humiliation, and degradation who actually enjoy such abuses.

These women's answers substantiate what many feminists have been saying for a long time: that pornography is filled with lies about what women enjoy sexually, and how they like men to relate to them. In addition, many of the women's answers reveal the negative impact of pornography on their feelings and attitudes contradicting the claim by many male researchers that women are as turned on by pornography as men are. The respondents' replies also provide anecdotal evidence that pornography promotes violence against women.

Types of Sex Acts Requested or Imposed
After Viewing Pornography

Some of the sex acts respondents said they were requested to perform included: "urinating in someone's mouth," "putting unnatural objects in my vagina," "doing a blow job," "having oral intercourse against my will," and "wanting rectal intercourse." Other examples follow:

> "A man wanted to pay me and another girl to do some kind of sex show. He asked me every time I came in contact with him. He said he would pay me $50 to let another girl go down on me."
>
> "One guy wanted to handcuff me to the bed. He was drunk. I was nervous and refused. I was afraid I wouldn't get loose."
>
> "It was oral genital contact with me standing and him kneeling. I was very uncomfortable with the impersonal way it was foisted on me. It was like a big performance."
>
> "He was more interested in getting into the whipped cream than me. It was kinky and insulting."
>
> "A friend pulled out a leather thong. He didn't hurt me, but he hit me with it. I didn't like it and told him to stop. [Was sexual intercourse involved?] Yes. He didn't force me into anything, but it offended my sensibilities."
>
> "A man friend once asked me if he could tie me up, but I didn't agree to it. He asked me if I minded, and I said I did. He didn't try to force me."
>
> "I was newly divorced when this date talked about S and M and I said, 'You've got to be nuts. Learning to experience pleasure through pain! But it's your pleasure and my pain!' I was very upset that someone thought I would want to sacrifice myself and have pain and bruises. It's a sick mentality. This was when I first realized there are many men out there who believe this."

As is clear from some of the unwanted experiences described above, many of the requests did not go beyond propositions because the women refused to cooperate. However, this does not mean that the women were not often very upset and disillusioned by these experiences.

Sometimes the respondents succeeded in stopping the unwanted sex acts before they were completed. For example, "He wanted to get involved with slapping around — the violent part which I don't like at all. He started to do it, but I got so afraid and angry, I insisted that he stop."

Other women consented to the men's proposals, but nevertheless found them upsetting. And at other times the women found that they got more than they had bargained for.

"My old man and I went to a show that had lots of tying up and anal intercourse. We came home and proceeded to make love. He went out and got two belts. He tied my feet together with one, and with the other he kinda beat me. I went along with it. But when he tried to penetrate me anally, I couldn't take it, it was too painful. I managed to convey to him verbally to quit it. He did stop, but not soon enough to suit me. Then one time, he branded me. I still have a scar on my butt. He put a little wax initial thing on a hot plate and then stuck it on my ass when I was unaware."

There were also many cases in which men imposed the sex acts they desired without the respondents' permission.

"He made me have sex in different positions that I found very intimidating. It was like monkey-see, monkey-do. I felt like an animal, like a dog fucking. It was impersonal, and there was no other body contact between us, just his organ and my organ."

"It was physical slapping and hitting. It wasn't a turn-on; it was more a feeling of being used as an object. What was most upsetting was that he thought it would be a turn-on."

"He forced me to have oral sex with him when I had no desire to do it."

"It was anal sex. First he attempted gentle persuasion, I guess. He was somebody I'd been dating a while and we'd gone to bed a few times. Once he tried to persuade me to go along with anal sex, first verbally, then by touching me. When I said, 'No,' he did it anyway — much to my pain. It hurt like hell."

"My boyfriend and I saw a movie in which there was masochism. After that he wanted to gag me and tie me up. He was stoned. I was not. I was really shocked at his behavior. I was nervous and uptight. He literally tried to force me, after gagging me first. He snuck up behind me with a scarf. He was hurting me with it and I started getting upset. Then I realized it wasn't a joke. He grabbed me and shook me by my shoulders and brought out some ropes, and told me to relax, and that I would enjoy it. Then he started putting me down about my feelings about sex, and my inhibitedness. I started crying and struggling with him, got loose, and kicked him in the testicles, which forced him down on the couch. I ran out of the house. Next day he called and apologized, but that was the end of him."

COMPARISON WITH OTHER STUDIES

Four Canadian researchers, Charlene Senn, Evelyn Sommers, Patricia Harmon, and James Check, have used Russell's survey question on upsetting pornographic requests in three different studies.

In Senn's sample of 96 female undergraduates obtained from a subject pool at the University of Calgary in 1984 to 1985, 24% reported being upset by requests to enact pornography (see Chapter 17). This amounts to approximately one-in-four of her respondents as compared with one-in-ten in our study.

Senn suggests that the differences in our samples likely account for the disparity in our findings. For example, her sample was much younger than ours, with an average age of 22 years compared to our average age of 43 years. However, when we separate the younger from the older age groups in Russell's survey, we find that 12% of the 18- to 19-year-olds reported upsetting pornographic requests and 13% of the 20- to 29-year-olds. These percentages are only half of the 25% who reported such requests in Senn's study.

Another explanation for the disparity offered by Senn is that pornographic materials and mainstream depictions of women have become increasingly violent in the past two decades (see Chapter 17). This increasing violence may result in more men "asking their partners to perform offensive acts today [in 1984/5] than when Russell conducted her study" (Chapter 17).

Contradicting this explanation is the fact that there have been far more governmental restrictions on pornography in Canada than in the United States. Hence, pornography in Canada in 1984 and 1985 might not have been significantly more violent than pornography in the United States in 1978 when Russell's survey was conducted. The results of research conducted by Patricia Harmon and James Check in 1987 also does not support Senn's explanation. Only 9% of a sample of 604 Toronto women residents obtained by random digit dialing answered yes to the question on whether or not they had ever been upset by requests to enact pornography. This figure is, of course, very close to our 10% figure (Harmon & Check, 1989).

The most plausible explanation for the higher 20% figure obtained by Senn is that her sample of 96 female undergraduates may have been more willing to disclose such experiences to her than women in relatively large scale community samples. Being a female graduate student at the same institution as her subjects probably created a superior level of trust than the interviewers in our study and Harmon and Check's were able to obtain.

The more taboo the topic being investigated in a social survey, the more necessary it is to train the interviewers to feel comfortable asking questions about it, and probing for honest answers. Training should also include educating interviewers about the issue (pornography, in this case) in an effort to minimize biases that would likely impede frank disclosures by respondents. This kind of training was not undertaken in the Harmon and Check study. Although Russell undertook such special training on sexual assault in her survey, regrettably she did not do so for the questions on pornography.

Sommers and Check asked this same question on pornography of 44 battered women who were living in shelters or participating in counseling at the time of their study (1987, p. 192), and a comparison group of 32 non-battered women obtained from psychology classes at York University in Toronto. Thirty-nine percent of the battered women reported that they had been upset by requests to enact pornography compared to only 3% of the control group (1987, p. 200).

Sommers and Check also found that the batterers consumed significantly more pornography than the non-batterers. They concluded that:

> Although the results of the present study do not provide direct evidence of a causal link between the use of pornography and violence against women . . . these observations are consistent with a link between pornography and violence against women and may ultimately add to the growing body of evidence showing that the use of pornography increases males' aggressiveness toward women. (1987, p. 205)

In their 1990 Toronto study, Harmon and Check looked at a much more broadly defined group of battered women, that is, those who reported "any physical assault against a woman by a male partner with whom she is, or has had an intimate romantic relationship. Assaults ranged from relatively minor pushes and shoves to severe beatings and attempted murder" (1989, p. 60). Of the 604 women interviewed, these investigators found that the "women who had been physically abused were three times more likely to have been upset by being asked to imitate pornography (10.4%) than were women who had not been abused (3.6%)" (1989, p. 64).

As interesting as the finding of a co-occurrence of physical abuse and pornography, is the finding that the more severely battered women reported far higher rates of unwanted requests to enact pornography (39%) than did the less severely beaten women (10.4%). In contrast, the two groups of nonabused women in these studies reported remarkably similar percentages of unwanted pornographic requests (3% of the student sample, and 3.6% of the Toronto sample). The 10% figure found in Russell's survey may be so much higher than the Sommers and Check percentages because the abused women were not removed from her sample.

In summary, from 9 to 20% of the women in three different samples disclosed that they had been asked to enact pornography. This percentage is from two to four times higher (39%) for severely battered women.

CONCLUSION

The results of the three surveys compared indicate that some men imitate, and others try to imitate, the sex acts they have seen in pornographic pictures, movies, or books. This refutes the notion that the impact of pornography consumption is merely cathartic. In addition, the frequent comment by respondents that women in pornography are portrayed as enjoying abusive or forceful sex may be the source of, or may reinforce, many men's beliefs that women's refusals to engage in sex should not be taken seriously. The normalization of abusive sex acts is but one of the many destructive messages in pornography.

This chapter demonstrates that exploring the impact of pornography on girls and women by means of a social survey is a worthwhile task. We have reported both quantitative and qualitative evidence — some definitive and some suggestive — that pornography is harmful to women. It is important that more in-depth research be conducted on this vital topic in the future. Comparison of the findings of three studies indicates that more effort must go into training interviewers to improve the way they question women about their experiences with pornography.

Part IV

FEMINIST STRATEGIES AND ACTIONS AGAINST PORNOGRAPHY

Guerrilla action in Santa Cruz, CA, to protest the sexist violence in Brian de Palma's movie, "Dressed to Kill," 1982. People were forced to step over the "corpse" if they chose to go to the movie.

Credit: Nikki Craft

CHAPTER 19

Wimmin's Fire Brigade Bombs Porn

Jas

Feminists in British Columbia, Canada, have been campaigning to force a chain of pornographic videocassette stores to close. The Red Hot Video chain has grown very rapidly in less than a year. By November it included thirteen outlets which stock some videos depicting incest, rape, and other forms of sexual violence against women. After months of pressuring the Attorney General, Allan Williams, to take action against the stores through Canada's obscenity laws and laws against hate propaganda, women were frustrated that although Williams had stated publicly that prosecution would be possible under existing B.C. laws, he had done nothing. Also, laws covering video materials are vague in B.C. — it is illegal to produce and import hardcore porn, but not to copy or distribute the films. The stores have taken advantage of the loopholes to escape prosecution.

Store operators claimed their films did not show rape, despite the fact that women had viewed numerous videos from the Red Hot chain that did. In addition, the store's catalogue, "The Red Hot Video Special Handbook," included listing under the headings "rape and gang-bang," "incest," "young girls," and "first sex experience." Later, store operators cited the guarantee of freedom of speech to defend the material, and also used the "porn is a harmless outlet for male aggression" argument.

BRIGADE'S ILLEGAL ACTIONS

A group of women called the Wimmin's Fire Brigade, realizing that the legal route was not achieving change, decided that illegal action was necessary. On November 22, 1982, the group fire-bombed three Red Hot Video outlets in the lower mainland of B.C. The Surrey store was com-

---

Reprinted by permission from *Off Our Backs*, p. 4.

217

pletely destroyed (along with three adjacent stores). The North Vancouver store was somewhat damaged, and in Coquitlam the outlet was left intact because the bombs were not ignited.

NO MORE VIOLENCE AGAINST WOMEN

The Brigade issued a statement which was received by newspapers in B.C. while the fire bombing was taking place. It read, in part:

> This action is another step towards the destruction of a business that promotes and profits from violence against wimmin and children. Red Hot Video sells tapes that show wimmin and children being tortured, raped, and humiliated. We are not the property of men to be used and abused. Red Hot Video is part of a multi-billion dollar pornography industry that teaches men to equate sexuality with violence. Although these tapes violate the Criminal Code of Canada and the B.C. guideline on pornography, all lawful attempts to shut down Red Hot Video have failed because the justice system was created, and is controlled, by rich men to protect their profits, and property. As a result, we are left no viable alternative but to change the situation ourselves through illegal means. This is an act of self-defense against hate propaganda. We will continue to defend ourselves!

ARRESTS IN JANUARY

Five people were charged and arrested in January in connection with the bombings. They were also charged with the previous June's dynamiting of the Cheekye-Dunsmuir hydro substation. According to *Kinesis*, the media coverage of the arrests has been biased and sensational, calling the group of two women and three men a "terrorist . . . extremist . . . anarchist cell," and assuming guilt automatically. *Kinesis* reports that "no evidence has been given to the defense counsel linking the five accused to the impressive arsenal of explosives and firearms that have figured so prominently in the press."

FEMINIST SUPPORT

At the time of the fire bombings, women's groups rallied to support the Brigade's actions. The B.C. Federation of Women (BCFW) issued this statement November 22:

While we did not participate in the fire bombings of November 22 in the Lower Mainland, we are in agreement with the frustration and anger of the women who did. We noted and appreciated their efforts to see that no one got hurt. Thirty-six women's liberation groups of the B.C. Federation of Women have made a decision to close Red Hot Video outlets this year. We insist that Allan Williams take action immediately to prevent rich men from profiting from Red Hot Video's hate literature about women and children. The women of B.C. are being driven to desperate acts. The Canadian and B.C. governments have failed to use existing laws to defend more than half the population from the horrors of propagandist industry. Pornography is the theory — rape is the practice.

The BCFW is the organized voice for women in B.C.

Lee Lakeman, a BCFW member, said, "We will certainly not desert these women who have taken the action. There's a difference between violence to live women and violence to a building."

The Feminist Coalition Against Pornography in Montreal released a solidarity statement:

Fire-bombing shops selling pornographic videotapes might seem at first glance an inappropriate way to fight the violence against women. But things are not that simple. The violence that is used in an attack on private property is qualitatively different from the violence that is used in videotapes aimed at glorifying rape, torture, and humiliation of women . . . We are the last to underestimate the importance of the right to freedom of speech. But for that right to have any meaning it must be conditioned by the respect for the rights of others — in this case, principally women. Pornography, by its systematic distortion of female sexuality and insult to our intelligence, denies all women the right to speak.

NOT ALL WOMEN AGREE

However, a representative of the North Shore Women's Center, J. Andrews, has said that she is anti-pornography, but believes the fire-bombings were "against everything we stand for. It's just why we are attacking Red Hot Video in the first place . . . we are appalled by violence."

Canada's Women Against Violence Against Women has begun to put pressure on another video company called Tricolor Video Inc. Strong anti-pornography organizing continues, including mass picketing of video outlets and petitioning.

POLICE RAID RED HOT

On January 7, police in B.C. raided twelve video stores (nine were Red Hot ones). They confiscated hundreds of tapes and brought formal charges against one store. Police also took possession of 5000 recorded and blank video tapes from the home of a Peter Struk.

Lately, Red Hot has changed the names of some of its outlets in an attempt to dodge publicity. But it has also closed two stores because of public pressure and a third outlet lost its lease.

The fight against Red Hot has brought the issue of pornography into the public eye in Canada. Radio and TV shops and mainstream newspapers have covered the controversy.

CHAPTER 20

Unmasking Male Privilege

Nikki Craft

In 1991 several of us founded a fly-by-night organization: the A.C.L.U. (Always Causing Legal Unrest). Now, we don't mean to be confused with the American Civil Liberties Union! It's only a coincidence that our acronyms are the same. We're NOT that group that supports the pornographers, the Nazis, the KKK, the tobacco industry, and the child pornographers. We're NOT those guys fixated on reciting defamatory, whining mantras about Andrea Dworkin. Instead, our ACLU is concerned that conservative values such as corporate trademark laws, private property rights, and individual privacy (as opposed to public safety and welfare), severely infringe upon and limit free expression, and they *enjoy* more rights (legally, socially, and politically) than women do in the public and private domain. Our motto is "We tear into sexism." And we do. We don't let laws of any kind get in the way of our free expression. No siree. That summer in Bellingham we went on numerous crime sprees. Since that time the ACLU has decorticated many copies of Bret Easton Ellis' novel, *American Psycho*, and other books that were "asking for it."

In July, I was arrested at the Mt. Baker Theater during a showing of the movie *Kill Me Again*. I was the one hurling candy at the screen during the sexually violent scenes. When they found out I was in the audience, rather than dealing with me, the theatre manager refunded everyone's admission. I returned the next night and they attempted to prevent me from entering. I went in anyway, bought two big boxes of Sugar Babies, and by the time the police arrived, I was already pelting the candy at the screen. The movie is about an "attractive" (of course) woman who pays to stage her own murder. She becomes sexually aroused in a cheap motel

Edited version of an article published under the same title in *the ICONoclast*, Summer 1991, pp. 5–9. © Nikki Craft 1991. *The ICONoclast* is available from P.O. Box 2085, Rancho Cordova, CA 95741-2085. Reprinted by permission of the author.

while a guy pours a gallon of blood over her semi-nude body while she coos, "I've always wondered what it would be like to die a *really* violent death." Then he stuffs her body into the trunk of a car. In the end, she dies. And nobody really cared, not even me. You know the plot: The bitch wants it, she deserves it, and in the end she gets it — with lots of violence, sex, blood, and car crashes to exercise the adrenals and other organs. The satisfaction I got from my Sugar Baby bombings, and the clatter they made when they bounced off the screen onto the linoleum floor, was well worth the night I spent in jail for that one. Charges were quietly dismissed after I left Bellingham.

I was also arrested for tearing up $11.00 worth of *Esquire* magazines. For this one I spent 23 (count them hatch-mark-on-the-wall style) days in the Whatcom County jail. The theme of *Esquire* that month was, "Your Wife: An Owner's Manual." Need I say more? My jailers would not release me on my own recognizance unless I agreed to abide by all the laws — everywhere. Because of my commitment to fighting pornography and in-equality with civil disobedience as political resistance, I would be hard pressed to make any agreement of that sort. Besides, as I told the prosecu-tor, he was kidding himself if he thought he could control me outside Washington. I was held there until the "authorities" finally realized that I would never comply, and then they threw me *out* of jail. The headlines in the local newspapers read: *"Feminist Thrown Out of Jail."* The article read: "Yes, Nikki Craft has been thrown out of a lot of places before, but never before has she been thrown out of jail . . . "

The high point of this action came at an unexpected time. By the time I went to trial I was exhausted. I was relieved when author and scholar Diana Russell arrived in Bellingham to testify as an expert witness. She was fresh energy with a clear, radical analysis to offer as a guiding force. [See Chapter 21 for a description of this action.]

Earlier that year, Lucy Colvin, Sharon Black, Steven Hill, Darcy Alexandra, Chad Knuckles, Sharon O'Connell, and I donned ski masks and converged on the downtown Masturbation Service Center (Great Northern Books, a local pornography shop). Throughout July and August, we stood, for hours at a time, photographing hundreds of men (and one or two women), who entered the porn shop. Those of us who took part in this community experiment were all dedicated activists who have always taken individual responsibility for our work, words, and deeds. Some of us wore the ski masks because we feared for our personal safety. But we had other political points to make, too.

We did it because we believe strongly that men supporting the pornog-raphy industry must be publicly identified — whether they are our next door neighbors, sexual harassers, prominent citizens, or convicted predatory sex offenders.

We took the photos with the intention of publishing them in our free speech leaflets. Several leaflets were published and posted throughout Bellingham. We gave these customers the public recognition they deserved for being porn users. The color photos are now framed and waiting to be included in an art exhibit called "When the Viewer Becomes the Viewed." We have yet to find a gallery willing to display the prints.

Neither the hordes of porn shop goers, First Amendment Liberal Fundamentalists, nor the local newspaper *The Bellingham Herald*, exactly jumped to defend our First Amendment Rights to publish our little newsletter. In fact, they tried in every way they could to stop us and even tore our posters down. The local newspaper censored and misrepresented us.

Men in the community harassed us on the street. Several, including Robert Sensarnie from Mission Beach, British Columbia, and one Christopher John Shelly from Everson, Washington, (a nudist and now convicted child molester) physically assaulted us. Both were found guilty of assault in separate trials. In the police report, Sensarnie said he attacked one of our demonstrators because he was upset that he was being photographed. In court, Sensarnie claimed the reason the assault took place was because I supposedly yelled at him, "Fuck you, nigger." I would never use that racist language. There were witnesses that will attest to the fact that Sensarnie lied in court that day.

Edward Ross, the same judge who sentenced me to 90 days in jail for ripping up four *Esquire* magazines, gave Sensarnie no fine and a suspended sentence for assaulting women. As Sensarnie left the courtroom, he was smiling and gloating. There was no media coverage of either the assaults or the trial. In fact, even though we had been physically assaulted by these males in front of the porn shop, *The Bellingham Herald* would not allow me to write in an editorial that "some of [them] are dangerous." I was also not allowed to say that some of them were "prominent citizens."

These days it's often difficult to tell if the media is being stupid or malicious, but in Bellingham that summer we encountered plenty of both. *The Bellingham Herald* ran one article and one editorial about our actions that did a real disservice to the community by misinforming them about our work and our intent, thereby threatening the safety and well-being of our group. The editors trivialized our work in an attempt to diminish our credibility because we chose to mask our identities for this particular action.

The Herald ran one editorial called "Credibility Lacking," where the editor (who was not individually identified) lambasted our tactics, calling us "shadowy figures" who refused to be identified. (It was well known within the community who most of us were because of our past involvements.) After we stated that we feared retaliation, one *Herald* reporter published our names anyway. In the same article, he respected the anonymity of the manager of the porn store. They have refused to allow us to identify the owner of the store in an editorial.

The article (about our demonstration on July 3, 1990) called "Women Harass Customers of 'Adult' Store" should have been more accurately titled "Men's Porn Shop Associate Assaults Anti-Pornography Activist." That day, Chris Shelly, a man identified by the manager of the porn shop as one who "does things" for the store (according to police reports, he was allegedly a dildo repairman), chased Sharon O'Connell and me down the alley behind the porn shop. He caught Sharon, furiously yanking off (and stealing) her ski mask from behind, pulling her hair in the process, and trashing her leaflets. Our experience with Shelly corroborates the testimony of Amy, Ginny and Ryan (the children he photographed and molested). We all know Shelly to be a male who resorts to physical force and violence to get what he wants, because he did it to us.

In the police report, he lied, claiming we were "closing in on him" — though no demonstrator was standing closer than twenty feet away when he began chasing us. There were many witnesses, so he ended up pleading guilty to assault charges. Then, a little over a month later on August 12, 1990, Shelly was again arrested, this time for child pornography, child molestation, and rape of a child, for an incident that took place at the local nude beach.

We were surprised to learn that in one discussion several police officers postulated that criminal charges (for assault) should not be pressed against Shelly. The police justified Shelly's attack because he had been enraged that he was photographed. Others in the community took this same view as well.

For years I have confronted voyeurs and nudist men photographing unclothed women and children at nude beaches, Naturist Society and American Sunbathing Association events. I have also challenged individual men all across the country who were buying pornography at stores where we demonstrated.

During the Bellingham action I was struck by the fact that the type of men who were in front of the porn shop bitching and complaining about how we didn't have the "right" to take their picture because they were entitled to their privacy, were the same type of men I had been encountering at the naturist/nudist events for years. These nudist men argued that if a woman had her clothes off on the beach, which was a public place, anybody (read any *man*) who wanted to take her photograph had the "right" to do so, even if the woman objected. The arrogance of these men, the hypocrisy of their actions, and their male supremacist political position is appalling to behold.

Men take for granted their right to be unexposed. When they go to leer at images of women at the porn shop they want no one to violate their privacy. It's even considered a social *faux pas* for men to look at each other once inside the porn shop. Our demonstrations intentionally violated a near sacred totem by shining a spotlight on these men, their behaviors and their habits. We wanted to create for them the opportunity to experience what it feels like to be psychologically invaded — not a comfortable feeling to be sure, but certainly no justification for physical assault.

We also wanted our masked presence to serve as a reminder to the community that women are often sexually violated by men who maintain their anonymity, some by wearing masks just like the ones we are wearing.

There is also a certain kind of justice in usurping from rapists and other sex offenders such a fierce symbol as a ski mask, usually reserved for the male domain, in order to yank these men from their anonymity and hold them publicly accountable.

We felt some vindication and pleasure by turning the tables so that men can experience the feeling of being vulnerable, exposed and threatened, albeit in a minuscule dose. In fact, we realize it will take much more radical actions, and more of them, to explore these various possibilities. Women's experience of being vulnerable, exposed, and threatened are far too common in their day-to-day existences and with few exceptions women's experiences of fear and restriction are unfathomable to men.

The very concept of privacy is nearly inconceivable to many women. The spread-legged images of women inside the porn store certainly allow women no privacy. In fact, the voyeuristic "turn on" of most pornography depends on the violation of women's privacy. Out on the street, many women unfortunately do not assume they have the ability, much less the right, to even go to the bus stop without being visually or verbally assaulted.

The "Unmasking Male Privilege" action was an inspiring, rejuvenating experience for all of us involved. It is particularly appealing because it afforded us our anonymity while exposing the real perpetrators. We urge other anti-pornography activists throughout the country to try it and examine some of the related possibilities. But it is not an action to take part in without plenty of fore-thought. Make sure there are at least five women present before you try this tactic in your community.

Photographing these men was stressful and confrontive on a level like no other action I have ever done before. On many levels, the repercussions can be awesome and the immediate hostility of the male patrons will be shocking to the experienced and inexperienced alike. One hour on the streets with your camera in hand and your mask in place, and you will get the point: this action exposes the patriarchy by getting right to the crux of the issue.

CHAPTER 21

Poking Around Under Rocks and Pornographers

Sharon O'Connell & Steven Hill

Why we had been taking photos of customers entering and leaving the Bellingham porn store, we were not quite sure. Somehow it just felt right. We knew that the porn store sold propaganda proclaiming that women are sexual objects and playthings for male consumption and penetration— propaganda that promotes violence against women. We also knew that it was a meeting place for all sorts of unsavory characters, including pedophiles and other sex offenders seeking like-minded men to support each others' sexual delusions about women and children. At the very least, we wanted our photos to expose this aspect of the porn store and the men who patronize it. And sometimes, if one pokes around and lifts up enough rocks, there's no telling what kind of surprises will crawl out from underneath.

Imagine our astonishment one August evening when one of our group (Citizens Opposed to Media Exploitation or C.O.M.E.) was reading the local *Bellingham Herald* and discovered the tiniest mention, tucked away on the back page in the police log, that a man named Chris Shelly had been arrested for child pornography, child molestation, and rape of a minor. Chris Shelly was none other than the man who had pled guilty to a charge of assaulting one of our members when we were taking photos of customers entering and leaving the porn store. This was the same Chris Shelly who, we were told by an employee of the porn store, "does things" for the porn store.

After doing some investigation we discovered that, at the time of his arrest, Shelly was in the company of porn store owner Ross Rowell and a third man named Marc Hubbard who was employed at the United States

Printed by permission of the authors.

Post Office. Hmm, we pondered. Child pornographer, porn store owner, postal employee . . . Egads! Had we stumbled on a child pornography ring in sleepy ol' Bellingham? Shelly's prosecuting attorney in the Whatcom County Prosecutor's Office agreed with us that this three-way triangle was "highly suggestive." Child pornography rings operate via informal underground networks that use the mail to deliver their illegal and highly profitable products — sexually explicit pictures of naked children. Thus began our 2-month campaign to publicly expose the connection between Shelly, Rowell, and the Post Office employee.

We distributed a series of leaflets all over Bellingham and Whatcom County, and mailed out informational letters to all the media in the region, as well as to the ministers of selected churches. We publicized the fact that eight guns were confiscated from Shelly's apartment as well as nude photos of children that he had hanging on his bedroom walls, plus eight-millimeter X-rated movies, numerous dildos and vibrators, a computer, and a printer. Shelly, sporting a bullet on his key chain, had taken approximately 20 photos of three children, all 12 years old (two girls, Shelly's niece and her friend, and one boy) against their wishes at a public nude beach. Shelly had told the children that he could sell the photos for a lot of money to "Ross, my friend." Despite all this incriminating information against Shelly, including Shelly's previous assault on our group, he was not required to post bail, but was free to walk the streets of our neighborhoods for the several months while he awaited trial.

The prosecutor's office was not anxious to pursue the prosecution of this possible child pornography ring. The prosecutor's office said it was up to the police to investigate the connection between Shelly, Rowell, and Hubbard, and to provide better evidence before they could prosecute. Meanwhile, the police said they didn't have the human or material means to pursue a child pornography ring because their resources were being pumped into the "war on drugs." In a more candid moment, one of the lieutenants told us that the higherups in the police bureaucracy don't care about this sort of thing.

Nor, apparently, did the local media. Despite our furnishing them with all the information, and despite their statements that they were interested in this case and were planning to quietly investigate it, the *Bellingham Herald* did not publish anything beyond the initial notification of Shelly's arrest.

Our informational leaflets were seen as controversial among the liberal crowd. While maintaining that they did not support child pornography (well, most of them), they called our leaflets slanderous and spouted slogans like "right to privacy" and "innocent until proven guilty." They did not seem to be concerned at all about the victimized children nor the children's heartbreaking testimony. They also did not seem to be concerned that the media had not covered this story, nor that Shelly, a thoroughly dangerous man, was free to walk the streets.

Ironically, this same crowd of Free Speechists and First Amendment Fundamentalists led the pack in ripping our informational posters off the walls and swiping our leaflets. They did everything they could to prevent the dissemination of our information. Apparently, they are all for free speech as long as it's saying what they think it's acceptable to say.

But we will not be deterred. We are about to embark on a new project to keep the pressure on the porn store and its customers. We plan to use the photos we took of men entering and leaving the porn store in the summer of 1990, in a photographic art exhibit entitled "When the Viewers Become the Viewed." This exhibit will give us the opportunity to turn the tables on the porn store and its customers. Viewers of our art exhibit will be able to take a hard look at something that is for the most part accepted as normal in our society: the mostly male customers of a pornography outlet before or after they have consumed (masturbated to?) images of female subordination.

There are all kinds of men in these photos: young men, old men, business men, blue collar men, sports aficionados advertising their favorite teams on their shirts and white tennis shoes—all of whom were caught unawares. Our exhibit will strip their anonymity from them. Those who argue that pornography provides a catharsis for men will be hard pressed to explain these men's hostility on being photographed. Some of them verbally abused and threatened us, and two of them assaulted us.

Our photography exhibit will be dedicated to our sister and inspired fighter on the front lines, Nikki Craft. Nikki's presence in our community touched off this maelstrom of feminist activism. Our goal has been to raise community awareness about the relation between pornography and acts of violence against women and children. We want a non-sexist, non-exploitative society in which women and children and all oppressed people are safe and truly free to grow to their fullest potential. An ambitious goal, to be sure, but a worthy one. Worthy enough to poke around in those silent places we all usually try so hard to ignore. Try not ignoring sometime, try poking instead, and see what you come up with. You may be surprised. And you may raise a few hackles at the same time.

Epilogue: Chris Shelly pled guilty on April 18, 1991, to child molestation in the first degree and sexual exploitation of a minor. He was sentenced to two terms in jail totalling 83 months, to be served concurrently.

Ross Rowell, the porn store owner, and Marc Hubbard, the postal employee, are still at large.

Four of the masked demonstrators who took photographs of the men entering and exiting from the pornography store in Bellingham, WA.

Credit: Nikki Craft

CHAPTER 22

From Expert Witness to Jail Inmate

Diana E. H. Russell

Nikki Craft's arrest in Bellingham, Washington, on May 24, 1990, for tearing up four *Esquire* magazines on sale in a local bookstore was described in Chapter 20. This chapter completes the story.

I was invited by Craft's lawyer, Deborah Moranville, to be an expert witness at her trial on August 22. However, the presiding judge, Edward Ross, would only allow me to testify when the jurors were absent from the court because my testimony "would confuse them." Perhaps he was afraid I might have succeeded in convincing them that Craft's actions were not malicious, but on the contrary, a thoughtful and courageous effort to bring to the apathetic public's attention the fact that there is still a widely held sexist notion that husbands own their wives, body and soul; and that validating such an idea contributes to the problem of violence against women.

Despite Moranville's argument that Craft's intent had not been malicious, the jury of four women and two men found her guilty of malicious mischief after a few minutes of deliberations. Conceding that 23 days in prison was an excessive punishment for her destruction of $10.80 worth of *Esquires*, Judge Ross nevertheless saw fit to sentence her to 67 additional days in jail if she refused to pay $10.80 for restitution to the owner of Village Books, Chuck Robinson. This additional punishment followed Craft's defiant statement in court that she would not pay restitution because she considered doing so to be an admission of guilt. Judge Ross's response reminded me of the rage many men manifest when the women in their lives refuse to obey their commands.

Craft countered by offering to pay $20, not for restitution, but for the purchase of feminist magazines by Robinson for sale in his store. However,

---

This is an expanded version of an article published in *The Oakland Tribune*, Oakland, September 28, 1990, and *Off Our Backs*, Vol. 20, No. 10, November 1990, p. 4.

Ross and Robinson — two men in transparent collusion — insisted that the
$20 would include restitution. Craft, believing that the men had agreed to
her proposal, accepted the terms, thus avoiding spending the next 2
months in jail.

After discussing what had happened in court with co-activist Sharon
O'Connell and myself, Craft was distraught to learn that she had misun-
derstood the final outcome. She insisted we drive straight to Robinson's
bookstore where she demanded he return her $20. Had he done so, she
intended to tell Judge Ross that she had never agreed to pay restitution,
and that she would rather go to jail for an additional 2 months than to pay
it. But Robinson refused to return the money.

Craft felt tricked and angry about what had happened. As O'Connell
drove us toward her home, where Craft and I were staying, Craft expressed
despair that so few other women seemed to be willing to undertake civil
disobedience despite her example of 49 arrests for resisting men's war
against women. But her despair turned to jubilation when O'Connell and I
said that we were willing to get arrested to show our disgust with Judge
Ross's unjust treatment of her. The three of us immediately began to plan
our action for that night. We were also able to recruit Sharon Black for the
venture. She was the only other local anti-pornography activist who was
free to join us at such short notice.

We decided to destroy pornography because we believe that it is a very
significant cause of violence against women. We also wanted to make it
clear that we were engaging in this action at that particular time to protest
the extreme sentence that Judge Ross had imposed on Craft. We wanted to
show him and the people of Bellingham that we would not be intimidated
by his macho handling of Craft's case.

Besides these reasons, I chose to engage in this action because I have
believed for a long time in the efficacy of civil disobedience as a form of
protest. And for a long time I have wanted to engage in such actions with
Craft, because I hoped thereby to acquire some of her skills at attracting
media interest and at thinking creatively about actions and the paraphernalia that accompanies them (costumes, posters, slogans, brochures, arti-
facts). I also wanted to learn from her daring, confident, and often humorous handling of adversaries, having followed her career as an active
opponent of violence-inducing pornography with great admiration.

Craft advised us on what to expect, for example, how long we were
likely to spend in jail. As I had to be present at a fund-raising event the
following day to help pay for my travel expenses to Bellingham, I didn't
want to spend more than a night in jail. Craft assured me that I probably
would not.

Craft decided to be our back-up person in this action, and to avoid getting arrested for the 50th time. She was due for another court appearance in Bellingham the following month for disrupting an appalling example of mainstream femicidal pornography entitled *Kill Me Again* by throwing candy at the screen. She wanted to be able to return to California to continue her other work after having already spent 3 months longer than the 2 days she had originally planned to stay in Bellingham. So Craft accompanied us on our adventure, but did not enter the two locations at which we engaged in our cathartic acts of creative destruction.

We started our night of action by destroying some pornographic magazines sold in a local grocery store—Rhea's Market. We wanted to protest the fact that pornography has become so acceptable today that grocery stores all over the United States carry it, making it accessible to any child or youth who enters them.

Remembering a *Hustler* magazine cover that portrayed a naked woman being minced to death in a meat grinder, and the demonstrations against this femicidal image, I took particular pleasure in my first experience of tearing up every copy I could find of that particular woman-hating magazine. Destroying copies of *Penthouse* and *Playboy* was almost as gratifying. Craft had advised us that if we tore up more than $250 worth of pornography between us, we could get charged with a felony, so we tried to restrain our eager hands from exceeding this limit.

A woman was standing alone at a cash register in the middle of the market as we entered just before the 10 P.M. closing time. The sounds of tearing paper and our excited whispers broke the silence. Soon the floor was covered in a sea of pictures of women's body parts. The woman made no effort to stop us, remaining strangely quiet throughout our rip-in. When we figured we were close to becoming felons (by exceeding the $250 limit), we ran out the door to our car, still wondering if she had noticed us. We found out later than she had reported us to the police, who told us that she had described us "to the T." The contrast with the way she and the men at our next action site handled us was striking.

We felt elated by our grocery store action, and, because we had accomplished it so easily, we felt more prepared to take on Ross Rowell's "Adult Shop"—inappropriately called Great Northern Books. Nevertheless, we entered this masturbation service station with considerable trepidation because Bellingham activists consider Rowell to be a dangerous man. Although tearing up some of his massive collection of hardcore magazines ($234 worth, according to the police report) was also a thrilling experience, we became alarmed when he locked us in his store.

O'Connell was particularly frightened because a man called Shelly, an incest perpetrator, child pornography consumer, and regular customer of Rowell's store, had assaulted her when she was demonstrating outside the store a few weeks earlier. So O'Connell started banging on the door, screaming, "Let us oouut! Let us Oooouuut!!" Meanwhile the police had arrived, and were banging on the door shouting, "Let us in! Let us in!!" Bizarrely, Rowell would not admit the police. Radio journalist Neil Clemens was outside the door as well, taping all this commotion for his radio show the next day. (He later received a journalism award for this dramatic program.)

Then Black started running toward the back door. I stood in the middle of the store wondering what to do. I didn't feel a need to escape, but I did not want to be left alone in this masturbation parlor with a bunch of angry men. A Bellingham post office employee, who brought hot meals to Rowell at the store every day, yelled furiously at us for destroying his beloved porn magazines. The atmosphere was highly charged.

When Black started to run for the door, Rowell threw the keys to the post office employee so he could block this potential escape route too. In his race to beat Black to the door, he fell over backwards just as he reached her and the door, then started yelling, "Assault! Assault! I'll have you for assaulting me!"

Before Black could escape, three policemen entered through the back door, and two or three more policemen entered the front door, after it was finally unlocked. Rowell and the "assaulted" man started to tell the police what we had done, and of course the evidence was clear for all to see: wonderful colorful piles of torn up magazines all over the floor. To us, the only beautiful pornography is torn-up pornography—the smaller the pieces, the more beautiful.

One of the policemen started reading our rights to us. "Would you guys *listen*!" another of them remonstrated. "We aren't *guys*," I protested. This only angered them more. Loud sexual sounds continued to emanate from Rowell's X-rated video on the counter as a penis kept vigorously thrusting between a woman's breasts. "Tell that man to turn off that disgusting tape!" O'Connell shouted angrily and repeatedly until Rowell did so. "Have you fully understood your rights?" asked the first policeman, having reached the end at last. "No," I answered, truthfully. "There has been far too much commotion to be able to hear them properly. Please start again," I requested.

By this time Rowell had started videotaping us. "Tell him to stop! Tell him to stop!" screamed O'Connell. She was the only Bellingham resident among the three of us, and she was afraid Rowell's video would make it easier for him to harass her at another time. She also felt our being videotaped in a porn store was sinister and voyeuristic.

Thoroughly exasperated and angry with our small anti-porn brigade, the policeman refused to reread our rights to us. Instead, he and his colleagues pulled out their handcuffs and impatiently cuffed us, then bundled us into separate police cars. I was surprised how uncomfortable it was to sit with my metal-cuffed wrists behind me, unable to lean back on the seat because of the pain it caused.

O'Connell, Black, and I were kept separated on our arrival at Whatcom County jail, read our rights once more, and asked if we would like to make a statement. I took the opportunity to make a little speech about how I believe pornography endangers women's lives, after which "my" policeman's anger and impatience changed to politeness and respect. "I agree with what you say," he commented. "But I have to do my job."

After providing three sets of fingerprints and a list of our belongings, we were rewarded with drab prison uniforms. Three hours after our first exhilarating porn tear-in, Black and I were escorted to a two-room women's cell. We settled on two unoccupied concrete slab-beds wondering when O'Connell would join us. We learned later that she had been released because, as a local resident, the police were not afraid she would skip town.

Devoid of a toothbrush or comb, and feeling too shy to use the only very public toilet that was situated in the cell, I made my bed, lay down on the concrete slab, and slept like a log.

The next day started early. Before I had finished eating my stodgy pancake breakfast, two prison officials insisted on taking my dishes. I had made the mistake of chatting with Black as I ate instead of quietly gobbling up my food. Ah, well, I'll know for next time. Meanwhile, I wondered how long it would be before we were allowed to have such luxuries as toothbrushes and combs.

On calling Craft on the telephone in the corner of our cell, she told me that our noisy lockup in the porn store had already been played on the air, and that some other radio station wanted to have us on a show that afternoon. Then Craft set us to work. With borrowed writing implements, we jotted down Craft's long list of media contacts to call collect (we weren't allowed to call any other way). I found it embarrassing to try to interest the media in our story in earshot of women, many of whom might feel hostile toward our action.

Some of the media representatives we called were unsympathetic. Others were quite intrigued. But to Craft's surprise, none of our efforts led to much. She had thought that the incarceration of a well-known professor–researcher–writer on violence against women would be news in Bellingham. But the newspaper editors in and around this conservative little town had had their fill of Craft and her supporters. They appeared to want us all to go home so they could enjoy their pornography in peace. Except for the two radio programs mentioned, there was virtually no other coverage of our action and our arrests.

Another prisoner in our cell shared her story with us of a shattering life of abuse by men that had landed her in jail. We became so engrossed in it that it was difficult to remember we were not supposed to be enjoying a period of R&R in jail, but continuing with our phone calls. By the time we were escorted to our arraignment on the afternoon of our first day, a few of the other women prisoners had also become more friendly toward us. Still without a comb or toothbrush, we sat with about 30 other prisoners, waiting to hear our fate.

Our public defender had heard me testify in court the previous day. He made it clear that he respected our efforts to protest pornography, and promised to try to get us released in time to participate in a radio program that afternoon. He always addressed me as "Professor," a rare experience even though that is what I had been for 21 years. In contrast, the prosecutor and judge always referred to me as Miss.

Black and I were charged with two counts each of malicious mischief, and Black was also charged with assault. Our trial dates were set for November, then we were released on our own recognizance. By this time the radio program was already underway, and O'Connell was having to handle it alone. But before it ended, the reporter called the jail, and I was able to answer some questions on the air.

When I heard a recording of this program later, I got a taste of the hostility of some Bellingham residents toward us. Many people love to tell us activists what we should be doing for their cause, as if they know better, and as if we are there to do their bidding. Few appear to question why *we*, rather than *they*, should be doing the actions they prefer. Men, in particular, seem to enjoy instructing women activists about superior forms of protest while sitting passively on their backsides.

According to our police report, we had torn up a minimum of $234 worth of magazines at the porn store, although "the possibility exists of higher loss due to the difficulty of matching torn parts." I found it hilarious imagining these policemen trying to piece together the different body parts of the women like a jigsaw puzzle in order to make a more accurate estimate of the total damages we had achieved.

Much to my surprise, I received a letter on November 2 giving me the option of having the charges against me dropped if I would sign a statement declaring that I would not destroy any "non-owned literature" (I assume this was their euphemism for pornography) "for a period of 90 days from the date of the agreement." I was told that O'Connell and Black had signed the statement, so I followed suit.

Comparing what happened to Craft as a result of her destruction of $10.80 worth of *Esquires* with what happened to us despite our far more destructive action shows the arbitrariness of the legal system. O'Connell suggested the following reasons for this unexpected outcome in a letter to me[1]:

1. Gibson [the Prosecutor] really does sympathize with us, and wanted to give us a break." [O'Connell explained that Gibson and some of the policemen "admit that porn plays a huge role in violence against women and are in sympathy with what we're trying to do."]
2. After their ordeal with Craft, they were leery of another such case.
3. Rowell didn't want the case to come to trial and bring him the extra notoriety.
4. Doug Hyldahl, our former Public Defender, is also Shelly's defender. [Shelly is the child molester who had assaulted O'Connell outside Rowell's porn store earlier, and who was being charged with another case of child sexual abuse.] Hyldahl had a conflict of interest and had to decide to either defend us or Shelly. In the process of working out this arrangement, the Prosecutor came up with this deal.

All in all, I found my 2 days in Bellingham fascinating, exhilarating, fun, cathartic, scary at times, but a great learning experience. No doubt there are many factors that account for this, including that I felt willing and prepared for the experience, unlike the nonpolitical jail inmates or the political prisoners who have not engaged in civil disobedience.

I wondered at the trepidation I used to feel about tearing up pornography. It felt so easy once I started. And our action felt so much more rewarding than the many demonstrations and Take Back the Night marches I had participated in. Four women participating in such protests cannot have as much impact as our action did. Civil disobedience is a powerful strategy, and one that feminists must consider doing more often.

Anti-pornography activists are frequently charged with censorship, despite the irony that we are practicing free speech when we express our convictions about the harmful effects of pornography. We resort to tearing up pornography not merely because we consider it misogynist propaganda, but because no one appears to listen to our screams when men act out its woman-hating invitations to violate and abuse us; and because no one listens when we use so-called legitimate channels of protest. We are so appalled and frightened by the violent man-made world in which we are forced to live, that we are willing to go to jail for our beliefs. In tearing up pornography we are merely exercising *our* right to freedom of speech just as those who burn the United States' flag are doing.

And as O'Connell points out, destroying pornography is also an empowering experience that strengthens us. It's a way of fighting back, of refusing to accept that pornography has become acceptable. It also fuels our ability to demand that men must change, and that "patriarchy has got to go"[2] because it is killing us.[3]

Do most people accuse the Anti-Defamation League of censorship when they object to anti-Semitism, or the NAACP when they object to manifestations of racism? No. It is only women who are routinely labelled censors when we protest sexism in pornography and other media. But the *Bellingham Herald* was the real censor in this case, not us. Only 12 lines of text on our action and subsequent arrest were published in this newspaper. Nor had their coverage of the controversy surrounding Craft's acts of civil disobedience in Bellingham been accurate or fair; even Judge Ross stated at Craft's trial that he had obtained an entirely inaccurate picture of her and what she was about from the media.

When Craft complained to *Bellingham Herald* editor Jack Keith about the sparse coverage of our arrest in his newspaper, and expressed her shock that the jailing of an international expert on pornography and violence against women would be totally ignored, he replied: "We get lots of famous people passing through Bellingham." "Well, they're not in your jails!" retorted Craft. In response to her criticism, Keith finally suggested that *I* write a guest editorial for the *Herald* about what happened.

Not only did Keith decline to publish my editorial, but he told me (and Craft) that the *Herald*'s decision makers had elected to put "an embargo" on any further coverage of our actions because the paper had been deluged with letters about the issues raised by such actions for such a long time.

"So you would stop covering cases of death due to drunk drivers if they kept happening for too long a time?" Craft asked Keith. "No," he conceded. But actions by feminists are a whole other kettle of fish in Keith's eyes. We are the enemy, not the misogyny we are attacking.

So, from the time of our arrest onwards, *The Bellingham Herald* blotted out all news and readers' comments about women's anti-sexist activities in Bellingham. Not because of a lack of public interest, but because there appeared to be *too much* interest! Sleepy Bellingham isn't used to being a hot bed of feminist militancy, and the *Herald* doesn't want it to continue to be so — even if it does sell newspapers.

Now *this* is what *I* call censorship!

CHAPTER 23

Torturing Women as Fine Art: Why Some Women and Men Are Boycotting Knopf

Robert Brannon

Enjoy reading fiction? Try to read if you can (skip if you can't) a few passages from a "serious" new American novel from a prestigious publisher, Knopf, a Division of Random House:

> "In my locker in the locker room at Xclusive lay three vaginas I recently sliced out of various women I've attacked in the past week." (Ellis, 1991, p. 370)

> "The mouth opens and not even screams come out anymore, just horrible, guttural, animal-like noises, sometimes interrupted by retching sounds. 'Scream honey,' I urge, 'keep screaming. No one cares, no one will help you . . .' and with the same pair of scissors I cut her tongue out, which I pull easily from her mouth. . . . Blood gushes out of her mouth and I have to hold her head up so she won't choke on it. Then I fuck her in the mouth, and after I've ejaculated and pulled out, I mace her some more." (Ellis, 1991, p. 246)

In case you aren't perceptive, the young male author has explained that this nightmare of women-abuse is "Equal amounts of black comedy and satire of the 1980s." "I used comedy to get at the absolute banality of the violence of a perverse decade," the author told the *New York Times* in April. "Look, it's a very annoying book. But that is how as a writer I took in those years."

Still following the plot? Here then is the story-in-progress of how this unprecedented celebration of sexual violence against women, *American Psycho* from Knopf–Random House, soared to the Best Sellers' list, made a

Slightly edited version of an article published under the same title in *On the Issues*, (1991, Fall), pp. 18–21. Reprinted by permission of the author.

239

few wealthy men a little wealthier, and has finally triggered a national boycott of Knopf, Inc., by people who are saddened and angered by the rising visibility and respectability of real and simulated sexual sadism.

HOW KNOPF EMBRACED TORTURE: THE STORY SO FAR

Several years ago, another large N.Y. publisher, Simon & Schuster, gave a 26-year-old "literary bad-boy" a $300,000 advance, rather unwisely as it turns out, to write a novel. This ivy-educated youth, Bret Ellis, eventually turned in a bizarre first-person account of a rich male yuppie who happens to be unbelievably sadistic in torturing and murdering women. Though there were other themes, and a few other victims (one child, one "bum," one dog), the literally dozens of savagely-detailed, gut-wrenching scenes of sexual tortures and dismemberment of young women were the basic refrain, the "art form" with which the author had chosen to work. So detailed is the narrative ("It takes very few blows, five or six, to smash her jaw open completely and only two more for her face to cave in on itself") that it reads as a how-to manual, with endless variations in raping and torturing women. The story's rich male hero, who also enjoys watching "rape-slasher" movies on his hi-tech VCR, is never apprehended.

An unsolicited manuscript of this nature would have quite certainly been rejected, but a "serious" novel for which a (non-refundable) $300,000 advance had already been paid was apparently a different matter. The assigned editor, Robert Asahina, saw "no major problems" (later citing the large investment) and asked for only a small, "structural" re-write. Division president Charles Hayward also saw nothing problematic here. On the authority of these men, the book was accepted and scheduled for publication. But at a Spring, 1990 company meeting, Asahina had to show a sample chapter to the rest of the staff. In the sample, a woman's breasts were hooked to a high-voltage battery and they exploded and burned; in another sequence, a starving, live rat was stuffed into a woman's vagina. Women employees, seeing the text for the first time, were stunned and horrified.

Xeroxes were leaked to feminist groups, the word spread, and SPY and Time magazines ran advance stories about how misogynist, sadistic, and badly-written the book would be. These caught the attention of Simon & Schuster's Board Chairman, Richard Snyder, who then called for and read the manuscript. On November 14, he announced that Simon & Schuster was exercising its legal right not to publish the manuscript it had earlier accepted and paid for, on the grounds of "taste."

The public explanation was a bit lame, but this was obviously an important decision. Within the company, it was a clear rebuke by corporate leadership to Hayward and Asahina for accepting such a manuscript. More importantly, it was a principled statement from a major publisher that sadistic woman-abuse had no place in serious literature. Women's groups and women in publishing collectively breathed a sigh of relief.

Just 48 hours later, however, *American Psycho* found a new sponsor. "Sonny" Mehta, President of Knopf, Inc., a Division of Random House, announced that Knopf's Vintage division would buy and publish the book. "It seems to me appropriate given the immense coverage and curiosity," said Mehta, "that we bring out *American Psycho*." Mehta had calculated that Knopf could make a nice profit from the "coverage and curiosity." In this decision, Mehta obtained the strong backing of current Random House CEO, Alberto Vitale.

And finally, to underline that Knopf/Vintage was not merely publishing Ellis' work, but actively sponsoring and promoting it, the company announced a five-city author's tour for Ellis to meet the public and read from his book. (Try to picture it: A well-dressed audience nods appreciatively as the tuxedoed author intones: "I slap her hard and hiss 'Dumb bitch,' spraying her face with spit but it's covered with so much mace she probably can't even feel it and so I mace her again and then I try to fuck her in the mouth once more but I can't come so I stop.")

Just two days after Simon & Schuster's announcement that this femicide was too repulsive for mainstream publishing, the decision had been effectively reversed. Mehta, Vitale, and the once-respected Knopf–Random House firm had seen a way to make a windfall profit; Ellis had been rescued from disgrace and handed an (estimated) $75,000 more by Knopf.

WOMEN FIGHT BACK

By early December, a letter to Mehta and Vitale from New York feminist leaders Gloria Steinem, Phyllis Chesler, Andrea Dworkin, Merle Hoffman, Kate Millett, Sidney Abbott and others exploded: "We are appalled by your poor taste, bad judgment, and inability to hear what feminists for at least 20 years have been saying about violence toward women, what causes it, and what it causes in return." And within weeks, from the west coast, Los Angeles National Organization for Women president Tammy Bruce announced a national boycott of all Knopf and Vintage publications.

Ms. Magazine editor Robin Morgan joined the boycott, even though her classic *Sisterhood is Powerful* has sold over half a million copies as a Random House/Vintage book, and is still selling. "I won't buy Random

House titles for the duration of this boycott, and I urge all women, if they want *Sisterhood* to really be powerful, to do the same," she said. (The boycott has now been officially defined to apply to all Knopf and Vintage titles except those few by feminist writers.)

President Molly Yard and other NOW leaders asked for a discussion meeting with Mehta: Mehta refused to speak with them. "Bret inadvertently offended a certain feminist sensibility . . . " Mehta explained to the press. In January, 1991, the National Board of NOW voted that the boycott of Knopf "encourages women and men of conscience to protest the massive and unrelenting violence against women." Additional motions applauding the boycott were passed at the NOW Young Feminist Conference, by New York State NOW, and by other feminist groups. The National Organization for Men Against Sexism has also strongly endorsed the boycott.

A LOOK AT THE ISSUES

While this brief history makes rather clear what the "sides" are, it does not answer a number of important questions that many have about this action. Isn't boycotting a publishing company rather unusual? What is the actual harm in publishing such a book, even if a lot of women don't like it? Here are some questions and answers about some of the deeper issues behind the Knopf boycott.

Torture in a Book Is Not the Same as Torture in Real Life. What's So Bad About Violence Against Women in Fiction? At the most obvious level, choosing to seek out, publish, and sponsor an author's tour on a theme that is clearly and predictably horrifying to more than half the population is hurtful and harmful to those people's feelings. It's a symbolic slap (or mace) in the face to women.

But beyond this, there is growing reason to believe that massive portrayals of sexual violence in "entertainment media" may be a contributing factor to the real and growing incidence of rape and domestic abuse of millions of women.

Rape and other crimes of sex-related violence are now known to be a much more frequent experience of women than was once thought. About one-fourth of all women in the U.S. have been raped, and the rate is apparently increasing. The government believes that 10–15 percent of all women who live with men are experiencing "severe and ongoing" battering; women are more likely to be murdered by their husbands than by other men.

In the past 15 years there has been a great deal of scientific research on the effects, especially on male viewers, of various sexual-and-violence themes in entertainment. The particular type that *American Psycho* most patently resembles (and often mentions in its pages) is the "slasher" (or "snuff") film. The hero asks at one point, "Have you seen 'The Toolbox Murders?' . . . it's really quite good." (This notorious "slasher" features many gruesome rape and murder scenes.) In another place he wants to rush home "to watch the video tape I rented this afternoon called 'Blood-thirsty' . . . Bobo will make you die, then eat your body." The book's deadly superficiality seems borrowed from the porno-snuff-slasher film, with anonymous, X-rated sex leading suddenly, without explanation, to the torture and murder of women.

So, You Believe That a Book Will Cause Women to Be Assaulted? No, the facts above don't necessarily mean that this book will directly cause additional assaults; however, it might. There are often "copy-cat" crimes against women after highly-publicized media portrayals.

The major concern is not that one novel will lead to more abuse in itself, but that it is part of a growing pattern of legitimation and proliferation of "chic" sexual woman-abuse, which has already appeared in fashion photography, Bloomingdale's catalogs, rock videos, movies made for teenagers, general Hollywood movies, and TV soap operas. Serious fiction is simply the latest frontier for this concentrated misogyny, but it's a part of a much, much bigger phenomenon that, taken together, contributes to the epidemic of rape and violence. And Knopf has chosen to jump in and make profits from this tragic situation.

But Didn't Ellis Have the Legal Right to Write Such a Book, and Knopf the Legal Right to Publish It? Absolutely. Ellis has the right to write anything he wishes, and to publish it himself or submit it to a commercial publisher. A publishing company never has to accept, but has a legal right to accept and publish, whatever it chooses. We have no "censorship," or prior regulation by any governmental authority, of what can be published. Knopf violated no laws.

Then Why Try to Punish Knopf, Just for Choosing to Publish It? Companies are responsible to the public for what they do. Publishing companies aren't sacred, they're corporations which exist to make money. Their future decisions will probably be based on the profitability of current decisions. Like other large corporations, such as Exxon and Union Carbide, they should be held accountable by the public if they are harming society. Women and their supporters have an equal right to express their views in the only language that corporations understand: By choosing not to give Knopf their money.

Is It Legal to Boycott a Publishing Company? Of course. A consumer boycott of a company or product is a tried and true, typically American, and totally capitalistic form of expression by consumers. Also, the U.S. Supreme Court has clearly held that boycotts are protected by the First Amendment, as a form of political expression.

Won't All This Backfire and Boost the Sales of the Book? Unfortunately, more of these books will probably be sold because of the controversy. Soon after its release, *American Psycho* hit the *NY Times* Best Seller list. Literary woman-abuse will be profitable, at least in the short term. However, the boycott is of all Knopf products, not just one book. Over the months to come, the boycott will begin to slowly erode the huge profits made on *American Psycho*, and to gradually push the total balance of Mehta's cynical decision into the red.

Can This Boycott Succeed in Changing the Publishing Industry? Perhaps. We must try to do something about the growing popularity and legitimacy of violence against women — to work together as human beings to stop it. In a boycott, time, word of mouth, and publicity become our allies. And, unlike waiting for Congress or the courts to act, a boycott empowers us, as individuals. Many people have felt powerless in recent years to stop the spread and commercial exploitation of sexual violence. We can each resolve for ourselves to not spend our money on books from Knopf and to tell them why.

In my own case, as a college teacher, I discovered that I had been assigning a textbook published by Knopf. The book was quite adequate, but there are good alternatives. Knopf makes a lot of profit from textbooks, and I've probably required 300–400 students to buy this text over the years. So I thought: "I've just joined the Knopf boycott." I will no longer buy or ask others to buy any book published by them, and that feels good. In this way, I'm adding my economic vote to stop the legitimation of sexual violence.

Now, the obvious conclusion. If you want to buy a book, please check first to see that it's not from Knopf or Vintage. Freedom of expression isn't only for corporations; you and I have a right to be heard, too. Let's just say "NO" to Knopf.

CHAPTER 24

There Are Better Ways of Taking Care of Bret Easton Ellis Than Just Censoring Him . . .

Tara Baxter Co-conspiring with Nikki Craft

When Tara Baxter became aware of American Psycho *she was, as any feminist would be, disgusted and furious. Unlike many feminists, she felt compelled to do something about it. After her arrest for reading aloud excerpts from the book (in a bookstore where it was for sale), she collaborated with long-time activist Nikki Craft on the essay which follows.*

Their attempts to get the essay published make an interesting story. The national radical-feminist publication off our backs *was as unwilling to print it as Baxter's home-town women's newspaper* Matrix. *Even the radical British feminist magazine* Trouble and Strife *was uncomfortable with the piece in its entirety (as it appears here) and wanted to make significant cuts.*

In each case, editorial concern focused on the imagery and advocacy of violence by women against men. Editors or collective members suggested that printing it might only "escalate the violence" pandemic among us; one went so far as to call it "hate speech."

There are several points of interest in this situation. First, I note that the passages quoted directly from Ellis's book are far more explicit, gloating, and hateful than Baxter's brief account of castrating a male assailant. If I were an editor, I would have been more concerned with the ethics of reprinting Ellis's hideous vivisection fantasies at such length, and with their impact on my readers. But in every case, it was the imagery of violence against men which aroused editorial caution.

At this time when there is strong pressure on feminists to accept a

Reprinted from *Nemesis: Justice is a Woman with a Sword*, A.C.L.U./Nemesis Publishing Concerns, © 1992. Reprinted by permission of the authors.

simplistic First Amendment position on anti-woman art and media —
when pornographers and other exploitative media moguls are winning
support by conflating their business interests with artistic freedom and
liberalism — it's rare to find a feminist editor or writer willing to take a firm
stand against anything at all. This is why I find Craft and Baxter's difficul-
ties so very intriguing.

There is not one publication or person in a thousand willing to curtail
the "rights" of pornographers (straight, gay, or lesbian) to churn out vio-
lent and exploitative materials by the hundredweight. But there seems to
be a sudden upsurge of moral concern among editors when a woman dares
to write about doing violence to men for feminist reasons, out of violent
political anger.

If Baxter and Craft had written an elaborate "erotic fantasy" about a
cruel dominatrix and her herd of panting male slaves, their work might not
only have seen print by now, but earned them money. Their point, howev-
er, was not to entertain or titillate the reader with a few easy paragraphs of
hot sex and warm blood. This essay is not a diversion, but an inquiry. It
asks us a very disturbing question about justice and vengeance, and wheth-
er women will ever have the first without claiming and exercising the
second.

The very possibility of female rage and revenge is frightening and
shocking to us — more shocking and frightening that any image of female
enslavement, suffering, or death. The oldest and most basic double stan-
dard in the world has kept this essay out of the feminist press. The image of
a woman killing a man — not for his or the reader's obscure sexual satisfac-
tion, but in cold vengeance — is blasphemy. Even those who defend the
worst excesses of pornography as the price of free speech will draw the line,
apparently, right here.

— De Clarke

Like many other people of conscience, I was appalled when I read the
best-selling *American Psycho* by Bret Easton Ellis. It's about a Wall Street
yuppie who, in his spare time, murders, tortures, and mutilates women,
children, animals, homeless people, and homosexuals. But like many other
male media hawks, Ellis reserves his most grisly detail for the recreational
killing of women. It's just another "How-To-Kill-Women" manual for that
ever-growing special interest group: the good ol,' all-Amerikan misogynists. That's entertainment, after all.

Ellis writes: "None of this comes close to killing her, so I resort to
stabbing her in the throat and eventually the blade breaks off in what's left
of her neck. . . . Finally, I saw the entire head off and holding the head up

like a prize. I take my cock and push it into her bloodied mouth and start fucking it until I come, exploding into it . . . " *(Pg 304)*

Ellis' endless psycho-babbling style is self imposing and ego-maniacal. Living and killing vicariously through our protagonist, Patrick Bateman — Ellis is methodical in his description of everything he wore and ate, his stereo equipment, and the music he listened to. With equal attention to detail, he tells us how he skinned alive, fucked, and killed women. Ellis is a pornographer; and this trashy dime-store novel is not worth the paper it's printed on — not worth the trees that gave their lives. For me, and others like me, it was not an entertaining novel. For some, unfortunately, it will be.

Ellis' first two novels were so inept that he needed to write something notably woman-hating to succeed this time. Even Norman Mailer (who parades his woman-hate as much as Ellis does), thinks Ellis is a poor writer. So, just out of curiosity, I ran Ellis' writing through a computer program called the *Flesch Index*, which gauged in his writing at a whopping "high school" level in readability and writing skill. It may be out of vogue to berate neophyte writers for misplaced commas — after all, it might kill their desire to write. But in the case of Ellis' borderline skills, his editors at Vintage would have been best to err on the side of a good grammar manual.

Here's another sample of Ellis' prose: "Her breasts have been chopped off and they look blue and deflated, the nipples a disconcerting shade of brown. Surrounded by dried black blood, they lie, rather delicately, on a china plate I bought at the Pottery Barn on top of the Wurlitzer jukebox in the corner, though I don't remember doing this. I have also shaved all the skin and most of the muscle off her face so that it resembles a skull with a long, flowing mane of blond hair falling from it, which is connected to a full, cold corpse; its eyes are open, the actual eyes hanging out of their sockets by their stalks. Most of her chest is indistinguishable from her neck, which looks like ground up meat, her stomach resembles the eggplant and goat cheese lasagna at II Marlibro or some other kind of dog food, the dominant colors red and white, and brown. A few of her intestines are smeared across one wall and others are smashed up into balls that lie strewn across the glass-top coffee table like long blue snakes, mutant worms. The patches of skin left on her body are blue-gray, the color of tinfoil. Her vagina has discharged a brownish syrupy fluid that smells like a sick animal, as if that rat had been forced back up in there, had been digested or something." *(Pg 344)*

Reading the book gave me the energy and inspiration to protest it. I asserted my own free speech by organizing a protest and "First Amendment Rights Read-In" outside B. Dalton Bookseller in a Santa Cruz shopping mall. After reading a statement about what I think should be done to Bret Easton Ellis, I started quoting the book out loud to a hostile crowd of blurry-eyed shoppers (some teenage boys applauded during the fuck/murder scenes; and others, oblivious, kept on walking). I wanted to appeal to "responsible" Amerikan consumers to let them know that B. Dalton profits off of the rape, torture, and mutilation of women.

And hey, guess what I found out — all these First Amendment yahoos out there get *really* irritated, and even *offended*, when you read the contents of these despicable books to 'em. And guess what else I found out — that free speech (you know, the First Amendment) don't mean much in the capitalists' shopping malls, where leafleting and protesting remains illegal. And guess what else — I got arrested.

In keeping with the stated sardonic values of the A.C.L.U. — that all private property rights infringe on my rights to free speech — I took one step backwards into the B. Dalton store. I continued reading, ignoring the warning from mall security that, if I didn't leave, I would be arrested. After about forty minutes of reading, a police officer showed up and informed me of my arrest. Out of nervousness, I couldn't stop reading that book, until, of course, the officer took it away, handcuffed me, and charged me with Trespassing.

Yeah, sure, the charge against me was Trespassing, but we know that society's real intent was to shut me up (a form of censorship) and to transmogrify me into an obedient and compliant female (yet another form of censorship).

Despite the smile on my face as I was being escorted out of the mall, I was scared as hell. I had never been to jail before — although, I had been waiting since I was thirteen years old to be arrested. At thirteen, I had seen the documentary *Miss or Myth?* about the protests of the Miss California pageant (appropriately dubbed "Myth California"). Ann Simonton's and Nikki Craft's use of civil disobedience in that film piqued my already present, teenage rebellion. When I would express my intention of getting arrested to my mother, she would tell me it would cost her $84 a night for me to stay in Juvenile Hall. She'd ask, "*Why not stay at the Holiday Inn, instead?*" Now, as I get older and wiser, I suspect she was just trying to keep me from beginning a life of crime at a much earlier age.

Because of my strong belief in the media's influence on people's behavior, I am *willing* to be arrested to illustrate my convictions (no pun intended). Because of feminist activists like Nikki Craft and Andrea Dworkin I came to believe at a very early age, in radical retaliation against the patriarchy. Amerikan psychos like Bret Easton Ellis (and all men like him) are an integral part of that patriarchy; and they need to be dealt with in a swift and appropriate manner.

On my way to the Santa Cruz County Jail, my arresting officer struck up a friendly conversation and complimented me on my orderly behavior. Then, amidst obvious routine questions, asked, "Why'd ya do it? What's this book about?" I gave him a brief description of my motives, assuming he wouldn't agree or care to understand. He assured me everything that was said between us was "off the record" (not that that should *ever* be trusted), and if I wanted to make a statement, he would read me my rights. After exercising my voice for so long reading aloud, I wanted to be quiet for awhile. I declined.

Once inside the jail, I was searched and my three layers of protective clothing were taken away from me. (I had on four; I was told it gets cold in jail). Then the questions came at me again. Not routine questions, but the genuinely curious ones. The officers were all surprisingly supportive and even laughed when I removed my "Question Authority" T-shirt. "I wore this shirt just for y'all," I quipped as I was carried away to a holding tank. To my surprise, I had my very own toilet, bench, and phone — that's all.

My (il)legal advisor, Nikki Craft, advised me to "call home" if I got arrested. I immediately phoned her. After singing a beautiful, operatic rendition of "Happy Birthday" for me, she told me how proud she was of my action, that it validated her life's work. I spent the rest of my five-hour stay in the holding tank, empowered by her words. It works both ways. For over twenty years now, Nikki has been urging us to "break any law that discriminates against women, and to ignore any social custom that keeps women in the place of second-class citizens." I had been one of the women who heeded her words. I was glad for what I did; and furthermore, I was glad I wasn't at the Holiday Inn.

I was arrested at 3:30 in the afternoon and released at 8:30 in the evening, just in time to watch the action on the 11 o'clock news. I went home and my mother was great. She joked about changing her last name and having a button made that read: "I am **NOT** Tara Baxter's Mother." We laughed at how absurd the charges were: "*You what?! You were arrested for reading a book out loud in a bookstore?!*" It did seem pretty silly. My fear subsided — momentarily.

The next day, my anxiety returned. After my crime wave was blazed across the front page of the *Santa Cruz Sentinel*, I wanted to hide in my room for several weeks (and I wasn't even grounded). "I WOULD LIKE TO SEE BRET EASTON ELLIS SKINNED AND TORTURED. — Tara Baxter, protester," was the larger-than-life pull quote.

My quote was taken out of context. What I had actually said before that was: "There are better ways of taking care of Bret Easton Ellis than just censoring him. I would much prefer to see him skinned alive, a rat put up his rectum, and his genitals cut off and fried in a frying pan, in front of — not only a live audience — but a video camera as well. These videos can be sold as 'art' and 'free expression' and could be available at every video outlet, library, liquor, and convenience store in the world. We can profit off of Ellis' terror and pain, just as he and bookstores are profiting off the rape, torture, and mutilation of women."

While this is how *I* feel, I knew that not everyone would agree. One local liberal compared me to the Ayatollah Khomeini wanting to have Salman Rushdie killed for his book . . . as if I wielded the power of a world leader.

My arraignment was three weeks later at the Hall of (alleged) Justice. I requested a jury trial, but my assigned public defender advised me to plead "no contest" to one of the charges of Trespassing. (The prosecutor usually adds several extra unjust charges, then kindly offers to drop one for a guilty plea to the other.) The lawyer, allegedly working on my behalf, proffered that if I just accepted the one year of probation the judge would likely offer me, I could walk out of the courtroom a "free woman."

In the next year, there are many laws that I intend to break to express myself politically. Probation asserts debilitating limits on activists committed to civil disobedience. It curtails the political expression of those of us who are always causing legal unrest. In 1854, Elizabeth Cady Stanton expressed a similar sentiment when she asked "What is physical freedom compared with mental bondage?" I informed my public defender that I would not only refuse probation, but I would not *ever* promise to obey the law. In fact, I told him, I would break the law at the first available opportunity. (Which I did.)

I am determined, like Nikki, to remain unrehabilitated — determined, also, to be a multiple offender. I want to offend misogynists over and over again. My legal representative eventually gave up trying to bring me into line, and informed the prosecutor of my plans. The prosecutor and my representative consulted and negotiated with the judge for what seemed like a long time to me. Occasionally, they'd look over at me with raised eyebrows. I enjoyed being an itsy-bitsy wrench in their wheel of injustice. Feeling unrepentant, I read Saul Alinsky's *Rules For Radicals* while I waited.

Finally, the judge called my name. He didn't even offer me probation, knowing that I would refuse it. Instead, he sentenced me to one day in jail with time served for the five hours I had already done. The judge smiled knowingly and said, "Good luck, Ms. Baxter. I trust we won't be seeing you back here anytime soon." I left that courtroom, knowing I'd be back. He knew it too.

At first, I felt I had gotten off real light, but after the fact (we all learn from the doing), I have figured out that if *real* justice had prevailed in that courtroom, I shouldn't have even been convicted (or tried for that matter). Remember, I was arrested for the "crime" of reading a book aloud in a bookstore. Besides, wasn't it Ellis who trespassed onto women's most basic right to live without the constant threat of hate crimes and femicide? Wasn't it Ellis who stomped all over women's autonomy with flagrant disregard for the consequences of his actions?

Since that fateful day, I've continued my work against misogyny-disguised-as-"art"-or-"speech." I've made friendly visits to five different bookstores in San Francisco, pouring blood on every copy of *American Psycho* I could get my hands on, (twenty-seven, to be exact).

I've also paid several not-so-friendly visits to a local Santa Cruz porn store, working with other women to invade male-supremacist space, like the Bellingham chapter of the A.C.L.U. did at their local "masturbation service center." I asserted my free expression by artistically applying white lotion to the video screens located in the private viewing closets — achieving that "Gee, I came on the screen" look. I also doused the video screens and door handles with blood — rendering them untouchable. The A.C.L.U. is committed to working to assure that men experience at least a bit of the fear women do.

One night, at about eleven P.M., I took pictures of men going in and out of the porn store, destroying their privacy and anonymity (just as pornography destroys the privacy of all women) and holding them accountable for their contribution to violence against women.[1] One man, clearly terrified by the fact that I took his picture, came at me, demanding that I give him the film. When I refused, he went off, (half-cocked?), grabbed me by the arm and shoulder and threw me up against the porn store wall. I lost my balance and fell into the brick planter in front of the store. My friend leaped between the man and me, so I could escape.

Three friends of mine, who had gone inside the porn store, immediately came out when they heard me yelling for the guy to back off. He yelled to us, "Oh, you dykes just need a good fuck. That guy up in Montreal killed women just like you bitches . . . " Fortunately, my friends came out of the porn shop just at that moment. I'm lucky that way, sometimes.

When he thought there were only two of us, he was one tough dude; but when he realized we numbered five, he lost his cool. As if in a dream, we slowly moved to form a semi-circle around him. My friends reached for him, quickly now, they grabbed his arms and legs, and threw him back up against the planter. When I heard how hard his head cracked against the wall, I knew this was going to get really intense. I yanked out my Buck knife and slid my thumb to one side of the four-inch long blade. With one quick movement, I flipped my wrist in a downward motion, and the knife slipped willingly from its sheath. One woman scrambled up onto the planter box and positioned her foot across his throat. She glared down, menacingly, at him, "You know, if they laid all the men on earth end to end so they circled the globe . . . " She snarled, at the same time spitting fiercely, "It might be a pretty good idea to leave 'em that way." By that time, he was shaking so hard he wasn't much good to anyone, least of all, himself. He frantically and impotently kicked at us, but with ease, my friend unzipped his pants. I saw two hands grab his dick, pushing the head down hard against the bricks. I, then, sliced it right off. It was a lot easier to do than I had thought it would be. His eyes widened; he gurgled as blood gushed from where his penis was. We even thought he liked it — maybe — like he knew he deserved it.

. . . Well, a bit of good fiction/fantasy never hurt anybody, eh? That's entertainment! In fact, women must begin to dream, to reach into their wildest imaginations to envision what can and should be done to sex offenders, femicidites, and all the misogynists who act out their own hatred against women everywhere, all the time.

So anyway, what *really* happened was this: I yelled for him to back off and he threw me up against the wall. My three friends emerged from the porn shop. He lost his cool. We formed a semi-circle around him. Once again, with a cracking voice, he demanded the film back. Not wanting to escalate or engage with this man anymore than we already had, we all kept quiet, except to let him know we had no intention of meeting his demands.

It was tempting to argue with this jerk (who, ironically, looked just like the boutique store clerk from "A Question of Silence"), but even if he was capable of *understanding*, we knew that he would never *agree* with our position. Moments (and I do mean moments) later, we left. Afterwards, one woman in our group said, "Hey, you know when that guy was begging for his picture? It would have been funny to say, 'Just give us your name and address and we'll send it to ya.'" We all laughed — even me; but my mind was still full of the assault I had just experienced.

At 18 years old, I can understand what Andrea Dworkin means when she says, women are living in a war zone. We get it when we fight back, and we get it when we don't. I'm sick and tired of hearing about women being hurt and victimized. I'm sick of women — living like hostages or victims of the Stockholm syndrome — turning the violence and the self-loathing back onto ourselves, and collaborating with the enemy.

Resistance — resistance (not visualization) of all kinds (don't listen to Sonia on this point[1]) — sends a strong message back to these men: an assertion that women will not tolerate their rapacious ways. The limits of tyrants are prescribed by the endurance of those whom they oppress . . . etc., etc. It's like the raunchy, male-bashing, feminist rappers, *Bytches With Problems*' Lyndah — The Teacher who belts out: "No means No, my brother. Are you deaf in your ear, mother fucker?" And as for the men like Bret Easton Ellis who don't get that message loud and clear . . .

I have been involved in self-defense for almost two years now, and have co-taught classes for a year. My experience has shown me that women must have access to every option available, including all forms of weaponry. For without access to *all* our options, we can't ever have real choice. And it's ever so important that when we finally get wise to what's happening, that some of us become shit-kickin', rabble-rousing, trouble-makers: Thelma and Louise-style.

In my classes, women always ask, terrified, "Well, what if the rapist has a knife?" I think it's long past time that *rapists* start worrying about whether or not a woman has a gun — or at the very least, about a woman's willingness and ability to do some serious damage to any man who fucks with her space.

As long as women are being raped, tortured, and murdered at the rate that we are, it is imperative that we seriously consider all the strategies that decorticate male dominance. One strategy, is refusing to accept violent, exploitative male fantasy wherever it may be expressed — whether in fiction, art, pornography, in the public sphere, or in our homes. Otherwise we collaborate in our own victimization by remaining silent during this war that men are waging against us.

The A.C.L.U. is committed to the concept that we must fight back together, so we won't be attacked alone. We advocate relentless resistance — of all kinds. Furthermore, we urge women to do more than visualize about how to do grave damage to any batterers, rapists, killers and/or child abusers who are within their arms reach.

If we, women, are to survive as a species, we must learn to fight back, and that means fighting back by any means necessary. Yes, there are more ways than one to skin Bret Easton Ellis, and men like him . . .

CHAPTER 25

From Witches to Bitches: Sexual Terrorism Begets Thelma and Louise

Diana E. H. Russell

"While women who stepped out of line in early modern Europe were tortured and killed as witches, today such women are re- garded as cunts or bitches, deserving whatever happens to them."
—Jane Caputi and Diana Russell, 1990

"We're not disrespecting women, we're disrespecting bitches."
—Easy E of N.W.A. (Niggas With Attitude), 1990

"Why is it wrong to get rid of some fuckin' cunts?"
—Kenneth Bianchi, 1981[1]

A cover feature of the December 1990 issue of *Hustler* magazine offers this advice:

> If you are going to gouge out an eye, do it slowly, taking care not to damage the optic nerve. Then you can leave the eyeball hanging on his cheek, still functioning. His brain will still receive the visual information, but he will be unable to turn away or close his eyelids as, for example, you mutilate his genitals. (Parfrey, 1990)

On the evening of October 22, 1990, the day that the December issue of *Hustler* magazine appeared on the racks in Norman, Oklahoma, a 10-year-old boy "was walking home from school through a wooded park, when he was approached by a man who said he was searching for his lost dog. The boy ran and hid behind a fallen tree, according to police, but the man found him and attacked him" (Montgomery, 1990).

Journalist Rick Montgomery reported that the way in which the brutal attack was carried out had been "spelled out in bold type on the first page" of the *Hustler* article. The boy's "right eye was stabbed and his genitals were slashed," and his eye had to be surgically removed.

The day after the assault, Norman police officers "contacted all merchants in the area who sold the issue" to express concern about the "inappropriateness" of the article. Most convenience store merchants removed *Hustler* from their shelves, along with all other so-called adult magazines. Merchants were "advised by police to read the magazine and decide for themselves whether to sell it or throw it away." Most voluntarily removed the issue.

Glaring examples of people imitating scenarios described or pictured in men's magazines capture public attention from time to time. The vast majority involve women. Feminist psychologist and anti-pornography activist Melissa Farley (1992) has described a series of nine photographs eroticizing violence against Asian women in the December 1984 issue of *Penthouse* (Ishigaki, 1984). In several pictures the women are bound tightly with heavy ropes cutting into their ankles, wrists, labias, and buttocks. Two of the photographs show clothed women bound and hanging from trees, heads lolling forward, apparently dead. In another photo a naked adolescent girl is pictured without pubic hair, permitting the viewer to see how tightly the rope cuts into her genitals. Two other photos feature bound women dumped on rocky cliffs, limp and dead, their genitals displayed. These photographs are accompanied by arty haiku "poems" exalting dominance and submission, a theme grotesquely illustrated by the eroticized torture and murder of these women.[2]

On the morning of January 30, 1985, a month after this December issue of *Penthouse* appeared on the stands, Jean Kar-Har Fewel, an 8-year-old Asian girl, was found dead, strung up in a tree in Chapel Hill, North Carolina. Some feminists, immediately perceiving a connection between Jean's murder and one of the pictures in *Penthouse*'s Asian bondage photo series, started protesting against this magazine. The alibi given by the man who was finally convicted of murdering the little girl was that he was reading pornography at the "adult" bookstore in Durham, North Carolina, at the time of her abduction. Cookie Tier, a feminist organizer then living in Durham, told me that this particular pornography store carried Asian bondage material prior to the murder (personal communication, January 12, 1991).

Two years earlier, *Hustler* magazine published a photo story of a woman being gang raped on a pool table (1983). The text described the victim being penetrated by pool cues as well as by penises. Shortly afterwards, a woman was gang raped in a bar in New Bedford, Massachusetts. At the trial, the victim was blamed for her rape because she had voluntarily entered the bar alone late at night. This typical, sexist defense strategy (which the nation witnessed again in the William Kennedy Smith rape case in Palm Beach, Florida, in 1991) was exceeded in its outrageousness only by the protests organized by the Portuguese community in defense of the rapists, who were members of their community. Over 10,000 demonstrators protested that the defendants were being treated in a racist manner (Clendinen, 1984).

The New York-based Women Against Pornography charged *Hustler* with responsibility for the New Bedford gang rape. WAP argued that *Hustler* owner Larry Flynt's publication of the pool table gang rape story merely to entertain and sexually excite his male readers very likely led to the New Bedford rape. Moreover, they attacked *Hustler* for routinely glorifying sexual violence against women.

Flynt responded by publishing a postcard of a nude woman on a pool table welcoming people to New Bedford, described as "the gang-rape capital of America" (*Hustler*, 1983). In New Bedford, the victim was also attacked by an entire community for pressing charges against her rapists. When four of the six indicted men were found guilty of aggravated rape (the other two were acquitted because "neither man assaulted the victim, although they cheered and yelled encouragement to the others," one woman said of the victim, "They should hang her" (Clendinen, 1984, p. A14).[3] The crowd of more than 300 largely Portuguese Americans cheered the defendants as they exited the court. One of them yelled, "She should have been home in the first place" (Clendinen, 1984, p. A14). The rape victim felt she and her children had to leave the area where her friends and extended family lived because she feared for her life. The New Bedford rape victim is believed to have subsequently committed suicide (Cookie Tier, personal communication, January 12, 1991). It is common for rape victims to feel raped again by the male-biased system of justice. In this case, she was also re-victimized by an entire community.

When copy-cat rapes or other crimes occur, media commentators invariably dismiss them as anecdotal evidence of a connection between pornography and violence against women, and therefore irrelevant to the debate about causation. The media generally insists they cannot be blamed for exercising constitutionally protected free speech, arguing that copy-cat rapists, killers, and the like must have been predisposed to commit such crimes. Even were this to be true, research shows that a majority of men in the United States are predisposed to be violent toward women,[4] so this claim is cool comfort indeed.

While I think it would have a chilling effect on freedom of speech to hold the media responsible for such copy-cat crimes in all cases, I think a distinction should be made between media that portray hate crimes to entertain and sexually arouse viewers, and media that portray hate crimes for other purposes (e.g., news, education) and that do not endorse or recommend the hate crimes.

No, I am not proposing censorship. I favor the policy proposed by MacKinnon and Dworkin in which victims of pornography (and all media, I would add) that portrays hate crimes merely to entertain and sexually arouse the viewers should be able to sue those responsible for any harm that results from this experience. But the media that portrays pornography and other hate crimes in order to educate viewers should not be held legally accountable, even when copy-cat crimes occur.

For example, after watching the TV version of "The Burning Bed," a male viewer reacted by setting his wife on fire. Because this movie was made and shown for educational purposes (as well as for entertainment), the TV station on which it appeared should not be held legally responsible for this crime. However, if a man had set fire to a woman after viewing a movie in which a man was portrayed as perpetrating such an atrocity simply to sexually excite viewers, I think the victim and/or her family should be able to sue those responsible for damages. Although people's motivation is often difficult to ascertain, this would be the task of the court, just as it is the court's task for other crimes for which motivation is a salient criterion.

THE ROLE OF PORNOGRAPHY IN THE CONTEMPORARY EPIDEMIC OF VIOLENCE AGAINST WOMEN

Data from my interviews with a probability sample of 930 adult women in San Francisco in 1978 revealed an alarming increase in the rape rate. While 44% of the women in this sample were victimized by rape and/ or attempted rape, this percentage rose to 59% for women between 30 and 39 years old, and to 53% for women between 18 and 29 years old. In contrast, "only" 22% of the 60 an older cohort of women reported such an experience (Russell, 1984).

It is evident, then, that rape is escalating at an alarming rate. Although no sound statistics are yet available on the rate of misogynist murders of women — or *femicides*[5] — it seems clear that serial femicides have increased dramatically over the last 25 years (Caputi, 1987, p. 1).

In Chapter 14, I presented a model and considerable empirical evidence that pornography can, and does, cause rape. But there are many other factors that also play a causal role in rape (for example, male sexual and sex role socialization, experiences of child sexual abuse in boyhood, male peer pressure). Similarly, other factors besides the increasing violence against, and degradation of, women in pornography also play a causal role in the contemporary escalation in rape and femicide, for example, the easy availability of guns, and the increasingly lethal types of guns that men have access to.

In recent years, men's power has been challenged by a rising tide of feminism and by increasing numbers of women entering the work force. Many men have responded to these trends by trying to force women out of the work force, sexually harassing them into a subordinate role. Anger at women's increasing refusal to allow men to remain on their pedestals and their growing unwillingness to place mens' needs above their own, inflames many men into lashing out at women in violent ways.

As well as this increase in sexual violence against women, I cited studies in Chapter 14 showing that portrayals of violence against women in pornography have also increased. What explains this? The content in pornography is shaped by men's needs and desires. And their needs and desires in a patriarchal society are to maintain power over women. Seeing women disempowered and subject to male control in pornography and other media can provide a source of sexual gratification to some men. At the same time, pornography can undermine male inhibitions against acting out the rage they feel toward women. Remember Dolf Zillmann's finding that viewing pornography decreases men's support for women's liberation and notions of equality in interpersonal relationships between the sexes (see Chapter 14).

Men are no different from any other ruling class in resisting any threat to their monopoly of power. Just as the whites in South Africa have repeatedly lashed out at black people who undermine the racially based power structure, so have men reacted to women's efforts at liberation. Ironically, as more women succeed in gaining access to power and money, increasing numbers of men are becoming even more violent toward women — although not necessarily toward the particular women who gain this access.

In summary, I am suggesting that there is an interactive causal relationship between pornography and men's desire to maintain their power in society, in their families, and in interpersonal relationships. Men's wrath at what they perceive as women's challenges to their power appears to have whetted the appetites of some for more vicious portrayals of violence against women in the media (pornography and mainstream media). Media violence also justifies and encourages increasingly brutal acts of violence against women outside the pornography industry. Law enforcement officials have noted a growing viciousness in slayings of women. Justice Department official Robert Heck reported, "We've got people [sic] now killing 20 and 30 people [sic] and more, and some of them just don't kill.[6] They torture their victims in terrible ways and mutilate them before they kill them" (Caputi, 1987, p. 2).

Atrocities against women are joked about and rendered normal fantasy fare: from comic books to Nobel prize-winning literature, from best-selling books to box-office smashes, from award-winning photography to highly acclaimed art, from expensive ad campaigns to prime-time TV movies, from popular computer games to phone-in sex, from so-called soft-core pornography such as *Playboy* and *Penthouse* to more hard-core materials like *Hustler* and the millions of magazines sold in porn stores.[7] The picture of the raped and murdered corpse of the dead woman heroine of "Twin Peaks" (a short-lived, but popular, TV series) was selected for the cover of *Esquire's* June 1990 issue. A handsome man is pictured leaning over to kiss the lipstick covered lips of a glamorized corpse, on whose face the title, "Savage Tales of Love," appears in large letters. Then there is Bret Ellis' best selling femicidal novel, *American Psycho* (1990), described by Robert Brannon in Chapter 23, and Tara Baxter and Nikki Craft in Chapter 24. As intolerable as Ellis' book is, *San Francisco Chronicle* book review editor Pat Holt points out that this kind of lurid celebration of misogynist violence has, in the last decades, "emerged with increasing regularity in commercial fiction" (1990). She cites the following examples:

> William Caunitz's first novel, *One Police Plaza*, begins with the blood-encrusted maggot-filled but otherwise beautiful body of a young woman who has been raped repeatedly with a curtain rod that cut apart her viscera until she died.
>
> In Thomas Harris' *The Silence of the Lambs*, the protagonist not only kills, guts and skins his female victims, but he also puts on their skins like coats to wear around the house.

The movie version of *The Silence of the Lambs* won the Best Picture Oscar in 1991, as well as numerous other awards and accolades.

Holt observes that, as in pornography, these lucrative women slashing books feature beautiful young women as their victims (Holt, 1990). Perhaps the only really unusual thing about *American Psycho* is that woman-hating violence has finally aroused some opposition. The National Organization for Women initiated a boycott of Knopf (see Chapter 23) which was publicly supported by nine prominent feminist authors, including Gloria Steinem and Kate Millett. In their letter of support, these authors point out that the president of Knopf, "would not have been so quick to buy the spoils of Simon & Schuster if the book's protagonist had dismembered and tortured a black, Jewish or Indian man" (Venant, 1990).

THE BEST OF TIMES, AND THE WORST OF TIMES

Prior to the Nazi holocaust, Jews in Germany had appeared to be more integrated into the gentile population than in most other European countries. Similarly, women in the United States today are considered to be better integrated into the economy with more occupational choices and greater individual and sexual freedom than ever before. Yet, as Jane Caputi has pointed out, we are living in a period in which women are the targets of an unrecognized reign of terror, comparable in magnitude, intensity, and intent to the persecution and annihilation of witches from the 14th to the 17th centuries (1987, p. 117).

Just as it was so much easier for American soldiers to rape or kill a "gook" or a "slope" during the Vietnam war, it is so much easier for men to rape or kill a "cunt," a "bitch" or a "whore" than a human being. A major role of pornography — much of it nonviolent — is to reduce women to cunts. Page after page of photographs in millions of pornography magazines sold daily throughout the United States focuses on this part of women's anatomy. Peter Sutcliffe, England's "Yorkshire Ripper," described his crimes as follows: "The women I killed were filth, bastard prostitutes who were just standing around littering the streets. I was just cleaning the place up a bit" (Caputi, 1987, p. 33).

Unlike the Jews in Nazi Germany, modern women are not being sent to death camps or exterminated in ovens. But women and girls — in the United States in particular — *are* being tortured in large numbers (rape certainly is a form of torture), and slaughtered in large numbers, sometimes after years of persecution by their husbands or boyfriends, or after enduring excruciating pain at the hands of unrelated kidnappers. Sometimes they are abruptly eliminated by a man who regards killing a woman as an insignificant act. For example, one rapist–murderer explained stabbing a woman 21 times: "I was thinking . . . I've killed two. I might as well kill this one too . . . " (Ressler, Burgess, & Douglas, 1988, p. 129). Sometimes women are massacred and dismembered by men who then sexually violate their corpses.

Some people might wonder if it is possible that gynocide could remain an unrecognized phenomenon at the time of its occurrence. Denial that the slaughter of women bears any relationship to gender is routine. The experts invariable dismiss the killing of women by men as the senseless acts of madmen, even when the killers (like Montreal murderer Mark Lepine, for example) clearly state that they are motivated by their hatred of women (Caputi & Russell, 1990). We now know the extent to which the Nazi holocaust was denied by most Germans while it was happening under their very noses, and it was also denied by the citizens and governments of the allied nations. Indeed, it is still being denied by many people today.

Although rape, torture, and murder of women has not quite been institutionalized in the United States, these forms of violence have been institutionalized in the media. Men in the United States are increasingly exposed to such images in pornography, many young boys from early childhood. Of course the media would not manufacture such images if ratings declined and/or sponsors withdrew support. But sexually violent images sell; they are an integral part of the multi-billion dollar propaganda machine. By pimping such images, the media promotes misogynistic attitudes and behavior. Watching movies of females being raped, tortured, and killed is now a favorite leisure activity for many Americans, particularly for teenagers.

A brochure advertising an R-rated movie featuring selected clips from favorite pornographic movies, contained the following inducement: "See bloodthirsty butchers, killer drillers, crazed cannibals, zonked zombies, hemoglobin horrors, plasmatic perverts and sadistic slayers slash, strangle, mangle, and mutilate bare breasted beauties in bondage" (Donnerstein, 1983). It is no wonder that sex killer experts Robert Ressler, Ann Burgess, and John Douglas have noted that: "These men learn early that they can get away with violent behavior. In essence they see nothing wrong with what they are doing. Many of them emphasize that they are doing exactly what everyone else thinks of doing" (1988, p. 40).[8]

An FBI study of 36 serial sex killers found that 81% of them ranked pornography as the highest of many possible sexual interests (Ressler et al., 1988, p. 25). Such notorious sex killers as Edmund Kemper (the "Coed Killer"), Ted Bundy, David Berkowitz (the "Son of Sam"), and Kenneth Bianchi and Angelo Buono (the "Hillside Stranglers") were all heavy pornography consumers (Caputi, 1987). Bundy maintained that pornography "had an impact on me that was just so central to the development of the violent behavior that I engaged in" (Dobson, 1989). Despite the widespread skepticism that greeted Bundy's statement on the eve of his execution, his assessment of the role pornography played in his sexual femicides is consistent with the testimony of many other sex offenders. Indeed, he also made the point that he had met many men "who were motivated to commit violence just like me. And without exception, every one of them was deeply involved in pornography . . . deeply influenced and consumed by an addiction to pornography" (Dobson, 1989).

DESENSITIZATION TO VIOLENCE AGAINST WOMEN

The role pornography plays in fostering males' desensitization to rape is a very serious one. Desensitized men are more likely to act out their rape desires. Moreover, the omnipresence of female "victims" as entertainment means that women rape victims (close to one woman in two in San Francisco) (Russell, 1984) have to live with increasingly insensitive reactions to their trauma, as well as well-founded fears of repeated assaults.

As already noted, Zillmann's research led him to conclude that, "heavy consumption of common forms of pornography fosters an appetite for stronger materials" (1985, p. 127). And like narcotics, the stimuli must be made more and more extreme for the violence to arouse the audience. Consequently, what was considered hard-core in the past has become soft-core in the present.

Pornography (hard-core and soft-core) and mainstream media are highly interrelated and influenced by each other. Since R-rated woman-slashing movies tend to portray even more violence than most X-rated pornographic movies, such R-rated material may well influence hard-core pornography and mainstream media to become more violent, while hard-core pornographic movies will likely play a role in making more and more explicit sex acceptable in the mainstream media. And as sex and violence become increasingly merged in the media, this fusion will likely have an ever greater impact on men's sexually assaultive behavior.

DEMOLISHING THE ANTI-PORNOGRAPHY-EQUALS-CENSORSHIP ASSUMPTION

The word "censorship" is hurled at us like a curse no matter what feminist anti-pornography activists do to protest pornography, and no matter how wildly inaccurate it is. This accusation skillfully manipulates public sentiment in an effort to silence us, an effort that has met with considerable success. This is a favorite strategy of the pornographers, the liberal establishment, and some feminists as well — evidence that anti-pornography feminists have been a significant obstacle to this multi-billion-dollar business. Hugh Hefner's memo to *Playboy* staff members, quoted in an epigraph for Chapter 1, calls feminists the "enemy." (The amusing side of this is that Hugh's daughter Christie Hefner, who runs *Playboy*, also calls herself a feminist.) And, as previously mentioned, Larry Flynt has used *Hustler* to attack well-known anti-pornography feminists Andrea Dworkin, Gloria Steinem, Susan Brownmiller, and Dorchen Leidholdt in the form of grotesque cartoons or full-page "Most Wanted" notices like those the FBI publishes for criminals.

Those of us who are not directly attacked by the pornographers are often silenced by pornography itself, contributing as it does to our being beaten and bullied and raped and sometimes even killed. All this represents an atrocious denial of *our rights*: rights to free speech, to assemble (because we cannot go out at night or even in daylight in some areas), to health and happiness, to safety, indeed, our very right to go on breathing. Why are the fundamental rights of women subordinate to men's rights to entertainment? According to Dworkin and MacKinnon it's because: "The pornographers have convinced many that their freedom is everyone's freedom" (Allen, 1985, p. 1).

This is not to denigrate the importance of the question of free speech. But "censorship," says Catharine MacKinnon, "is an exercise of *government* power to prevent the free expression of ideas" (Mancusi, 1985, p. A17). Although a few feminists have supported the banning of certain forms of pornography, the vast majority have never recommended government censorship. Those feminists who testified before the Attorney General's Commission on Pornography presented evidence on the profound danger that pornography poses for women, not on why pornography should be censored. Some of us recommended to the Commission (I, for one) the well-known proposal made by MacKinnon and Dworkin that victims of pornography be allowed to sue the pornographers for any harm done to them by the pornography. Once again, erroneous accusations of censorship are slung at those who support this simple attempt at protecting women's rights (Censorship . . . , 1984, p. D16).

WHAT TO DO AND NOT TO DO

Because we now live in a pornographic culture, and because we now know that exposure to pornography leads to a greater acceptance of such materials (see Zillmann & Bryant, 1984), it is no wonder that our anti-pornography movement in the United States is at a very low point. Several groups have died, including San Francisco-based Women Against Violence in Pornography and Media (the first feminist anti-pornography group in the United States), and the Minneapolis-based Organizing Against Pornography, among others.

The women's movement has been working to combat rape since the early 1970s. But rape has been increasing dramatically during this period, as well as during the decades before (Russell, 1984). We have to recognize the stunning failure in our rape prevention efforts. But what headway can we expect to make as long as there is a multi-billion dollar pornography industry promoting the idea that rape is an entertaining, self-fulfilling, masculinity-enhancing act with no negative consequences for men, an act that women deserve and secretly even enjoy? The answer is that we should expect to make no headway whatsoever.

Despite the numerous rigorous and replicated studies now available in the United States that show the harmful effects of pornography—particularly on women—the claim is repeatedly made that all the studies are inconclusive. This is because a society's response to scientific findings depends on politics, not on the validity of research. Just as the pro-tobacco lobby continues to maintain that there is no solid proof that smoking causes lung cancer, so much larger forces in this country make the equivalent claim for pornography. We saw the power of this pro-pornography public relations campaign swing into operation in 1986 after the Attorney General's Commission on Pornography concluded that pornography is harmful, particularly to women (see Chapter 1). Those who were hired to ridicule this conclusion likely had no idea how to even evaluate the research they were ridiculing. They knew that the validity of the research was not what mattered. Successfully manipulating public opinion did. So they simply made it appear that all the Commissioners were right-wing, religious fanatics, and dismissed the research as inconclusive. Shockingly, the best-known researchers did not contradict this view (see Chapter 15 for a detailed documentation of this statement).

So, we cannot deceive ourselves that more definitive research verifying the harmful effects of pornography will break through the wall of many men's self-interested attachment to material that denigrates women, particularly at a moment in history when men feel threatened by women's rejection of their traditional subservient role.[9] If so many males were not blinded by their attachment to pornography, many might come to view it differently after simply listening to the survivors of pornography speak about how they have been hurt by its manufacture and/or by men who consume it. For those who are unable to listen to women or to believe us, mere logical consistency should suffice in order to recognize the harm. Progressive people accept that racist, anti-Semitic, and homophobic propaganda promote racism, anti-Semitism, and homophobia. Why then would sexualized bigotry be harmless, even cathartic?

It makes absolutely no sense that the easy availability and widespread acceptability of photographed women-abuse — including acts that constitute sex crimes — would lower the rate of sex crimes. This is as absurd as believing that blanketing cities with photographs of people enjoying and simulating enjoyment in snorting coke and smoking crack, and suffering no ill effects, could lower the rate at which these drugs are consumed.

Quite aside from the relationship between pornography and violence against women, we also now know that pornography undermines the goals of the women's movement not only by fostering sex role stereotypes, but by turning people against the movement itself (Zillmann & Jennings, 1984, p. 134). This is true for both male and female subjects. Knowing the results of this one experiment should turn every feminist into a rabid anti-pornography activist as it is clear that we have been overwhelmed by the success of the anti-woman propaganda directed at undermining our struggle for a society free of sexual violence.

One of the functions of pornography is to boost the male ego when it is under attack. Another function is to foster misogyny so that men will make more efforts to keep women from gaining power both in personal relationships and in society at large. The answer to the question, "What is to be done?" is that women must become much more militant in our attacks on pornography and mainstream media's violence against women, as well as on all other manifestations of sexism. I believe that we will not progress in our struggle to stop rape, other violent sexual assault, and child sexual abuse, as long as we ignore the fact that pornography continues to foster and sanction the reign of terror women live under.

If a lot more women were to start engaging in civil disobedience, I believe we would discover that there is a great deal we can accomplish, despite the hideously reactionary period we are suffering through in 1992. Consider how much Nikki Craft—one dedicated woman—has achieved during her years of radical activism. Think about all the creative political work she inspired during a relatively short stay in Bellingham, Washington, in 1990. Craft manages to persuade feminists that direct action is a viable tool. Santa Cruz, where she lived for many years, will never be the way it was BC—before Craft—particularly while Ann Simonton continues to engage in the same kind of creative and militant activism there.

Many women in the movements for civil rights, peace, and animal rights engage (or have engaged) in civil disobedience—together with male participants. However, only a small minority of women have employed this strategy as feminists. In the "Take Back the Night" marches in which I have participated recently, I sense a growing feminist rage. I hope some of this rage will be channelled into civil disobedience, and I also hope that pornography will be one of the major targets. One practical advantage of attacking pornography is its visibility. Pornography is much easier to target than rape or child sexual abuse, for example. There are all those movie houses, video stores, porn districts, vending machines, grocery stores, magazines, books, ads, computer games, and so on, where pornography can be seen, and attacked.

In my book, *Exposing Nuclear Phallacies* (1989), I argue that civil disobedience may have lost some appeal as an effective strategy because the victories of the Civil Rights movement in this country seemed so short-lived and insufficient. But the struggle of women opposed to sexism has some advantages over that movement. When minority men and women engaged in civil disobedience, the goodwill of the white majority determined whether or not their demands were met. But this goodwill often did not exist. In contrast, women from all classes and ethnic groups not only constitute a majority of the population, but we are integrated into the male world, particularly in the family, so we cannot be isolated or ghettoized the same way members of minority groups have been.

Sonia Johnson, whose past actions include chaining herself to the White House fence, observed that each woman who had participated in civil disobedience was "euphoric" and "high with admiration for herself" as a result (1987, p. 21). This was my experience when I was arrested for tearing up pornography in Bellingham, Washington (see Chapter 22). Johnson describes the effects of a civil disobedience high experienced by a group of activists: "They all felt bigger and nobler, capable of so much more than they had thought. Each had caught a glimpse of her true stature and was ready to grow into it as fast as possible" (1987, p. 21). Because women have been socialized to obey the law and to obey men, practicing civil disobedience can be exceedingly liberating.

But just as there came a point in the South African liberation struggle when the African National Congress found it necessary to embrace violent resistance, so some women in the United States believe that the time for nonviolent resistance is over. Baxter and Craft's article on what they would like to do to Bret Easton Ellis (see Chapter 24) exemplifies the growing interest of some women in fighting back against male violence with violence.

Women have been "turning the other cheek" for centuries. This nonviolent response has failed to stop or reduce the continuing escalation and increasing savagery of male violence against women. Growing numbers of women are questioning the widely held belief that violence breeds violence, and, in particular, that "female violence . . . will only escalate male violence" (Clarke, 1992a). One Craft-made button reads, "Men don't take us seriously because they're not physically afraid of us." D. A. Clarke expresses the same idea as follows, "Men commit the most outrageous harassments and insults against women simply *because they can get away with it*: they know they will not get hurt for saying and doing things that, between two men, would quickly lead to a fist fight or a stabbing. There are no consequences for abusing women" (1992a). It follows from this view that, "If the risk involved in attacking a woman were greater, there might be fewer attacks" (Clarke, 1992a).

Janice Raymond points out that, "Women are expected to react and pick up the pieces of violence against women but not to act offensively" (1990, p. 5). The rape crisis centers and battered women's shelters are consistent with this tradition. Raymond notes that after Marc Lepine assassinated 14 women in Montreal, no one appeared to worry that women might retaliate: "National, religious, racial, and ethnic terrorism generates public expectation of reprisals, but not gender terrorism" (1990, p. 5).

The film *Thelma and Louise* touched a nerve in many women throughout the nation. This may be the first time that a mainstream movie has shown an ordinary woman shooting the would-be rapist of her friend, and many of us loved it, as well as the other acts of violence of these two women. It resonated with the gut feelings of many women that violent resistance to male violence has become warranted. "Protected by Thelma and Louise," reads another Craft-made button, displaying a picture of these two movie heroines with their guns drawn. "Thelma and Louise Live," reads another.

Articles on women buying guns and learning to use them have been appearing in newspapers (e.g., Hagar, 1992). Craft and Baxter have started manufacturing buttons with messages on them like, "Dead Men Don't Rape;" "So Many Men, So Little Ammunition;" "Men and Women Were Created Equal, and Smith and Wesson [a kind of gun] Make Damn Sure It Stays That Way;" "How Dare You Assume I'm Non-Violent;" "Stop Sucking; Start Biting;" "Feminine Protection," accompanied by a picture of a gun; "Dead Men Don't Use Pornography;" "The Best Way to a Man's Heart Is Through His Chest," also accompanied by a picture of a gun; "Visualize Yourself Blowing Up a Porn Store;" "When Justice Is Gone — There's Always Force;" "If You Misuse It . . . You Should Lose It;" "Cut It Out, or We'll Cut It Off;" "Batterers Beware! The Woman at Your Feet Today Will Be at Your Throat Tomorrow;" "If I Could Get Away with Murder, I'd Get My Gun and Commit It."[8]

In a speech commemorating the victims of Marc Lepine, Andrea Dworkin told her audience, "Like many women, I have a long history of violence against me, and I say, to my increasing shame, that anyone who has hurt me is still walking around" (1991). She goes on to say that women have to take public power away from men, and "If we have to fight back with arms, then we have to fight back with arms" (1991). In her novel *Mercy* (1990), Dworkin's character Andrea, after years of victimization by men, articulated what she referred to as "a political principle" that went as follows: "It is very important for women to kill men." When Dworkin did a reading from *Mercy* at a Berkeley bookstore on September 21, 1991, I was struck by the empathetic rage of the mostly female audience in response to passages supportive of women's violence against men, whether or not the violence was in self-defense. At the end of Dworkin's reading, a woman ripped up a copy of *Penthouse* that a male member of the audience was conspicuously brandishing about. Then a second woman delivered a hard kick to his butt that sent him sprawling across the bookstore floor.

Does this incident shock the reader? It didn't seem to shock the women in the bookstore. But Clarke notes that:

> The very possibility of female rage and revenge is frightening and shocking to us — more shocking and frightening than any image of female enslavement, suffering, or death. . . . The image of a woman killing a man — not for his or

the reader's obscure sexual satisfaction, but in cold vengeance – is blasphemy. Even those who defend the worst excesses of pornography as the price of free speech will draw the line, apparently, right here. (1992b)

Clarke wrote these words in reaction to three feminist publications' refusal to publish the article by Baxter and Craft attacking Bret Ellis included in this volume: *Off Our Backs, Matrix*, and *Trouble and Strife* (a British feminist magazine). "In each case," wrote Clarke,

> editorial concerns focussed on the imagery and advocacy of violence by women against men. Editors or collective members suggested that printing it might only "escalate the violence" pandemic among us; one went so far as to call it "hate speech." . . . If I were the editor, I would have been more concerned with the ethics of reprinting Ellis' hideous vivisection fantasies at such length, and with their impact on my readers. But in every case, it was the imagery of violence against men which aroused editorial caution. (1992b)

Craft and Baxter reacted to *Matrix's* refusal to publish their article and accompanying letter on the grounds that it was "hate speech" with rage, protesting that: "Your decision in 'choosing' not to print our [article and] letter is as politically despicable as censoring the rage of African-Americans against honkies during the civil rights movement (unpublished letter to *Matrix*, November 8, 1991). Referring to the escalation in male violence against women that has occurred, and to the fact that "the women's movement has tried nearly everything to stop men from hurting women," they argued that, "by taking part in the conspiracy to limit women's options (and even a discussion about women's options) with regards to self-defense, you too are contributing to this escalation of violence against women."

After quoting the passage from *Mercy* in which Dworkin's character concludes that "it is very important for women to kill men," Craft and Baxter write,

> There are many women who share this political idea, but lack the where-with-all to act according to their acquired wisdom and their principles. Like Utah Phillips said, "The Earth isn't dying, it's being killed. And the killers have names and addresses." Same goes for rapists and batterers, too. Let's work together to give women every tool they need to go after their abusers. Women deserve, at the very least, the permission (in the loosest sense of the word) to think the unthinkable in regards to their own self-defense (unpublished letter to *Matrix*, November 8, 1991).

I, too, believe that when women, whose lives are in jeopardy because they are unable to avoid or escape abusive relationships with men, kill their abusers, they should not only be *supported* by feminists, but heroinized by us. JoAnn Little is one woman I can think of who was heroinized for killing her rapist. But I would wager that, had her rapist been her husband, lover, date, friend, political colleague, acquaintance, or stranger, rather than a prison guard, the political left would not have taken up her cause.

The furthest that most feminists have been willing to go until now in supporting women who kill abusive partners is to argue that their act was understandable and excusable; that they should not be prosecuted or they should be pardoned and released from prison because they are victims of the "battered women's syndrome." This is not the place to go into my objections to this concept (see Russell, 1982). The point is that we should positively celebrate these women for killing their abusers, not just explain to the patriarchy the extenuating circumstances for their acts. We should also applaud them for saving other women and girls from becoming the victims of these men. (Note, the policy of encouraging women to leave their abusers rarely stops these men's abusive behavior. If women manage not only to survive but to get rid of their abusers, it usually means these men have found other women to victimize.)

Of course, women who kill their abusers often have to suffer heavy consequences for their acts. This is all the more reason to heroinize them for their courage and/or altruism. Meanwhile, the women's movement must continue to organize, as militantly as necessary, to insist on our right to defend ourselves. As I wrote elsewhere, women have been taking life-and-death risks for centuries (Russell, 1989). Simply by being women, we risk being raped. Some risks we cannot avoid. Some we sometimes can, such as continuing to live with a violent man. Women need to stop taking avoidable personal risks and, instead, take more political risks. Only by taking more political risks now will we eventually need to take fewer personal risks.

Notes

CHAPTER 1

1. This quotation comes from a memo to staff members at *Playboy*, cited by Jacobs, 1984.

2. I have incorporated into my definition of pornography several of Robert Brannon's suggestions, as well as my definitions of the concepts within it. Personal communication, March 11, 1992.

3. This is an FBI euphemism for the frequent practice by the police of discounting rape cases reported to them.

4. The fact that a sizable proportion of the killing is womanslaughter is essentially obliterated by this term.

5. Another feminist organization—Women Against Violence Against Women (WAVAW)—had already become a national action group in 1976. But while some WAVAW members in some cities engaged in anti-pornography actions, the organization as a whole focused primarily on sexist images of women on record covers.

6. Letter by Steve Johnson dated June 5, 1986, sent to me by MacKinnon, July 27, 1986.

CHAPTER 2

1. Since this writing, a judgment has been brought against Linda for "contract failure" during what she says was her period of imprisonment, and her payments for *Ordeal* have been attached. The book may end by financially benefiting Traynor's former lawyer. The punishment goes on.

CHAPTER 10

1. Offering a similar argument about the relationship between race and masculinity, Paul Hoch (1979) suggests that the ideal white man is a hero who upholds honor. But inside lurks a "Black beast" of violence and sexuality, traits that the white hero deflects onto men of color.

CHAPTER 13

1. While the severity of on-the-job victimization of street prostitutes can be dismissed by professionals and lay people alike as occupational hazards (discussed in Silbert & Pines, 1982a), those rapes suffered which were totally unrelated to their work (discussed by Pines & Silbert at the Proceedings of the International Interdisciplinary Congress on Women, December 1981), and the childhood abuses which preceded entrance into prostitution cannot be so easily dismissed. (Childhood abuses are extensively discussed in Silbert & Pines, 1982b; Silbert & Pines, 1981).

2. The quotes were transcribed responses taped during the interview.

CHAPTER 14

1. This woman was a victim of incest through pornography who testified at the Minneapolis Hearings. Catharine MacKinnon, personal communication, 1986.

2. I use the term *males* rather than *men* because many rapists are juveniles.

3. In 1984 Malamuth reported that in several studies an average of about 35% of male students indicated some likelihood of raping a woman (1984, p. 22). This figure has decreased to 25 to 30% since then, for reasons Malamuth cannot explain (personal communication, July 1986).

4. Unfortunately, this is the only part of the story that Malamuth has described in print.

5. A "scene" was defined as "a thematically uninterrupted sequence of activity in a given physical context" (1986, p. 25). Only scenes involving sex, aggression, or sexual aggression were coded.

6. It is a mystery why Donnerstein finds no effects for non-violent pornographic movies while Zillmann reports many significant effects.

CHAPTER 15

1. I use the term "woman-slashing" instead of "slasher" to emphasize the gender of the victim.

CHAPTER 17

1. For a different version of these findings, see Senn, C. Y., & Radtke, H. L. (1990). Women's evaluations of and affective reactions to mainstream violent pornography, nonviolent pornography and erotica, *Violence and Victims*, 5(3), 143–155. I would like to thank Diana Russell, Meredith Smye, and Michele Dore for

their helpful comments on the manuscript. It is only with their assistance that I was able to complete this project. Special thanks also go to Lorraine Radtke under whose supervision I conducted the research.

2. This concept of voyeurism is a difficult one as to some extent any photograph of sexual activity (or of any other activity) may be construed as voyeuristic. It was my intent to include in the nonviolent pornography category, those images that explicitly create "peeping tom" types of scenarios and are therefore creating more than the usual level of voyeurism in the image.

3. These were the exact definitions used in the research. I would now improve the definition of violent pornography to explicitly include "bondage" as this was a problem arising out of the ratings. Some raters had classified bondage images as nonviolent pornography, while others had classified them as violent pornography.

4. These women were volunteers and were acquaintances of the researcher. Their departmental affiliations were psychology, political science, and sociology.

5. I am not suggesting that the definitions suggested here are perfect. I would revise them in future research to clear up some ambiguities. I would explicitly mention bondage and bestiality in the violent pornography category.

6. The belief that women are not aroused to sexual images has been used to suggest that women are aroused only to more "complex" stimuli (involving romance or love) or that women have higher sex guilt than men (Kinsey, Pomeroy, Martin, & Gebhard, 1953).

7. Jeffreys is responding to the civil libertarian literature specifically, however the same can be said of the psychological literature. For example, Byrne et al. (1974) calls the factor which includes sexual arousal "positive affect" even though it also contains anxiety.

CHAPTER 18

1. Grant number R01MH28960.

2. For more detailed information on the methodology, see Russell 1984, or 1986, or 1990.

3. Social class was measured by the respondent's father's occupational status and education, her mother's occupational status and education, her own occupational status and education, her husband's occupational status and education (when relevant), and her total household income at the time of the interview.

4. See Russell's documentation of this phenomenon, for which she coined the term "revictimization," and her theoretical explanations of these findings (Russell, 1986, pp. 157–173).

5. This definition is broader than the one used in Russell's survey. For purposes of comparing my findings on the incidence and prevalence of rape with those of the official U.S. statistics at the time my survey was conducted, incidents of oral and anal intercourse were not included, nor was forcible penetration with a foreign object.

6. This analysis of pornography and wife rape is an edited version of a section in Russell, 1982, pp. 84–85; 1990 edition, pp. 83–85.

7. The following questions on pornography, asked of over half our sample, yielded very abstract and disappointing results: "Has pornography had any effect on your ideas or feelings about sex?" If yes, "What sort of effect has it had?" Hence we discarded them half-way through the field work period, replacing them with the request that respondents who said they were upset by seeing pornography explain why.

A few women also explained why they were *not* upset by seeing pornography, or why they liked it. As the goal of Russell's study was to evaluate the prevalence and impact of various forms of sexual abuse, we did not analyze these answers.

CHAPTER 22

1. Letter dated October 21, 1990.

2. "Hey, hey! Ho, Ho! Patriarchy has got to go!" is a popular contemporary demonstration chant.

3. Personal communication, December 5, 1991.

CHAPTER 24

1. In *Going Out Of Our Minds*, Sonia Johnson insists that, "What we resist persists," (*pg. 27*). We passionately disagree when she says: "Civil disobedience and resistance are collaborative . . . [and that] in protests we give away our own power, paradoxically giv[ing] it up to the very group we are trying to take power from." She adds: "Since it is apparent that ultimately we cannot use force to stop force, using the powers and deep mind, which are women's terrain anyway seems the obvious next step."

Political activists realize that "Radical action" is more — much more — than "changing the way you *think*." Sonia's self-defense tips literally drive us crazy and out of *our* minds. She writes: "I actually knocked a man back away from me in a parking lot, with the strength of my eyes focused on him. Knocked him *back*! Then, you see, since I didn't *need* to, I didn't hit him."

CHAPTER 25

1. Schwartz with Boyd, 1981, p. 37.

2. Three of these pictures have been reprinted in Russell's *Pornography: Turning men on to violence against women*, 1993.

3. Three of the rapists were sentenced to from 9 to 12 years, the fourth to

from 6 to 8 years, all in the same maximum security prison (Clendinen, 1984, p. A14).

4. See Chapter 14 for evidence in support of this statement.

5. The term femicide refers to the escalating phenomenon of men killing women *because* they are women (Caputi & Russell, 1990; Radford & Russell, 1992; Russell & Van de Ven, 1984).

6. Men who write about violence against women are among the few who use gender neutral terms — just when it is least appropriate.

7. Segments of the following few paragraphs were written by Jane Caputi and myself when drafting.

8. Note the gender neutral terms.

9. I am not saying that no more research should be conducted. There are many important topics to explore. I am merely saying that I consider that the harmfulness of pornography has been established.

10. These buttons are available in some bookstores. Or write to Nikki Craft, Box 2085, Rancho Cordova, CA 95741-2085.

References

Abel, Gene; Barlow, David; Blanchard, Edward; & Guild, Donald. (1977). The components of rapists' sexual arousal. *Archives of General Psychiatry, 34*, 895–903.

Abel, Gene; Mittelman, Mary; & Becker, Judith. (1985). Sexual offenders: Results of assessment and recommendations for treatment. In Mark Ben-Aron, Stephen Hucker, & Christopher Webster (Eds.), *Clinical Criminology: The assessment and treatment of criminal behavior* (pp. 191–205). Toronto: Clarke Institute of Psychiatry, University of Toronto.

Allen, Donna. (1985). Face pornographers' unequal first amendment rights, women work to be heard: Seek support for their right. *Media Report to Women, 13*(3), 1, 7.

Anonymous. (1979). *Sluts of the S.S.* New York: Star Distributors.

Anonymous. (1981a). *Abuse: Black and battered*. New York: Star Distributors.

Anonymous. (1981b). *Soul slave*. New York: Star Distributors.

Attorney General's Commission on Pornography: Final Report. (1986). (vols. 1–2). Washington, DC: U.S. Department of Justice.

Bachy, Victor. (1976). Danish 'permissiveness' revisited. *The Journal of Communication, 26*(1), 40–43.

Baker, C. David. (1978). Preying on playgrounds: The exploitation of children in pornography and prostitution. *Pepperdine Law Review, 5*(3), 809–846.

Baker, Edward. (1978). *Tricked into white slavery*. South Laguna, CA: Publisher's Consultants.

Baron, Larry & Straus, Murray. (1984). Sexual stratification, pornography, and rape in the United States. In Neil Malamuth & Edward Donnerstein (Eds.), *Pornography and Sexual Aggression* (pp. 185–209). New York: Academic Press.

Bart, Pauline; Freeman, Linda; & Kimball, Peter. (1985). The different worlds of women and men: Attitudes toward pornography and responses to 'Not a Love Story'—a film about pornography. *Women's Studies International Forum, 8*(4), 307–322.

Bart, Pauline & Jozsa, Margaret. (1980). Dirty books, dirty films, and dirty data. In Laura Lederer (Ed.), *Take back the night: Women on pornography* (pp. 204–217). New York: William Morrow.

Bell, Laurie (Ed.). (1987). *Good girls/bad girls: Feminists and sex trade workers face to face*. Toronto: Seal Press.

Bem, Sandra. (1981). Gender schema theory: A cognitive account of sex typing. *Psychological Review, 88*, 354–364.

Beneke, Timothy. (1982). *Men on rape*. New York: St. Martin's.

Berry, Ronald. (1978). *Soul food*. Los Angeles: Sutton House Publishing.

Bogdanovich, Peter. (1984). *The killing of the unicorn: Dorothy Stratten, 1960–1980*. New York: William Morrow.

Brady, Katherine. (1979). *Father's days: A true story of incest*. New York: Seaview Books.

Brian, T. *v.* Pacific Bell. (1989, May 22). *California Reporter* 258, pp. 707–716.

Briere, John; Corne, Shawn; Runtz, Marsha; & Malamuth, Neil. (1984). The rape arousal inventory: Predicting actual and potential sexual aggression in a university population. Paper presented at the American Psychological Association Meeting, Toronto.

Briere, John & Malamuth, Neil. (1983). Self-reported likelihood of sexually aggressive behavior: Attitudinal versus sexual explanations. *Journal of Research in Personality, 17*, 315–323.

Briere, John; Malamuth, Neil; & Check, James. (1985). Sexuality and rape-supportive beliefs. *International Journal of Women's Studies, 8*, 398–403.

Brownmiller, Susan. (1975). *Against our will: Men, women and rape*. New York: Simon & Schuster.

Bryant, Jennings. (1985). Unpublished transcript of testimony to the Attorney General's Commission on Pornography, Houston, TX, pp. 128–157.

Burstyn, Varda (Ed.). (1985). *Women against censorship*. Vancouver: Douglas & McIntyre.

Burt, Martha. (1980). Cultural myths and supports for rape. *Journal of Personality and Social Psychology, 38*(2), 217–230.

Byrne, Donn; Fisher, Jeffrey; Lamberth, John; & Mitchell, Herman. (1974). Evaluations of erotica: Facts or feelings? *Journal of Personality and Social Psychology, 29*(1), 111–116.

Byrne, Donn & Lamberth, John. (1971). The effect of erotic stimuli on sex arousal, evaluative responses, and subsequent behavior. In *Technical Report of the Commission on Obscenity and Pornography*. Vol. 8. Washington, DC: U.S. Government Printing Office.

Caputi, Jane. (1987). *The age of sex crimes*. Ohio: Bowling Green State University.

Caputi, Jane & Russell, Diana. (1990, September/October). Femicide: Speaking the Unspeakable. *Ms.*, 1(3), 34–37.

Ceniti, Joseph & Malamuth, Neil. (1984). Effects of repeated exposure to sexually violent or non-violent stimuli on sexual arousal to rape and nonrape depictions. *Behaviour Research and Therapy, 22*(5), 535–548.

Censorship is no one's civil right. (1984, May 27). *New York Times*, p. D16.

Check, James. (1985). *The effects of violent and nonviolent pornography*. Ottawa: Department of Justice, Canada.

Check, James & Guloien, Ted. (1989). Reported proclivity for coercive sex following repeated exposure to sexually violent pornography, nonviolent dehumanizing pornography, and erotica. In Dolf Zillmann & Bryant Jennings (Eds.), *Pornography: Research advances and policy considerations* (pp. 159–184). Hillsdale, NJ: Lawrence Erlbaum.

Check, James & Malamuth, Neil. (1985). An empirical assessment of some feminist hypotheses about rape. *International Journal of Women's Studies, 8,* 414–423.

Check, James & Malamuth, Neil. (1986). Pornography and sexual aggression: A social learning theory analysis. *Communication Yearbook, 9,* 181–213.

Check, James & Maxwell, Kirstin. (1992, June). Children's consumption of pornography and their attitudes regarding sexual violence. Paper presented at the Canadian Psychological Association Meetings, Quebec.

Clark, Lorene & Lewis, Debra. (1977). *Rape: The price of coercive sexuality.* Toronto: Women's Educational Press.

Clarke, De. (1992a). A woman with a sword: Some thoughts on women, feminism, and violence. *Nemesis: Justice is a woman with a sword.* A.C.L.U./Nemesis Publishing Concerns.

Clarke, De. (1992b). Retaliation: The feminist taboo. *Nemesis: Justice is a woman with a sword.* A.C.L.U./Nemesis Publishing Concerns. (Available by writing to PO Box 2085, Rancho Cordova, CA 95741-2085)

Clendinen, Dudley. (1984, March 27). Barroom rapists are given sentences of up to 12 years. *New York Times,* p. A14.

Cline, Victor (Ed.). (1974). *Where do you draw the line?* Provo, UT: Brigham Young University Press.

Court, John. (1977). Pornography and sex crimes: A reevaluation in light of recent trends around the world. *International Journal of Criminology and Penology, 5,* 129–157.

Dakin, Crystal. (1977). *Black head nurse.* New York: Star Distributors.

Davis, A. (1975, June). Joanne Little: The dialectics of rape. *Ms, 3,* 74.

Defeated by pornography. (1986, June 2). *New York Times,* p. I16.

Dial-a-porn restrictions allowed to take effect. (1992, January 28). *San Francisco Chronicle,* p. A4.

Diamond, Irene. (1980). Pornography and repression: A reconsideration of who and what. In Laura Lederer (Ed.), *Take back the night: Women on pornography* (pp. 187–203). New York: William Morrow.

Dietz, Park & Evans, Barbara. (1982). Pornographic imagery and prevalence of paraphilia. *American Journal of Psychiatry, 139,* 1493–1495.

Dobson, James. (1989). Transcript of interview with Theodore Bundy. (Focus on the Family, Arcadia, CA 91006).

Donnerstein, Edward. (1983). Unpublished transcript of testimony to the Public Hearings on Ordinances to Add Pornography as Discrimination Against Women. Committee on Government Operations, City Council, Minneapolis, MN, pp. 4–12.

Donnerstein, Edward. (1984). Pornography: Its effects on violence against women. In Neil M. Malamuth and Edward Donnerstein (Eds.), *Pornography and sexual aggression* (pp. 53–84). New York: Academic Press.

Donnerstein, Edward. (1985). Unpublished transcript of testimony to the Attorney General's Commission on Pornography Hearings, Houston, TX, pp. 5–33.

Donnerstein, Edward. (1990). PBS-TV interview on pornography with David G. Meyers.

Donnerstein, Edward & Berkowitz, Leonard. (1981). Victim reactions in aggressive erotic films as a factor in violences against women. *Journal of Personality and Social Psychology, 41*, 710–724.

Donnerstein, Edward & Linz, Daniel. (1985). Presentation paper to the Attorney General's Commission on Pornography, Houston, TX.

Donnerstein, Edward; Linz, Daniel; & Penrod, Steven. (1987). *The question of pornography: Research findings and policy implications.* New York: Free Press.

Dworkin, Andrea. (1981). *Pornography: Men possessing women.* New York: Perigee Books.

Dworkin, Andrea. (1988). *Letters from a war zone: Writings, 1976–1989.* New York: E. P. Dutton.

Dworkin, Andrea. (1990). *Mercy.* New York: Four Walls Eight Windows.

Dworkin, Andrea. (1991). *Mass murder: The sexual politics of killing women.* Speech at the Université de Montreal, December 7, 1990.

Dworkin, Andrea & MacKinnon, Catharine. (1988). *Pornography and civil rights: A new day for women's equality.* Minneapolis: Organizing Against Pornography (distributed by Southern Sisters, Inc., 441 Morris St., Durham, NC 27701).

Ebert, Roger & Siskel, Gene. (1980). *Sneak Previews* (PBS-TV), Transcript #304.

Einsiedel, Edna. (1986). Social science report. Paper prepared for the Attorney General's Commission on Pornography, Department of Justice, Washington, DC.

Eisenstein, Hester. (1983). *Contemporary feminist thought.* Boston: G. K. Hall.

Ellis, Bret Easton. (1991). *American psycho.* New York: Knopf.

Erlich, Reese. (1989, August 13). Computer porn at the office. *The World, San Francisco Examiner*, pp. 7–8.

Esquire. (1990, June). Cover picture.

Farley, Melissa. (1992). The rampage against *Penthouse*. In Jill Radford & Diana Russell (Eds.), *Femicide: The politics of woman killing* (pp. 339–345). New York: Twayne Publishers.

Fausto-Sterling, Anne. (1989). Life in the XY corral. *Women's Studies International Forum, 12*(3), 319–331.

Feshbach, Seymour & Malamuth, Neil. (1978, November). Sex and aggression: Proving the link. *Psychology Today, 7*(6), 111–117, 122.

Finkelhor, David. (1984). *Child sexual abuse: New theory and research.* New York: Free Press.

Fisher, William & Byrne, Donn. (1978). Individual differences in affective, evaluative, and behavioral responses to an erotic film. *Journal of Applied Social Psychology, 8*(4), 355–365.

Foucault, Michel. (1980). In Colin Gordon (Ed.), *Power/knowledge: Selected interviews and other writings, 1972–1977.* New York: Pantheon.

Frost, Richard & Stauffer, John. (1987, Spring). The effects of social class, gender, and personality on physiological responses to filmed violence. *Journal of Communication, 37*(2), 29–45.

Gallup, George Jr. (1986, August 14). Ban urged on depiction of sexual violence. *San Francisco Chronicle*, p. 6.

Garcia, Luis; Brennan, Kathleen; DeCarlo, Monica; McGlennon, Rachel; & Tait, Sandra. (1984). Sex differences in sexual arousal to different erotic stories. *Journal of Sex Research, 20*(4), 391–402.

Gardner, Tracey. (1980). Racism in Pornography and the Women's Movement. In Laura Lederer (Ed.), *Take back the night: Women on pornography* (pp. 105–114). New York: William Morrow.

Gilman, Sander L. (1985). Black bodies, white bodies: Toward an iconography of female sexuality in late nineteenth-century art, medicine, and literature. *Critical Inquiry, 12*(1), 205–243.

Goldstein, Michael & Kant, Harold. (1973). *Pornography and sexual deviance.* Berkeley: University of California Press.

Goodchilds, Jacqueline & Zellman, Gail. (1984). Sexual signaling and sexual aggression in adolescent relationships. In Neil Malamuth & Edward Donnerstein (Eds.), *Pornography and sexual aggression* (pp. 233–246). New York: Academic Press.

Gould, Stephen Jay. (1981). *The mismeasure of man.* New York: W. W. Norton.

Hagar, Laura. (1992, January 10). Guns and roses. *Express, 14*(13), 1, 10, 12, 14, 16–19.

Hall, Jacqueline Dowd. (1983). The mind that burns in each body: Women, rape, and racial violence. In Ann Snitow, Christine Stansell, & Sharon Thompson (Eds.), *Powers of desire: The politics of sexuality* (pp. 329–349). New York: Monthly Review Press.

Halpin, Zuleyma Tang. (1989). Scientific objectivity and the concept of "the other." *Women's Studies International Forum, 12*(3), 285–294.

Harmon, Patricia & Check, James. (1989, March). *The role of pornography in woman abuse* (Report #33). Toronto: LaMarsh Research Programme on Violence and Conflict Resolution, York University.

Hite, Shere. (1981). *The Hite Report on male sexuality.* New York: Alfred Knopf.

Hoch, Paul. (1979). *White hero black beast: Racism, sexism and the mask of masculinity.* London: Pluto Press.

Holt, Patricia. (1990, November 17). Book cancellation raises questions: Pornography, censorship issues surround 'Psycho.' *San Francisco Chronicle*, pp. C3, 7.

Hunter, Nan & Law, Sylvia. (1987–1988). Brief Amici Curiae of feminist anticensorship taskforce, et al., in American Booksellers Association *v.* Hudnut. *University of Michigan Journal of Law Reform, 21*, 69–136.

Hustler. (1983, January). Dirty pool. Vol. 9, p. 7.

Hustler. (1983, August). Greetings from New Bedford, Mass: The Portuguese gang-rape capital of America. Vol. 10, p. 2.

Ishigaki, Akira. (1984, December). Sakura. *Penthouse.* Vol. 16, p. 118.

Jacobs, Karen. (1984). Patterns of violence: A feminist perspective on the regulations of pornography. *The Harvard Women's Law Journal, 7*, 5–55.

Jeffreys, Sheila. (1990). *Anticlimax: A feminist perspective on the sexual revolution.* London: The Women's Press.

Johnson, Sonia. (1987). *Going out of our minds: The metaphysics of liberation.* Freedom, CA: Crossing Press.

Kanin, Eugene & Parcell, Stanley. (1977). Sexual aggression: A second look at the offended female. *Archives of Sexual Behavior, 6,* 67–76.

Kitzinger, Celia. (1987). *The social construction of lesbianism.* London: Sage.

Koss, Mary & Dinero, Thomas E. (1989). Predictors of sexual aggression among a sample of male college students. In V. Quinsey & Robert Prentky (Eds.), *Human sexual aggression: Current perspectives, Annals of the New York Academy of Sciences, 528,* 133–147.

Koss, Mary; Gidycz, Christine; & Wisniewski, Nadine. (1987). The scope of rape: Incidence and prevalence of sexual aggression and victimization in a national sample of higher education students. *Journal of Consulting and Clinical Psychology, 55,* 162–170.

Koss, Mary & Oros, Cheryl. (1982). Sexual experiences survey: A research instrument investigating sexual aggression and victimization. *Journal of Consulting and Clinical Psychology, 50,* 455–457.

Kutchinsky, Berl. (1970). Sex crimes and pornography in Copenhagen: A survey of attitudes. *Technical Reports of the Commission on Obscenity and Pornography,* Vol. 7. Washington, DC: U.S. Government Printing Office.

Kutchinsky, Berl. (1973). The effect of easy availability of pornography on the incidence of sex crimes: The Danish experience. *Journal of Social Issues,* 29(3), 163–181.

Lederer, Laura (Ed.). (1980). *Take back the night: Women on pornography.* New York: William Morrow.

Leidholdt, Dorchen. (1981, March 15). Where pornography meets fascism. *WIN Magazine,* pp. 18–22.

Linz, Daniel; Donnerstein, Edward; & Penrod, Steven. (1987). The findings and recommendations of the Attorney General's Commission on Pornography: Do the psychological facts fit the political fury? *American Psychologist, 42,* 946–953.

Longino, Helen E. (1980). Pornography, oppression, and freedom: A closer look. In Laura Lederer (Ed.), *Take back the night: Women on pornography* (pp. 40–54). New York: William Morrow.

Lorde, Audre. (1980). Uses of the erotic: The erotic as power. In Laura Lederer (Ed.), *Take back the night: Women on pornography* (pp. 295–306). New York: William Morrow.

Lovelace, Linda. (1981). *Ordeal.* New York: Berkeley Books.

Lovelace, Linda. (1986). *Out of bondage.* Secaucus, NJ: Lyle Stuart.

MacKinnon, Catharine. (1987). *Feminism unmodified: Discourses on life and law.* Cambridge, MA: Harvard University.

Malamuth, Neil. (1981a). Rape fantasies as a function of exposure to violent sexual stimuli. *Archives of Sexual Behavior, 10,* 33–47.

Malamuth, Neil. (1981b). Rape proclivity among males. *Journal of Social Issues,* 37(4), 138–157.

Malamuth, Neil. (1984). Aggression against women: Cultural and individual causes. In Neil Malamuth & Edward Donnerstein (Eds.), *Pornography and sexual aggression* (pp. 19–52). New York: Academic Press.

Malamuth, Neil. (1985). Unpublished transcript of testimony to Attorney General's Commission on Pornography, Houston, TX, pp. 68–110.

Malamuth, Neil. (1986). Do sexually violent media indirectly contribute to antisocial behavior? Paper prepared for the Surgeon General's Workshop on Pornography and Public Health, Arlington, VA.

Malamuth, Neil & Check, James. (1981). The effects of mass media exposure on acceptance of violence against women: A field experiment. *Journal of Research in Personality, 15,* 436–446.

Malamuth, Neil & Check, James. (1985). The effects of aggressive pornography on beliefs in rape myths: Individual differences. *Journal of Research in Personality, 19,* 299–320.

Malamuth, Neil & Donnerstein, Edward. (Eds.). (1984). *Pornography and sexual aggression.* New York: Academic Press.

Malamuth, Neil; Haber, Scott; & Feshbach, Seymour. (1980). Testing hypotheses regarding rape: Exposure to sexual violence, sex differences, and the "normality" of rapists. *Journal of Research in Personality, 14,* 121–137.

Malamuth, Neil; Heim, Margaret; & Feshbach, Seymour. (1980). The sexual responsiveness of college students to rape depictions: Inhibitory and disinhibitory effects. *Journal of Personality and Social Psychology, 38,* 399–408.

Malamuth, Neil & Spinner, Barry. (1980). A longitudinal content analysis of sexual violence in the best-selling erotic magazines. *Journal of Sex Research, 16*(3), 226–237.

Mancusi, Peter. (1985, June 2). Free to express—or suppress? *Boston Globe,* p. A17.

Marr, Manuel. (1977). *Black ghetto teens.* New York: Star Distributors.

Maxwell, Kirstin & Check, James. (1992, June). *Adolescents' rape myth attitudes and acceptance of forced sexual intercourse.* Paper presented at the Canadian Psychological Association Meetings, Quebec.

McKenzie-Mohr, Doug & Zanna, Mark. (1990). Treating women as sexual objects: Look to the (gender schematic) male who has viewed pornography. *Personality and Social Psychology Bulletin, 16*(2), 296–308.

McNair, Douglas; Lorr, Maurice; & Droppleman, Leo. (1971). *ETTS manual for the profile of mood states.* San Diego, CA: Educational and Industrial Testing Service.

McNall, Scott G. (1983). Pornography: The structure of domination and the mode of reproduction. In Scott McNall (Ed.), *Current perspectives in social theory* (Vol. 4, pp. 181–203). Greenwich, CT: JAI Press.

Medea, Andra & Thompson, Kathleen. (1974). *Against rape.* New York: Farrar, Straus & Giroux.

Miller, Jean Baker. (1976). *Toward a new psychology of women.* Boston: Beacon Press.

Mixer, Samuel. (1977). *Bondage fling*. Los Angeles, CA: Sutton House.

Montgomery, Rick. (1990, November 2). *Hustler* article blamed for mutilation of boy, 10. *The Kansas City Star*, p. C-1.

Mosher, Donald. (1971). Sex callousness toward women. *Technical Reports of the Commission on Obscenity and Pornography, 8*. Washington, DC: U.S. Government Printing Office.

Osgood, Charles; Suci, George; & Tannenbaum, Percy. (1957). *The measurement of meaning*. Urbana: University of Illinois Press.

Page, Stewart. (1989). Misrepresentation of pornography research: Psychology's role. *American Psychologist, 42*(10), 578–580.

Page, Stewart. (1990a). The turnaround on pornography research: Some implications for psychology and women. *Canadian Psychology, 31*(4), 359–367.

Page, Stewart. (1990b). On Linz and Donnerstein's view of pornography research. *Canadian Psychology, 31*(4), 371–373.

Palac, Lisa. (1991, March 27). Videotape at home: Is Big Brother finally in your bedroom? *San Francisco Weekly*, pp. 12–13.

Palys, T. S. (1986). Testing the common wisdom: The social content of video pornography. *Canadian Psychology, 27*(1), 22–35.

Parfrey, Adam. (1990, December). Mayhem manuals. *Hustler*, 1–2, 56–58, 67–68.

Parker, Rozsica & Pollock, Griselda. (1981). *Old mistresses: Women, art and ideology*. London: Routledge & Kegan Paul.

Pinsky, M. (1975, April). In the heat of the night: Joanna Little case. *Progressive, 39*, 9.

Public Hearings on Ordinances to Add Pornography as Discrimination Against Women (1983). Committee on Government Operations, City Council, Minneapolis, MN.

Rachman, S. & Hodgson, R. J. (1968). Experimentally-induced "sexual fetishism": Replication and development. *Psychological Record, 18*, 25–27.

Radford, Jill & Russell, Diana (Eds.). (1992). *Femicide: The politics of woman killing*. New York: Twayne Publishing.

Raymond, Janice. (1990, Summer). Misplaced Editorial. *Valley Women's Voice*, p. 5.

The Report of The Commission on Obscenity and Pornography. (1970). New York: Bantam Books.

Ressler, Robert; Burgess, Ann; & Douglas, John. (1988). *Sexual homicide: Patterns and motives*. Lexington, MA: Lexington Books.

Riddington, Jillian. (1983). *Freedom from harm or freedom of speech?: A feminist perspective on the regulation of pornography*. Ottawa: National Association of Women and the Law.

Robeson, Eli. (1981). Knife point. *Folsom Magazine* (2).

Rubin, Lillian. (1990). *Erotic wars*. New York: HarperCollins.

Rush, Florence. (1980). Child pornography. In Laura Lederer (Ed.), *Take back the night: Women on Pornography* (pp. 71–81). New York: William Morrow.

Russell, Diana. (1975). *The politics of rape*. New York: Stein & Day.

Russell, Diana. (1980). Pornography and violence: What does the new research say? In Laura Lederer (Ed.), *Take back the night: Women on pornography* (pp. 218–238). New York: William Morrow.

Russell, Diana. (1982, 1990 [2nd edition]). *Rape in marriage.* New York: Macmillan.

Russell, Diana. (1984). *Sexual exploitation: Rape, child sexual abuse, and workplace harassment.* Beverly Hills, CA: Sage.

Russell, Diana. (1985, September). The impact of pornography on women. Testimony prepared for the Attorney General's Commission on Pornography Hearings, Houston, TX.

Russell, Diana. (1986). *The secret trauma: Incest in the lives of girls and women.* New York: Basic Books.

Russell, Diana. (1988). Pornography and rape: A causal model. *Political Psychology, 9*(1), 41–73.

Russell, Diana. (1989). *Exposing nuclear phallacies.* New York: Pergamon Press.

Russell, Diana. (1993). *Pornography: Turning men on to violence against women.* Berkeley, CA: Russell Books.

Russell, Diana & Van de Ven, Nicole (Eds.). (1984). *Crimes against women: Proceedings of the international tribunal.* San Francisco: Frog in the Well.

Sakura: Photographs by Akira Ishigaki (Photo spread of Asian women). (1984, December). *Penthouse.*

SAMOIS Collective (Eds.). (1981). *Coming to power: Writings and graphics on lesbian S/M.* Palo Alto, CA: Up Press.

Sandalow, Marc. (1987, December 11). Phone-porn trial opens with ruling for defense. *San Francisco Chronicle,* p. A11.

Schiro v. Clark (1992). United States Court of Appeals, Seventh Circuit. 963 Federal Reporter, 2d Series, 962–976.

Schmidt, Gunter. (1975). Male-female differences in sexual arousal and behavior during and after exposure to sexually explicit stimuli. *Archives of Sexual Behavior, 4*(4), 353–367.

Schwartz, Ted & Boyd, Kelli. (1981, August). Inside the mind of the 'Hillside Strangler.' *Hustler.* p. 36.

Scully, Diana. (1985). *The role of violent pornography in justifying rape.* Paper prepared for the Attorney General's Commission on Pornography Hearings, Houston, TX.

Senn, Charlene. (1991). *The impact of pornography on women's lives.* Unpublished doctoral dissertation, York University, Toronto.

Senn, Charlene. (1992, June). Women's contact with male consumers: One link between pornography and women's experiences of male violence. Paper presented at the Canadian Psychological Association Meetings, Quebec.

Senn, Charlene & Radtke, Lorraine. (1985). Women's evaluations of violent pornography: Relationships with previous experience and attitudes. Unpublished manuscript.

The Sexuality Issue Collective. (1981). Sex issue. *Heresies, 3*(4), Issue 12.

Silbert, Mimi. (1982). Prostitution and sexual assault: Summary of results. *Biosocial: Journal of Behavioral Ecology, 3,* 69–76.

Silbert, Mimi. (1984). Treatment of prostitute victims of sexual assault. In Irving R. Stuart & Joanne G. Greer (Eds.), *Victims of sexual aggression: Treatment of children, women and men* (pp. 251–269). New York: Van Nostrand Reinhard.

Silbert, Mimi & Pines, Ayala. (1981). Sexual abuse as an antecedent to prostitution. *Child Abuse and Neglect, 5,* 1–5.

Silbert, Mimi & Pines, Ayala. (1982a). Occupational hazards of street prostitutes. *Criminal Justice and Behavior, 8,* 397–399.

Silbert, Mimi & Pines, Ayala. (1982b). Victimization of street prostitutes. *Victimology: An International Journal, 7,* 122–123.

Silbert, Mimi & Pines, Ayala. (1983). Juvenile sexual exploitation in the background of street prostitutes. *Social Work, 28*(4), 285–289.

Silbert, Mimi & Pines, Ayala. (1984). Pornography and sexual abuse of women. *Sex Roles, 10*(11–12), 857–868.

Smith, Don. (1976, August). *Sexual aggression in American pornography: The stereotype of rape.* Paper presented at the American Sociological Association Meetings, New York City.

Smith, Don. (1977). The social content of pornography. *Journal of Communication, 26,* 16–33.

Snitow, Ann; Stansell, Christine; & Thompson, Sharon. (Eds.). (1983). *Powers of desire: The politics of sexuality.* New York: New Feminist Library.

Sommers, Evelyn & Check, James. (1987). An empirical investigation of the role of pornography in the verbal and physical abuse of women. *Violence and Victims, 2*(3), 189–209.

Sontag, Susan. (1977). *On Photography.* New York: Farrar, Straus & Giroux.

Spelman, Elizabeth V. (1982). Theories of race and gender: The erasure of black women. *Quest, 5*(4), 36–62.

Steinem, Gloria. (1980). Erotica and pornography: A clear and present difference. In Laura Lederer (Ed.), *Take back the night: Women on pornography* (pp. 35–39). New York: William Morrow.

Stock, Wendy. (1983). The effects of violent pornography on the sexual responsiveness and the attitudes of women. Doctoral dissertation, State University of New York at Stony Brook.

Stoltenberg, John. (1989). *Refusing to be a man: Essays on sex and justice.* New York: Penguin USA/Meridian.

Technical Report of the Commission on Obscenity and Pornography. (1970). (vols. 1–9). Washington, DC: U.S. Government Printing Office.

Teish, Luisah. (1980). A quiet subversion. In Laura Lederer (Ed.), *Take back the night: Women on pornography* (pp. 115–118). New York: William Morrow.

Theodorson, George & Theodorson, Achilles. (1979). *A modern dictionary of sociology.* New York: Barnes & Noble.

Tuan, Yi-Fu. (1984). *Dominance and affection: The making of pets.* New Haven, CT: Yale University Press.

Valverde, Mariana. (1985). Pornography. In Connie Guberman & Margie Wolfe,

(Eds.), *No safe place: Violence against women and children* (pp. 131–161). Toronto: Women's Press.

Vance, Carol (Ed.). (1984). *Pleasure and danger: Exploring female sexuality.* New York: Routledge & Kegan Paul.

Venant, Elizabeth. (1990, December 14). Ellis' grisly novel: Literati battle over its violence. *San Francisco Chronicle,* p. B1, 6.

Viets, Jack. (1987, October 15). Molesting case leads to $10,000 dial-a-porn suit. *San Francisco Chronicle,* p. A23.

Vivar, Mona A. (1982). The new anti-female violent pornography: Is moral condemnation the only justifiable response? *Law and Psychology Review, 7,* 53–70.

Walker, Alice. (1984). Coming apart. In Alice Walker, *You can't keep a good woman down* (pp. 41–53). New York: Harcourt Brace Jovanovitch.

Washington, Spencer. (1983). *Animal sex among black women.* North Hollywood, CA: American Art Enterprises.

Wilson, John. (1978). *Black fashion model.* South Laguna, CA: Publisher's Consultants.

Zillmann, Dolf. (1985). Unpublished transcript of testimony to the Attorney General's Commission on Pornography, Houston, TX, pp. 110–157.

Zillmann, Dolf. (1989). Effects of prolonged consumption of pornography. In Dolf Zillmann & Jennings Bryant (Eds.), *Pornography: Research advances and policy considerations* (pp. 127–157). Hillsdale, NJ: Lawrence Erlbaum.

Zillmann, Dolf & Bryant, Jennings. (1984). Effects of massive exposure to pornography. In Neil M. Malamuth & Edward Donnerstein (Eds.), *Pornography and sexual aggression* (pp. 115–138). New York: Academic Press.

Zillmann, Dolf & Bryant, Jennings. (1988). Pornography's impact on sexual satisfaction. *Journal of Applied Social Psychology, 18*(5), 438–453.

Zillmann, Dolf & Bryant, Jennings (Eds.). (1989). *Pornography: Research advances and policy considerations.* Hillsdale, NJ: Lawrence Erlbaum.

Zillmann, Dolf; Bryant, Jennings; & Carveth, Rodney. (1981). The effect of erotica featuring sadomasochism and bestiality on motivated intermale aggression. *Personality and Social Psychology Bulletin, 7*(1), 153–159.

Zillmann, Dolf; Bryant, Jennings; Comisky, Paul; & Medoff, Norman J. (1981). Excitation and hedonic valence in the effect of erotica on motivated intermale aggression. *European Journal of Social Psychology, 11,* 233–252.

Index

About the Editor

Diana E. H. Russell obtained her B.A. from the University of Cape Town, South Africa in 1958; a Postgraduate Diploma from the London School of Economics and Political Science (with Distinction) in 1961; an M.A. from Harvard University in 1967; and a Ph.D. from Harvard University in 1970. She received the Mostyn Lloyd Memorial Prize awarded to the best student studying for the Postgraduate Diploma at LSE in 1961.

Dr. Russell is a professor emerita of sociology at Mills College where she taught sociology and women's studies for 22 years. She is the author of *Rebellion, Revolution and Armed Force: A Comparative Study of Fifteen Countries with Special Emphasis on Cuba and South Africa* (Academic Press, 1974); *The Politics of Rape* (Stein & Day, 1975, distributed by Scarborough House); author and co-editor of *Crimes Against Women: The Proceedings of the International Tribunal* (first published by Les Femmes, 1976, reprinted by Frog in the Well, 1984); author of *Rape in Marriage* (Macmillan, 1982; 2nd edition by Indiana University Press, 1990); *Sexual Exploitation: Rape, Child Sexual Abuse and Workplace Harassment* (Sage Publications, 1984); *The Secret Trauma: Incest in the Lives of Girls and Women* (Basic Books, 1986); *Exposing Nuclear Phallacies* (Pergamon, 1989); *Lives of Courage: Women for a New South Africa* (Basic Books, 1989); and co-editor of *Femicide: The Politics of Woman Killing* (Twayne, 1992).

The Secret Trauma won the 1986 C. Wright Mills Award. This award is given annually by the Society for the Study of Social Problems for outstanding social science research that addresses an important social issue.

Dr. Russell has been active in the women's liberation movement since 1969. She started teaching the first course in women's studies at Mills College at that time. She was one of the main organizers of the 1976 International Tribunal on Crimes Against Women. She has been arrested three times for her political activism, in South Africa (1963), in England (1974), and the United States (1990).

In 1976 Dr. Russell became one of the founding members of a feminist anti-pornography group called Women Against Violence in Pornography and Media (WAVPM). She remained active in this organization — the first feminist anti-pornography group in the United States — for many years.

Dr. Russell has lectured widely, in the United States and abroad, about the political situation in South Africa, rape, incest, child sexual abuse in general, pornography, and all forms of violence against women.

Dr. Russell is currently at work on a self-published book—*Pornography: Turning Men on to Violence Against Women*—over half of which is devoted to examples of visual pornography together with her critical evaluation of these materials. This book can be ordered from Russell Books, 2018 Shattuck Avenue, Box 118, Berkeley, CA 94704, after June 1993. Dr. Russell is also working on an interview-based book about incest in South Africa, plus a second volume on femicide.